The Life of Thomas Cooper Written by Himself

Thomas Cooper

THE LIFE OF THOMAS COOPER

WRITTEN BY HIMSELF

MDCCCXCVII

TO HIS DEAREST FRIEND

THE REV. FREDERICK JAMES JOBSON. D.D.

EX-PRESIDENT OF THE WESLEYAN METHODIST
CONFERENCE,

THIS AUTOBIOGRAPHY IS INSCRIBED,

WITH AFFECTIONATE REGARD AND HEARTFELT GRATITUDE

BY THE AUTHOR.

CONTENTS

CHAPTER I.
CHILDHOOD: 1805-1811. LEICESTER—EXETER— GAINSBOROUGH.

THE world expects, and almost demands, that some men write their autobiography. It ridicules the vanity and impertinence of other men who put the recollections of their own lives into print. Hundreds of people have told me that I ought to write a record of my own life. But, very likely, thousands will wonder that I have had the assurance to write it, or could imagine that anybody really cared to have it written. And, doubtless, to many people, my record will be worthless; yet I hope others will find something in it they may deem not altogether without value.

Having come to the resolution to write my own memoirs, I see no necessity for confining myself to the drawing out of a lean outline. If the account of a man's life be worth writing at all, it must be worth writing with fair completeness. So I shall fill up the outline as fully as I judge it wise to fill it up. I shall do so more especially when it will gratify myself. For, if there be any gratification to be derived from the reading of my book, I think I ought to share it. And I most positively declare that if I had thought a share of such gratification would be denied me, I would not have written the book at all. Thus the reader will see that I have let the truth out, at once: I have written the book chiefly to please myself. And that, I suspect, is the chief reason why anybody writes an autobiography.

Coleridge (in his "Literaria Biographia") thinks it "probable that all thoughts are in themselves imperishable; and that if the intelligent faculty should be rendered more comprehensive it would only require a different and apportioned organization—the body celestial instead of the body terrestrial—to bring before every human soul the collective experience of its whole past existence." One could desire to have such a power of tracing every thought to the earliest part of one's conscious existence. Not for the purpose of inflicting the recital of all one's thoughts upon others, but for the purpose of being able to tell the truth. What were the exact motives for the performance of certain actions in our lives, we often cannot state unerringly in our later years. It is not simply because memory fails that we cannot give the veritable statement; but because the moral and intellectual man has changed. We no longer think and feel as we thought and felt so many years ago; and, perhaps, we wonder that we did some things and spoke some words we did and spake at certain times. We are inclined to set it down that our motives then were what they would he now. We see the past, as it were, through a false glass; and cannot represent it to ourselves otherwise than as something like the present.

I am setting out to write my memoirs with the rigid purpose of telling the truth to the best of my knowledge. But I cannot expect to accomplish what none of us can accomplish, unless "the intelligent faculty should be rendered more comprehensive." I shall fail in rehearsing some things correctly, no doubt; but it shall not be wilfully, or from intention.

Most likely I shall become tedious to some readers when I am gratifying myself most fully. But any reader who is displeased with my narrative can pass over the pages in which he feels no interest; or close the book and take to his daily broadsheet, if he prefers it.

I cannot despise the good old-established practice of autobiographers and all other biographers: that of commencing with the venerable theme of ancestry. What though a man cannot aver he believes himself to be descended, either in a right or a wrong line, from John of Gaunt, or William the Conqueror,—may not his parentage be named, however humble, if it be honest?

By my father's side, I am descended from Yorkshire Quakers. My father became fatherless when he was a boy; and his Quaker grandfather apprenticed him to a dyer in Long Acre. His youth being thus spent in London, and without parental guardianship, he gave up the strictness of life in which his childhood had been trained, and ceased to belong to the Society of Friends. He left England, and went to India, but soon returned, travelled about the kingdom practising his trade as a dyer, and became acquainted with my mother at Gainsborough, in the county of Lincoln.

My mother's race bore the old Saxon name of Jobson, and were small farmers and carriers in Lincolnshire; and some of them fishermen on the sea-coast.

I was born at Leicester, on the 20th of March, 1805; but my father was a wanderer by habit, if not by nature; and so I was removed to Exeter when I was little more than twelve months old. I fell into the Leate, a small tributary of the Exe, over which there was a little wooden bridge that led to my father's dye-house, on the day that I was two years old—and, as my mother always said, at the very hour that I was born, two years before. After being borne down the stream a considerable way, I was taken out, and supposed to be dead; but was restored by medical skill. It may seem strange to some who read this—but I remember, most distinctly and clearly, being led by the hand of my father, over St. Thomas's bridge, on the afternoon of that day. He bought me gingerbread from one of the stalls on the bridge; and some of the neighbours, who knew me, came and chucked me under the chin, and said, "How did you like it?—How did you fall in?—Where have you been to?" The circumstances are as vivid to my mind as if they only occurred yesterday.

A more pleasing remembrance is that of having being taken at five o'clock on Christmas-day morning to hear the great organ of St. Peter's Cathedral. I was not then three years old. And I remember, quite as well, how Mother Hundrell, the milkwoman, used to give me white bread thickly covered with cream; that delicious cream for which I often longed, years after, when I became a hungry, ragged boy, and was far away from bland Devonshire.

I learned to read, they said, almost without instruction; and at three years old I used to be set on a stool, in Dame Brown's school, to teach one Master Bodley, who was seven years old, his letters. At the same age I could repeat by heart several of the fables of Æsop—as they were called—contained in a little volume purchased by my father. I

3

possess the dear relic, though tattered and torn, and minus the title-page,—together with my father's old silver watch, the silver spoon he bought for me, at my birth—I don't think I was born with one in my mouth—and the darling little hammer he bought for me at Exeter, and with which I used to work, in my childish way, when tired of reading and rehearsing fables and other stories, and hearing my father rehearse his, in turn.

All this pleasant, sunny life of early childhood was soon to pass away. My mother became a widow when I was but four years old, and left grand old Exeter for her native Lincolnshire. She settled down at Gainsborough, close by the Trent, which there divides Lincolnshire from the county of Nottingham. At Gainsborough I remained till I was nearly nine-and-twenty years old, a period of nearly twenty-five years.

My mother took up the trade of a dyer, for she had learnt the "art and mystery" thoroughly from my father; and she was at that time very strong, and in the prime of life, being in her fortieth year. And the business of a dyer, as it was then practised, needed strength.

My earliest recollections of Gainsborough begin with my taking the small-pox, which I had so severely that I was blind nineteen days, was worn till the bones came through my skin, at the knees, hips, and elbows, (the scars are yet renewed!) and was thrice believed, for some moments, to be dead. Measles and scarlet fever came close upon my weak recovery from the more fell disease. A whole year was thus filled up with dread affliction; and at five years old, when I began to go out of doors a few paces, I felt—child though I was—the humbling change that had come over me. I was no longer saluted cheerfully and with a smile, as at Exeter; no longer flattered and called a "pretty boy." Some frowned, with sour-natured dislike, at my marred visage; while others looked pitiful, and said "Poor thing!"

Within doors, there was no longer a handsome room, the cheerful look of my father, and his little songs and stories. We had now but one chamber and one lower room; and the last-named was, at once, parlour, kitchen, and dye-house: two large coppers were set in one part of it; and my mother was at work, amidst steam and sweat, all the day long for half of the week, and on the other half she was as fully employed in "framing," ironing, and finishing her work. Yet for me she had ever words of tenderness. My altered face had not unendeared me to her. In the midst of her heavy toil, she could listen to my feeble repetitions of the fables, or spare a look, at my entreaty, for the figures I was drawing with chalk upon the hearthstone.

As soon as I was strong enough, I was sent to a dame's school, near at hand, kept by aged Gertrude Aram: "Old Gatty," as she was usually called. Her school-room—that is to say, the larger lower room of her two-storied cottage—was always full; and she was an expert and laborious teacher of the art of reading and spelling. Her knitting, too—for she taught girls as well as boys—was the wonder of the town. I soon became her favourite scholar, and could read the tenth chapter of Nehemiah, with all its hard names, "like the parson in the church,"—as she used to say,—and could spell wondrously.

I had very little play out of doors, for that year of dire diseases had rendered me a very weakly and ailing child. So my dear mother bought me penny story books, in store; and I used to complete my enjoyment of them by getting them by heart, and repeating them. And then I fell upon the project of drawing with slate and pencil; but became still more attached to cutting out shapes in paper. With a pair of scissors, I used often to work for hours, making figures of men, horses, cows, dogs, and birds.

On fine Sundays, my mother began to take me into the fields, and to Lea Plantation, to gather flowers, which we kept in water, and I could worship them for several days. And on rainy Sundays, my mother would unwrap from its careful cover a treasure which my father had bought, and which she took care to bring with her from Exeter—Baskerville's quarto Bible, valuable for its fine engravings from the old masters; and I was privileged to gaze and admire while she slowly turned over that superb store of pictures, and sometimes repeated what my father had said about them.

After the novelty of her starting as a dyer had worn off, my mother found her enterprise answer but poorly. The few pounds she possessed when she reached Gainsborough, had been expended in purchasing coppers, and having them set, and in other necessary outfits of her business; indeed, it had not been sufficient for these. She toiled hard to reduce the debt she had thus contracted; for she was not a woman to sink for lack of effort. Pasteboard boxes, made entirely by hand, were then in very general use both as small work-boxes among tradesmen's wives and daughters, and as larger conveniences for holding servant's clothes. My mother took up this manufacture, in addition to her business as a dyer. She went from door to door in the town to try to sell her boxes; but finding little encouragement she began to journey to the surrounding villages and farm-houses, carrying her burden—the smaller boxes within the large, often to the amount of twenty or thirty—on her head. When the village or hamlet was near, as were Lea, Bole, and Morton, I went with her.

I cannot forget what occurred one day when I was about six years old, and was accompanying my mother in one of these journeys. The rent was due, and our landlord was a hard man, and my poor mother had toiled for a fortnight to make up an extra lot of boxes. She, at length, set out for Lea, a village two miles off, to try to dispose of her manufacture. I trudged by her side, taking hold of her apron to enable me to keep up with her, as she walked stoutly but sadly on, with the burden on her head.

We were not half-way towards Lea, when we were met by Cammidge, a master chimney-sweeper, and his two apprentices bending under huge soot bags. He began to try to entice my mother into an agreement for me to be his apprentice, and took out two golden guineas from his purse and offered them to her. She looked anxiously at them, but shook her head, and looked at me with the tears in her eyes; and I clung tremblingly to her apron, and cried, "Oh, mammy, mammy! do not let the grimy man take me away!" "No, my dear bairn, he shall not," she answered; and away we went—leaving the chimney-sweep in a rage, swearing, and shouting after my mother that she was a fool, and he was sure to have me, sooner or later, for that she could not escape bringing herself and me to the workhouse. My mother never went thither, however; nor did she ever ask parish help to bring me up.

When my mother went on more distant journeys, I was left, for the day, in the care of such of the neighbours as would consent to have me. Two of these I well remember. One was old Will Rogers, who kept a lodging-house where small pedlars and beggars slept; and the other was Thomas Chatterton, a pensioned soldier, who had lost his eyesight in Egypt. Many fragments of the fairy, and witch, and ghost-stories, told by the beggars and wandering pedlars, remain in my memory; but I have a far more vivid recollection of the blind soldier's relations of the way in which he stepped out of the boat up to the waist in water, in the Bay of Aboukir, and how they charged the French with the bayonet, and under cover of the cannon from the ships drove the enemy back from the shore, and effected a triumphant landing.

When I was in my seventh year—that is to say, in the autumn of 1811—my mother had the courage to leave her small house in "Penny's Yard," as it was called, and remove into the long street of the town which runs parallel with the river Trent, and is called "Bridge Street."

CHAPTER II.
BOYHOOD: THOMAS MILLER: 1811— 1814.

AS our new house fronted the street, the boxes my mother made were exposed for sale in the little bow-window, and she had greater publicity for her dyeing business. The coppers were now set in a back room, and thus the front room was kept neat and clean. Our new habitation was one of the four, the back doors of which opened into a close square of small dwellings called "Sailors' Alley." In this square resided the mother of Thomas Miller. He was about two years younger than myself, but was stronger and healthier, and now became my playmate. We lived in the house in front of Sailors' Alley till January 1816; and Miller and I were more or less together daily, till that time.

On account of my feeble state of health, my mother ceased sending me to aged Gatty's school; and when I began to grow stronger, I felt unwilling to return to a dame's school. Besides, there was a report that a large new Free School was about to be built; and as Miller's mother purposed sending him thither, my mother also had me placed on the list of applicants to be scholars. The school was not opened till August, 1813; but in the meantime I was sent to the Methodist Sunday school. My mother had frequently taken me with her to the Methodist chapel, from the time that I was able to walk about, after that year of diseases; but now I was taken with the other Sunday scholars, regularly, to the chapel, on Sunday mornings. I can recall the face and figure and manner of the preachers I heard in those very early years: quaint-looking Joseph Pretty; and gentlemanly John Doncaster; and young, dry, solemn-looking and solemn preaching Isaac Keeling—(he was equally dry when he was old, but 'he had a rare canister of brains,' as an old, intelligent Methodist used to say of him); and *young*, fervid, and seemingly-inspired John Hannah; and hearty, plain, original, and often-eccentric John Farrar.

When the new Free School opened, I had to leave the Methodist Sunday School, for my mother had succeeded in getting me made a

"Bluecoat" scholar; and boys on that foundation were compelled to attend the parish church twice on Sundays. Miller, I may observe, was not a Bluecoat, but a "White Hart" boy. These were the names of two charities left by deceased Gainsborough gentry, for the education of poor children. Bluecoat boys were allowed a coat and cap, blue with yellow trimmings, yearly. White Hart boys had simply their education.

The system of Bell and Lancaster, or the 'monitorial,' was pursued in the new school; and the course of instruction was limited to reading the Scriptures, writing, and the first four rules of arithmetic, simple and compound. Our frequent practice in spelling, and the working, over and over, of the four introductory rules of arithmetic, formed at least, a good preparation for larger acquirements. I liked the school, and, above all, I liked the grand organ at the church, the stately church itself, and the stately service.

The day after Christmas Day was a high day with us as Bluecoat boys. We then received our yearly new coat and cap, at the house of Dr. Parnell. "Gervase Parnell, Esquire," was his full name and title; and a finer specimen of the old-fashioned gentleman, with powdered head and tail, and his gold-headed cane, you would nowhere see. When we had received our new dresses at his house, he presented us with twopence each; and then away we went in procession to collect our "Christmas-boxes." We used to begin with Mr. Sandars, the corn-merchant, whose house was nearest the bridge; and then went through the town to Morton, calling at the houses of the merchants and gentry, whose names of Furley, and Etherington, and Torr, and Morehouse, and Barnard, and Garfitt, and Flowers, and Coats, and Metcalfe, and Smith, and Dealtry, and Brightmore, are far more familiar to me, now sixty years have passed away, since I first knew them, than any names that I learned but yesterday. Our last call in the town was upon the Rev. Mr. Fothergill, the vicar; and then away we went to Morton, and from Morton we sped away to Thonock Hall, the seat of old Miss Hickman, the lady of the manor, and heiress of Sir Neville George Hickman, Bart.

Money was always given to us, and, at some houses, bread and cheese and beer. I cannot say we always shared alike in what was thus kindly given; for I remember how, one severe snowy season, the big lads who carried the money-box persuaded some of us, who were weak and shivering with cold, to go home with a very few halfpence each, while they went on, and roguishly kept the larger share of the money for themselves. Fear of punishment, however, usually kept the big lads tolerably honest.

Twice in the year, Easter and Michaelmas, we were examined in our catechism by the vicar, preparatory to repeating it in the church, in presence of the congregation. We had given us a shilling, each, on these occasions, and always received smiles and kind words from the vicar. I well remember that we all esteemed Doctor Parnell and Parson Fothergill, with their grand powdered heads, and stately bearing, to be the two most veritable and genuine gentlemen in Gainsborough, albeit some wicked people said of the reverend vicar, that he was the best judge of the quality of a bottle of port, the best hand at loo or whist, and the best patron of the play and the ball-room, in the whole town. His curate, Mr. Pridham, was a stern Evangelical, and preached openly against the vicar's tastes, without naming him; but the vicar let the curate preach on, year after year, without remonstrance, and without forsaking his own favourite habits.

One little step of preferment that I obtained during the last year I was a Bluecoat boy, was a source of both pride and pleasure. I was chosen, with half a dozen other boys, to join the choir in the church; and my place was now no longer on the low benches in the middle aisle, but in the church gallery, close to the organ. I could thus see the large church organ played, as well as hear it ; and how I wondered at the changing face of the organist, young Mr. Hand—a great musical enthusiast—as he touched the keys! The other boys laughed at him—but I could not.

My preferment to the singing-loft had a more important result. It brought to our house the father of the organist, old Mr. Hand, a gentlemanly person, though he had a wooden leg. He was a great player on the dulcimer. The instrument was soon brought to our house; and I became so enamoured of it, that my mother eventually purchased it for thirty shillings. A few lessons, by the ear, I had from the old gentleman; and soon was able to play, by the ear, any tune I knew, or heard sung or played in the street. How often I have wished that the dulcimer had been a violin, or a pianoforte, and that I had been taught music by the notes,—had been taught to read music at that age. Such wishes are vain; but I have them, and of various forms.—"Oh that I had been trained to music—or painting—or law—or medicine—or any profession in which mind is needed; or that I had been regularly educated, so that I might have reached a University!"—I say, I often catch myself at these wishes still—even at sixty-six; but they are not so fervent as they were some years ago—for I remember that life here will soon end with me.

I have many pleasant remembrances of the time that we lived in the house in front of Sailor's Alley. Miller—my close companion—began, like myself, to cut shapes in paper, and to draw and colour. Our greatest incitement to drawing was the exhibition of pictures on the outside of the wild-beast shows at the Mart—a festival which occurs at Gainsborough twice in the year, Easter and Michaelmas. To run and look at these pictures, and come home, and imitate the figures of elephants, lions, tigers, leopards, zebras, and gorgeously-coloured tropical birds, formed a busy occupation for Miller and myself, during each Mart week; and to copy and improve upon our pictures was an enthusiastic employment for many weeks after.

These years—from 1811 to 1814—were among the hottest of the war period. And while our little town was kept in perpetual ferment by the news of battles, and the street would be lined with people to see old Matthew Goy, the postman, ride in with his hat covered with ribbons, and blowing his horn mightily, as he bore the news of some fresh victory,—Ciudad Rodrigo, or Badajoz, or Salamanca, or Vittoria, or St. Sebastian, or Toulouse,—Miller and I were pencilling soldiers and horses, or, imaginarily, Wellington and 'Boney'—for we never heard the word "Napoleon," at that time of day.

For our animal-drawing, we had another stimulus, in aged Abraham Haxby, who lodged with Miller's mother, and who had, in his youth, been a soldier in the war against the Dutch, in India. He used to tell us most delectable tales about elephants and tigers; nor were his descriptions of guavas, bananas, figs, jacks, and cashew-apples— your hat full for the value of a farthing!—less delicious. Miller and I often vowed we would go to that grand fruit country when we grew to be men!

Another companion was Job Holland. Job was a very simple, honest, good-natured lad, older than myself, and had no taste congenial with mine, save that of bird-nesting. Indeed, it was Job who taught me to love that delightful recreation; delightful, not so much for itself, as for the adventures and wanderings connected with it. With Job, and soon with others, I rambled over every field and lane, hill and wood, within three miles of Gainsborough. Saturday afternoons, and the long evenings in the season, were usually devoted to these rambles, except when my mother restrained me.

From George Wimble, whose father was a fisherman and herb-gatherer, I learned the names of agrimony, and wood-betony, and wood-sage, and mountain-flax, and centaury, and other herbs which were to be found in the neighbourhood, and were used as medicines, by the poor. But I often longed to know the names of flowers, which none could tell; for I gathered, fondly, every wild-flower in its season—a delicious pleasure, which, thank God! is fresh with me still, now age is reached, and I am familiar with the forms and know the names of every English flower.

In the autumn season, two or three weeks of gleaning holidays were usually granted to the Free School children. These weeks I usually spent at Market Rasen, a small town in Lindsey, twenty-one miles from Gainsborough, with my uncle, Luke Jobson, my mother's brother. He rented some twenty-four acres of land, under Squire Tennyson of Tealby; and also followed the occupation of a weekly carrier, as did his father, Luke Jobson, before him—his father, Luke Jobson, whose father Henry Jobson, was an innkeeper at

Northampton. I can go no higher with my genealogy on the maternal side.

How vividly the picture of my uncle Luke's large thatched cottage, at Market Rasen, remains in my memory! The outer room had a wide open chimney. My uncle's arm-chair was under it, and you could see the swallows' nests in the chimney, as you sat in the chair. On the chimney-front hung a curious old picture, painted on oak— displaying a cat playing bagpipes to dancing mice, in one corner, and a gamester, shaped like an ape, playing at cards with clowns, in another. Above was the legend:—

"Gamesters and puss alike doe watch,
And plaie with those they aime toe catch."

In the inner room, or parlour, was a heavy antique clock; and on the walls hung the "Twelve Golden Rules of Good King Charles," and "Death and the Lady," a long, serious dialogue in verse.

In my uncle's fields, and on the adjoining moors, I saw wild birds, and wild four-footed creatures in abundance; weasels, ferrets, fomarts, moles, hedgehogs, were often taken, and owls and hawks shot. The kestrel often hovered overhead; and now and then the glede, or kite, would soar aloft. The country was wilder at that time of day; and, of course, fuller of interest to me, in the centre of Lindsey, than it was at the Trent border.

The ride in the carrier's cart, too, between Rasen and Gainsborough, had its delights. One time, we set off from Rasen late at night, and drew up in an open field, sometime before the morning broke, to let the horses graze a little. I have a most lively recollection of awaking in the cart, and looking out in amazement at what seemed to be hundreds of small, dull, strange-looking lights, scattered over the wide field. My uncle told me they were glowworms; and he had never seen so many together before. Nor have I ever had such a vision of wonder as that, since boyhood.

Each Friday in the week—the day that my uncle came to Gainsborough as weekly carrier—I was closely attendant upon him, when school hours were over, having to read the directions on his letters and parcels—for he was never put to school; and to his dying day "Knew never a letter i' the book, save round O," as he used to say. He made much of me (I again use the old Lincolnshire language, for I love it!); always gave me a few coppers for my writing paper, lead pencils, and water-colours; and, indeed, showed every disposition to indulge me. I thus became greatly attached to him; and to the present moment regard his memory—plain, unlettered man, though he was— with fondest affection. I think I ought not to dismiss his humble name without saying that in his manhood he was strong and handsome, and was a pattern of industry. He had contrived to hoard up three hundred spade-ace guineas in a stocking-foot; but from illness in the close of life did not advance in wealth, yet he left a small property to be divided by his heirs.

My mention of the strange vision of the field of glowworms reminds me of another natural phenomenon I witnessed when a boy. I saw a shower of live frogs. I record this, because I have read, not only in that beautiful old book of Ray's, "The Wisdom of God in the Creation," but in later books affecting great fidelity to facts in science, that such a sight is impossible. I am as sure of what I relate as I am of my own existence. The minute frogs, jumping alive, fell on the pavement at our feet, and came tumbling down the spouts from the tiles of the houses into the water-tubs.

CHAPTER III.
BOYHOOD: GAINSBOROUGH MEMORIES: 1814-1816.

THE happiest hours of all I had in early years were spent alone, and with books. When childhood was past, and I ceased to feel so much absorbed in the Fables, and little story books, the immortal "Pilgrim's Progress" was my book of books. What hours of wonder and rapture I passed with Bunyan when a boy! He was always new; and though a "numberman," or travelling-bookseller, kindly left me his curiosities, now and then, because my eagerness interested him, I returned with increased relish to Christian and Faithful, Great Heart and Giant Despair, after reading odd numbers of Baines's "History of the War," and "Pamela," and "The Earl of Moreland;" and the stories of Turpin and Nevison, the famous highwaymen, and Bampfylde Moore-Carew, the King of the Gipsies.

The first rhymes that I can remember to have read with a sense of delight were those of the old ballad of Chevy Chase. I used to repeat them, when alone, until they used to make me feel as warlike as did the sight of Matthew Goy when he rode into the town with the news of a victory; or the array of the Gainsborough Loyal Volunteers, when they marched through the town, on exercise-days, to the sound of fife and drum.

Talking again of the War, reminds one, naturally, that it was followed by the Peace. The Peace of 1814—"the General Peace," as it was emphatically, called, was celebrated in ambitious style at Gainsborough. There was a general holiday; and there was a grand emblematical procession. A car, drawn by six horses, held figures representing Wellington, Blucher, Platoff, the Czar Alexander, and other high personages, together with the fallen emperor labelled "Going to Elba." There were bands of music in the streets, a thanksgiving sermon and anthems at church, and feasting parties at the inns, during the day; with a general illumination, bonfires, crackers, and squibs, at night.

The next day, Miller and I laid our young heads together, and enlisted Bob Mason, and Tom Aram, and George Laister, and Joe Cawthrey, and Joe Carver, and Bill Tyson, and Jack Barton, and George Wimble, and other lads we knew, to accompany us on an adventurous expedition to Lea. Papers were coloured and inscribed, and ribbons procured, and flags formed; and away we went to Lea, to try our fortunes. I was" Wellington," and was so labelled on the front of my blue cap; and Miller was "Emperor of Russia;" and Mason was "Blucher; " and Jack Bafton was "Prince Platoff;" and Joe Cawthrey was "General Salt" (Soult was always so named, in our hearing); and Tom Aram (dear old Gatty's grandson) was "Buonaparte" (for, as I said before, we knew nothing of the name "Napoleon"); and the other lads were named after other military or regal celebrities.

We went to Squire Western's, and Farmer Swift's, and Farmer Ashford's, and Mr. Longden's, and Sir Charles Anderson's; stood and sung "Awake, my soul, and with the sun," and "Glory to Thee, my God, this night," and other hymns we had learned at school, or in the church; gave three cheers, after shouting "Peace and Plenty! God save the King!" as we had heard them shout on the procession-day; and then one of us held his cap for coppers, with a low bow. We were well received. The beloved and venerated Sir Charles himself stood and smiled to hear us; and called us "very good boys," as he gave us a real silver half-crown! Many a time, in after-life, has some old playmate pleasurably reminded me of our boyish expedition to Lea, to celebrate the General Peace.

Bob Mason was a lad to whom Tom Miller and I were much attached; and yet he was utterly unlike either of us. Tom and I were all for learning, and excitement, and for doing something to win fame; but Bob, from a child, was for trying to get money. I well remember the talk he raised in the town, and the wonder in our boyish circle, by one feat. Bob crept about the wharves by the Trent, picking up rags, bones, and bits of old iron to sell, until he became possessed of fourpence. He then begged his passage to Hull, a distance of fifty miles, in the sailing packet of that day; bought a bag of cockles with the fourpence, begged his passage (and the carriage of the cockles) back to Gainsborough; borrowed a wheelbarrow and a quartern "skep," or measure, hawked his cockles about the town for sale, and realized half-a- crown! Bob could not be nine years old at that time, for he was younger than Miller or myself.

Dear Bob! I remember well how our friendship suffered a lapse by an unlucky incident. During a heavy snow season, I had made a large snow man, in Sailor's Alley, and he mischievously attempted to demolish it; when I suddenly struck him with a shovel I had in my hand, and with which I had been eagerly labouring. He received the blow on his forehead, which immediately streamed with blood; and I threw down the shovel, and grew sick with alarm, while neighbours ran out and clamorously threatened me with imprisonment and the gallows, and I know not what. Poor Bob's head was bound up for a week; and I remained in great trouble, and wept daily in repentance and fear till he grew well.

I had deeper troubles than this, let me say, during these years of boyhood, notwithstanding their many pleasant recollections. My dear mother had all along hard work to get a decent living, and pay her way. Rent, and taxes, bad harvests and dear bread, rendered it difficult for her to make a livelihood. At one time wheaten flour rose to six shillings per stone, and we tried to live on barley cakes, which brought on a burning, gnawing pain at the stomach. For two seasons the corn was spoiled in the fields, with wet; and, when the winter came, we could scoop out the middle of the soft, distasteful loaf; and to eat it brought on sickness. Meat was so dear that my mother could not buy it; and often our dinner consisted of potatoes only. We were glad, indeed, when, in the dreadful winter of 1813-14, Mr. Maw, Mr. Bowen, Mr. Palian, and a few other benevolent Quakers, started a subscription, which was joined by the gentry and wealthier tradesmen; and soup, biscuits, potatoes, and red-herrings, were served out, gratuitously, twice or thrice a week to the poor.

There was a tax-gatherer, too, at that time, who had a bad reputation for oppressing the poor, by going beyond the rigour of the law; and for lawless connection with women whom, it was said, he favoured, in advising the Parish Vestry to make them improper sharers in various old charities. This oppression was often spoken of very bitterly by my mother and Miller's mother, as we heard them whispering of his temptations, while they sat with their pipes at the fire. Miller's mother had seen better circumstances; but she was now a widow, and had to sew sacks for Brumby's factory. She worked early and late for bread for herself and her two boys; but would run in now and then, at the back door, and join my mother for a few whiffs at the pipe. And then away they would go again to work, after cheering each other to go stoutly through the battle of life.

They bent their wits, on one occasion, to disappoint the tax-gatherer. He was to "distrain" on a certain day; but beds, chairs, and tables, were moved secretly in the night to blind Thomas Chatterton's; and when the tax-gatherer came next day to execute his threat, there was nothing left worth his taking. The poor were often driven to such desperate schemes to save all they had from ruin, in those days; and the curse upon taxes and the tax-gatherer was in the mouths of hundreds—for those years of war were terrific years of suffering for the poor, notwithstanding their shouts and rejoicings when Matthew Goy rode in, with ribbons flying, bringing the news of another "glorious victory!"

Sometimes Miller's mother and mine were excused paying some of the taxes by appealing to the magistrates, a few of whom respected them for their industry, and commiserated their hardships. But the petition did not always avail. Sir Charles Anderson of Lea, William Hutton, Esq., of Gate Burton, and Gervase Woodhouse, Esq., of Owston, were protectors of the poor; but the other magistrates were inexorable in enforcing the law, and the letter of it. One can scarcely wonder at this, considering how heavy the pressure of taxes must have been in those expensive years; and how loudly some would have complained if all were not constrained to join in bearing the burden of war.

My poor mother waged war stoutly with difficulties during these years. She not only made rounds with her boxes to the surrounding villages, but walked weekly with them to the market at Epworth, in the Isle of Axholme, where she also took in goods to dye. I began now to go longer journeys with her; and twice or thrice, during fine weather, she took me all the way to Epworth—a distance of twelve miles; and a journey of wonders it seemed to me, for we had to cross the river Trent in the ferry-boat, at Stockwith, and to walk some miles along the bank of the river; and we saw sea-gulls, and a heron—a something to talk of!

I cannot dismiss this part of my boyish history without recording a few other reminiscences of that glorious Trent. I and my young companions used sometimes to bathe, not in the wide stream, but in a little arm of it, at Ash Croft, a part of the marsh called Humble Carr, in which lies "Can'dish Bog," the spot where Cromwell pistolled young Colonel Cavendish, and beat his troop. The young royalist hero has a monument, with a stone lion at his feet, in the neighbouring little church at Lea. I was ever a timid bather, and never learned to swim; but I remember how cheerily and boldly many of the boys took to the water, and how the greater number of these became sailors.

The shipping-trade of Gainsborough was great at that time. There was not a busier scene on a small scale in England, than the loading and unloading of vessels on the Trent in those years. Numerous large brigs, and many sloops and keels, with a great number of "ketches," or flat-bottomed boats from Staffordshire, crowded the river. Sailors enlivened the streets of the little town by their merriment; and the whole living appearance of the town presented a very pleasing contrast to the dulness and desertion of trade which have characterised it since railways destroyed the trade on the river.

The "Heygre" was our great excitement on the Trent. It used to be a very stirring sight when the tide was at the full. The huge rolling waves then dashed the shipping from their moorings, if they were not well moored and managed; and boats were often crushed to pieces. The capture of porpoises on the river sometimes raised a crowd on the banks and at the wharves, to see the sailors signalise their courage and activity. But the most striking incident, in my recollection, connected with the Trent, was the breaking-up of the ice, after the thirteen weeks' frost, in 1814, during which waggons loaded with coal had been drawn over the ice, and a bullock roasted on it. The breaking-up came in a moment, and shook the town. For a whole day and night, the broken pieces of thick ice rushed through the arches of the bridge, putting people in fear that the whole structure would give way; and, with the roar of thunder, the ice tore away past the town, driving many a stout vessel from its moorings and dashing many a small boat to pieces! And then came the great flood which extended for miles over the marshes, and covered that part of the street in which we lived for two or three weeks—during which time Miller and I had a constrained holiday, and drew on paper the men and boats, as we looked out of our chamber window, for the lower floors were all flooded.

The last incidents which have left their pictures in my memory, connected with our house in front of Sailors' Alley, are the return of sailors from service in the navy to their wives and families, and their stories of the press-gang, and life on board "men of war," as the huge ships were called; the coming home of soldiers, also, from the war; and, in the beginning of 1815, the curious exhibition of Martin Jackson, a half-lunatic, who went through the streets with a helmet on his head, and a piebald dress, on which were fastened papers, inscribed, "No Corn Bill!" While remembering his odd, threatening gestures and his broken talk about "Parliament House" and "Lunnon," it was some years before I gathered the fact that Martin Jackson was making a demonstration against the infliction of the Bread Tax. Plain Gainsborough folk understood little about politics at that time; but I remember that some shook their heads shrewdly, and said "Martin is right, in spite of all his craziness! "

In the same eventful year, there arose the cry of "The Devil is broke loose!" Napoleon left Elba—re-won the French throne—lost all at Waterloo—and was finally exiled to St. Helena. An important change came over our humble fortunes. Our house had become the property of a new landlord. He determined to pull it down and build a better; and so my mother had to prepare to quit.

CHAPTER IV.
BOYHOOD: SCHOOL-DAYS ENDED: 1816—1820.

TO avoid the payment of a high rent and of heavy taxes, my mother again withdrew from the public street, and retired into the obscurity of Old George Yard. She found a large empty stable, in which there was a good well; and as plenty of water was such a desideratum in her dyeing business, she bargained with the landlord of the stable to have it transformed half into a dye-house, and half into a rude dwelling-house. The bricklayers and joiners went to work; and the place was ready for our tenancy by the middle of January, 1816.

We were now within a few yards of a popular day-school for boys, kept by John Briggs, and which was chiefly patronised by tradesmen and better-paid workmen. I had grown weary of the monotonous teaching at the Free School; so my mother readily consented to my leaving it and entering the neighbouring day-school. Here there was no longer the bare routine of the four fundamental rules of arithmetic. There were big lads who had advanced to "Mensuration," in Bonnycastle's book. The new master tried my powers as a cipherer, and decided that I should begin with "Reduction," in Walkinghame's "Tutor's Assistant."

I remained with dear Daddy Briggs from May 1816 to May 1820. He took no school-fees of my mother, but employed me as an assistant, for about an hour each day, in teaching the younger children. He treated me less as a pupil than as a companion; and I became much attached to him. Yet he was never, really, a teacher to me. I made my way, easily, without help, through Walkinghame, part of Bonnycastle, and got a little way into Algebra before I left school. But the chief advantage I derived from Daddy Briggs's school was in being introduced to the companionship of lads of better culture than I had known before, and in obtaining the loan of their books to read—their Enfield's Speaker, and Mayor's British Plutarch, and the abridgment of Goldsmith's Histories of England, Greece, and Rome. And then, in addition to their school books, one boy had a "Robinson Crusoe," and another possessed "Philip Quarll," and another had "Salmon's Geography," containing the Lord's Prayer in thirty languages. Here was a world of new reading and new information!

The number-man began also to intimate that the bookselling firm he represented were printing an improved order of books. So I soon had the reading of Barclay's quarto Dictionary—or such parts of it as were readable; of Kelly's quarto Geography; and my mother took in, in numbers, "Dialogues between a Pilgrim, Adam, Noah, and Cleophas."

Soon I found, too, in going to buy my pencils and water-colours at Mrs. Trevor's, that she kept a circulating library; and from her shelves I drew the enchanting "Arabian Nights," and odd plays of Shakspeare, Dryden, and Otway, and Cook's Voyages, and the Old English Baron; and the Castle of Otranto, and Guiscard; and the Bravo of Venice; and Hardenbras and Haverill; and Valentine's Eve; and the Castles of Athlin and Dunbayne; and the Scottish Chiefs— and a heap of other romances and novels that would require pages even to name.

The visit to Gainsborough of Moses Holden, of Preston, to deliver lectures on astronomy, was a memorable event to me. I cannot remember who gave me the sixpence which enabled me to hear the first lecture; but I recollect that I drew out the figures of the zodiacal constellations, and of the solar system, and coloured them by memory, from the exhibition of Mr. Holden's orrery,—went round the neighbourhood, and showed them, and obtained pennies plenty to enable me to hear the remaining lectures. This was in my twelfth year.

I had no means for getting much enlargement of the elementary knowledge of astronomy thus obtained; and I was easily misled, by a notable old man of the name of Charles White, but who was more commonly known among the poor as the "Wise Man of Retford," to turn aside into the devious paths of astrology. He lent me a book or two, and talked so mysteriously of the "higher knowledge" he possessed above that contained in the books, that I became eager to learn it. Fortunately, he passed away; and I was weaned from the foolish passion for a time.

Save that childish enthusiasm I had felt while reciting "Chevy Chase," I do not remember that poetry really touched any chord in my nature, until, in my thirteenth year, by some accident there fell into my hands one of the cantos of "Childe Harold's Pilgrimage" and the drama of "Manfred." I had them in my hands for only a few hours, and I knew nothing of their noble author's life or reputation; but they seemed to create almost a new sense within me. I wanted more poetry to read from that time; but could get hold of none that thrilled through my nature like Byron's. I had read the "Paradise Lost;" but it was above my culture and learning, and it did not make me feel, though I read it with interest, as a mere story.

What strange mixtures there are in the experience of some of us! During these years I was still practising drawing, and playing my dulcimer, and gathering flowers, and trying to find out their names by Culpepper's Herbal, and reading anything and everything I could lay hold of; and in addition to all these, I was becoming thoroughly impregnated with the spirit of Radicalism. There was a shop of brush-makers very near to us, and they were most determined politicians. They read "The News"—the most radical paper of that day; and they were partisans of Cobbett and Wooler and Hunt; and they used to lend me Hone's Caricatures; and "The News," weekly, and talk to me of the "villanous rascals," Lord Castlereagh, and Lord Sidmouth, and Lord Eldon, and the Prince Regent, until I hated the Liverpool Ministry, and its master, bitterly, and believed that the sufferings of the poor were chiefly attributable to them.

Another change was at hand, and it was a signal one. It cannot be supposed that, with a nature so emotional as mine, I had listened to the earnest prayers of my teachers in the Methodist Sunday School, and joined in the singing so delightedly, both in church and chapel, and heard sermons, without having religious impressions. From a child I felt these. Often, during our reading of the gospels, verse by verse, as we stood in class, at the Free School, the Saviour seemed almost visible to me as I read of His deeds of mercy and love. The singing of our morning and evening hymns, and repetition, on our knees, of the Lord's prayer, had always a solemnizing effect upon me. And, doubtless, seeds of spiritual good were sown thus early in my mind, never to be really destroyed.

But it was not until my fourteenth year that I was strongly impressed with the necessity of repentance and forgiveness of sin. One Sunday morning, I ran out, with a crowd of the neighbours, to hear two men who were singing aloud as they walked along the street, in their way to the market-place,—"Turn to the Lord and seek salvation!" They were called "Ranters," by the crowd; but I soon learned that they termed themselves "Primitive Methodists." These men remained in the town for some weeks, and preached in the open air, and held meetings in houses; and the crowd, young and old, were greatly affected. Soon a society was formed, and they began regularly to preach in the very small chapel which John Wesley himself caused to be built, in a small square, in Little Church Lane; but which had been occupied as a warehouse for some time.

I became a member of the society, in company with at least a dozen other lads, some of whom were older and some younger than myself. I cannot describe my anguish and sorrow for sin. And, apparently, it was an equally serious case with each of the lads. My grief continued for many weeks, until I could find no delight in my books, or drawing, or dulcimer, and could read nothing but the Bible, and was getting into secret places twenty times in a day, to pray for the pardon of my sins.

Many loudly earnest preachers came and preached in the little chapel; and prayer-meetings were prolonged till midnight, often. And many upgrown sinners professed to find the pardon of their sins. The change of heart and life was real in some. I remember well an elderly man, an inveterate cockfighter, being humbled, and becoming a true penitent. This man lived, for many years afterwards, a consistent Christian life. Nor was his case a solitary one. On the other hand, there were some fearful backslidings.

Some of the boys, at length, professed to find the pardon of sin. For a day or two, I believed I had received it; but as I felt conscious that I sinned, I supposed I must "act faith," as they said, to find it again. And this "acting of faith" became, in the course of some weeks, so irksome to my mind, that my mere common sense revolted at the practice. We were told to "believe"; but I understood the teaching to mean that we were to believe ourselves into the persuasion that we were forgiven; and I could not avoid the conviction that this was not receiving pardon by the witness of the Holy Spirit—but pardoning ourselves.

So I began to grow weary of creeping into corners twenty times in a day to repent for sin—for I thought I was always sinning—and of believing myself again forgiven. I shrunk from the practice, at last, in sheer disgust; but neither did that bring ease of mind. I began, gradually, to get back to my music and my reading; but some of the members of the Society—poor men who knew little of books, but who found happiness in prayer, and in hearing others read and preach about the goodness of God—demurred to my reading any book but the Bible, unless it was a "truly religious book." My mind rebelled completely now; and I ceased to frequent the little chapel, and began to go to the Methodist (Wesleyan) chapel instead, where I listened to the argumentative preaching of Thomas Ingham, and the warm, genial discourses of William Stokes.

In March, 1820, I was fifteen years old, and had not left Briggs's school. My mother had tried, at my entreaty, to get me apprenticed to a painter, and had endeavoured to get me entered as a clerk at one or other of the merchants' establishments; but in every case a premium was demanded, and my poor mother had none to give. I became really uneasy, at last. The neighbours "told their minds" to my mother, saying she would make me a good-for-nothing, idle creature; and why did she not apprentice me to some humble trade? And then they looked bitter things at myself.

I had one dear companion in the school, Henry Cook, who was a born sailor—if there ever were one; and Henry began to say to me, "Go to sea! I shall. You say you mean to see all the foreign countries in the world. That's the easiest way to see 'em all. Be a sailor; and then you can sail round the world, like Captain Cook." I asked my mother if I might be a sailor; but she told me I must not think of it. The neighbours, however, caught hold of what I had said; and they harassed my mother with the proposal till she said I might go.

Henry Cook's father had a friend who wanted a cabin-boy; and so I left my broken-hearted mother, and went down in the packet to Hull, to go on board the brig which lay in the harbour. I was on board nine days, while they were loading with corn and other merchandise. The coarse language, the cursing and swearing, and brutality, I witnessed day after day, not only on board the brig, but on the other vessels that were crowded around us, rendered me so wretched that I told the master of the vessel I wished to go home. He told me, in profane terms, that I might go, for I should never be fit to be a sailor.

So I found my way home again, to the weeping delight of my dear mother. But the old difficulty stared us in the face the very next day. Indeed, my own position was more uneasy than ever. The neighbours began to mock at me, and scout me for a coward. Many of them had relatives at sea; and was I made of something more than flesh and blood that I could not go to sea?

One day in June, I met Tom Aram in the street. He had become a shoemaker's apprentice, he said; and he liked his place much, and they wanted another lad—Would I come? Tom was an old crony, for he was dear old Gatty's grandson, as I said before; and we had known each other from the time that we were four years old. I told him I would ask my mother.

She seemed hurt by the proposal. She had witnessed all my tendencies from my infancy, and had fostered and cherished all the buddings of intelligence, and formed a very different ideal for her child's future than that of his becoming a lowly labourer with the awl. But I entreated her to yield to me, and told her I could not endure the daily torment of being pointed at as an idle good-for-nothing. At last she yielded—saying, "The Lord's will be done! I don't think He intends thee to spend thy life at shoemaking. I have kept thee at school, and worked hard to get thee bread, and to let thee have thy own wish in learning, and never imagined that thou wast to be a shoemaker. But, the Lord's will be done! He'll bring it all right in time."

So on the 10th of June, 1820, I sat down, in Clark's garret, to begin to learn the art, craft, and mystery of shoemaking.

CHAPTER V.
SHOEMAKER LIFE: EARLY FRIENDSHIPS: 1820-1824.

JOSEPH CLARK, with whom Aram and I sat in the garret, to be taught shoemaking, was a lively young fellow of four-and-twenty, who had been in London for improvement, and had returned to his native town to conduct business for his widowed mother. His residence in London had given him some degree of polish, and also given him a passion for the theatre. I was a favourite with him, at once; and the favouritism was so injudicious that Aram was disgusted, and ran away to sea. I remained little more than a year with Clark; for he was capricious in temper, and would almost smother me with kindness for some weeks, and the following month treat me haughtily.

He was useful to me, however, in other directions than in teaching me the use of the awl. He had read some of the poetry of Byron, spoke of it passionately, and lent me the poems of Burns. The pathos of Burns took possession of my whole nature almost as completely as the fire and force of Byron. I soon learned to sing "Ye banks and braes o' bonny Doon," and "Auld lang syne," and "Robin Adair;" and formed tunes of my own for some of the songs—such as "Their groves o' green myrtle" and "Awa wi' your witchcraft o' beauty's alarms."

Clark also rehearsed to me what he had seen and heard of London actors, and repeated the criticisms of the Londoners on the personations of Shakspere's characters by Kemble and Young and Mrs. Siddons, and later performers. All this directed me to a more intelligent reading of Shakspeare, for myself; though I did not yet feel the due impression of his greatness. My first poem—for it was sure to come, sooner or later—seemed almost to make itself, one evening, as I walked in the valley below Pingle Hill. I give it here, be it remembered, as the first literary feat of a self-educated boy of fifteen. I say self-educated, so far as I was educated. Mine has been almost entirely self-education, all the way through life.

A MORNING IN SPRING.

See, with splendour, Phoebus rise,
And with beauty tinge the skies.
See, the clouds of darkness fly
Far beyond the western sky;
While the lark upsoaring sings,
And the air with music rings;
While the blackbird, linnet, thrush,
Perched on yonder thorny bush,
All unite in tuneful choir,
And raise the happy music higher.
While the murmuring busy bee,
Pattern of wakeful industry,
Flies from flower to flower to drain
The choicest juice from sweetest vein;
While the lowly cottage youth,
His mind well-stored with sacred truth,
Rises, devout, his thanks to pay,
And hails the welcome dawn of day.
Oh that 'twere mine the happy lot,
To dwell within the peaceful cot—
There rise, each morn, my thanks to pay,
And hail the welcome dawn of day!

From that time forth I often struck off little pieces of rhyme, and made attempts at blank verse; but all such doings were really worthless, and I kept no record of them.

I found that I must not expect any regular apprenticeship as a shoemaker; for Clark often quarrelled with his mother, and threatened to leave her, and go back to London. In one of his haughty fits, I took offence and left him. From about the age of sixteen and a half to seventeen, I sat and worked with another small master; and then, for another year, sat in a shop with others, and worked for the Widow Hoyle. My work, of course, was very imperfect; and so, when it was rumoured that "Don Cundell" had come to the town, and took young men under his instruction, I told my mother that I must become one of his pupils. "Don," in my time, was the title always given to a first-rate hand; and usually to one who was known to all the members of the trade who had "tramped," or travelled for improvement.

Under Don Cundell I learned to make a really good woman's shoe; but could not get any work from the best shops, because I had not served an apprenticeship to the trade. When Cundell left the town, I retired to a corner of my mother's humble house; and, as long as I continued at shoemaking, I worked for the Widow Hoyle, who sold her goods in the market, cheap, and therefore could only pay low wages. To the end of my short shoemaker's life, I could never earn more than about ten shillings weekly. But what glorious years were those years of self-denial and earnest mental toil, from the age of nearly nineteen to nearly three-and-twenty, that I sat and worked in that corner of my poor mother's lowly home! How I wish I could begin life anew, just at the end of them, and spend the after years more wisely!

But I am outrunning the dates of my story, and must go back. Soon after the age of fifteen, I formed the valuable friendship of Christopher Macdonald. He was several years older than myself, and was married. He was a Methodist; but he was a reader and a thinker, and, while he commended me for asserting my mental freedom, he directed my mind into more solid reading. He lent me Robertson's Histories of Scotland, America, and Charles the Fifth, and Neale's "History of the Puritans," and urged me to get a better acquaintance with theology; while he did not discourage my enthusiasm for the great poet of his fatherland, or for the Waverley Novels, with which I began now to get acquainted. Under his kindly influence, I continued to be an attendant on the Methodist ministry, and thus enjoyed the intelligent and deeply spiritual preaching of Laurence Kershaw. But my friend left Gainsborough; and I thus lost the benefit of his restraining, wise, and affectionate counsel.

Our little town was thrown into a most novel state of intellectual excitement, when I was in my seventeenth year, by a poetical war, about the propriety of singing a hymn to Arne's grand melody of

"Rule Britannia." The most classical combatant was a Unitarian and a schoolmaster; but the rhymester, who was the popular favourite, was Joseph Foulkes Winks, a draper's assistant, and son of a respectable tradesman of the town. When the rhyming rage cooled, Winks did not cool. He called together a number of friends and acquaintances, proposed that we should take the "Eclectic Review" and circulate it among ourselves; that we should form a "Mutual Improvement Society " for reading and discussion; and, above all, that we should be determined to establish an Adult School, on Sundays, for teaching the poor and utterly uneducated to read. Macdonald and I joined him in these enterprises; and so did Enoch Wood, a youth of about my own age, with whom I had often walked, arm in arm, to church, when we were Bluecoat boys. In my later life, I have seen Enoch's name, for many years, in the Methodist Minutes, as Dr. Enoch Wood, Superintendent of Canadian Missions.

The zeal and energy of Winks, in the conduct of that adult school, were very noble; and the school was instrumental in effecting a great deal of good. But when Winks left the town, the elder men who formed the committee decided to close the school, under the profession that they could not raise funds for the necessary expenses.

Our Mutual Improvement Society was also too short-lived; but its weekly meetings were valuable to me. It was, in reality, a little debating club, where the members were allowed to write and read their speeches on the question agreed upon the preceding week, or to speak off-hand. I never attempted to speak without preparation; but invariably read my essays. This weekly essay-writing was an employment which absorbed a good deal of my thought, and was a good induction into the writing of prose, and into a mode of expressing one's thoughts.

The adult school and the little debating society led to another friendship, which was the dearest of all my early friendships, but was severed, after a few years, by death. Henry Whillock was a grocer's apprentice in the town, and was remarkable for his refined and gentlemanly manners. He had been brought up as a dissenter; and was of serious and pious habits when we first became acquainted, as teachers in the adult school. But I soon found, to my delight, that he was a lover of poetry, and possessed "The Corsair," "Lara," and "The Bride of Abydos," and the very canto of "Childe Harold's Pilgrimage" I had formerly read; with "The West Indies," "Greenland," and other poems of James Montgomery.

Our friendship had become so strong, when the adult school was closed, and the Mutual Improvement Society had expired, and my good friend Macdonald had left the town, that we began to consider it a settled point that we should spend part of every Sunday together. If it were fine, we walked in the woods, or by the Trent; and if it were too cold to walk, we met in a small room belonging to one of the neighbours. Strangely enough, we both had dabbled in astrology in our boyhood, and we spoke of it, now, till we grew enamoured with the desire to prove the truth of it—which we thought was possible. Whillock's parents allowed him plenty of pocket-money; and he immediately expended, I think, two pounds, in the purchase of Sibley's famous quarto book, with plates, on Astrology and Divination.

And for many weeks, as regularly as the Sunday afternoon returned, we were seated in that little room, drawing of horoscopes, with the assistance of almanacs (White's "Ephemeris") and the "Table of Houses," and reading out of the pretentious volumes of Dr. Sibley, the opinions of the great sages of the science, the old alchemists, and Gadbury, and Lilly, and Booker, and the diviners of a later period. Our minglement of poetry with this strange study was but natural. The more important result was, that it led to conversations about religion and history; and brought us, at length, to the threshold of confession that we had been fools to spend our time and intelligence over Sibley's big books. So Whillock disposed of them, and purchased forty volumes of the English Essayists, and Langhorne's Plutarch; and we began to devote our Sunday afternoons to conversations on more rational themes, until at last, I fear, we began to be too rational. Elihu Palmer's "Principles of Nature," and a translation of Volney's "Ruins of Empires," and also a so-called translation of Voltaire's "Philosophical Dictionary," were offered to

Whillock by a travelling bookseller, very pressingly, and at low prices, one day, and he bought them.

Our curiosity was soon whetted; and we eagerly ran through the books. I do not think that Palmer's book took any hold of us. Its style of composition seemed stilted; and we thought, I remember, that he assumed certain heterodox conclusions, without proof. Neither did the other books make us unbelievers, in the usual sense of the word; but we began to conclude that there must be *some* fable, at least, in the Old Testament; that the exterminating wars of the Israelites could not have been commanded by Jehovah, nor all the deeds of the "Judges," and so on. We had grown very loose in our attendance on public worship; and now we gave it up altogether, and spent the greater part of each Sunday in earnest conversation.

I do not mean to indicate that our conversation now was wholly on subjects such as I have just mentioned. Far from it. We still exchanged thoughts on the history and poetry that we read, and showed to each other our attempts in rhyme and blank verse, and encouraged each other in the ambition and belief that we should run a successful career of authorship, as poets and prose-writers, in the years to come!

Henry Whillock's apprenticeship ended, he left Gainsborough, went to Nottingham, and put the little fortune he inherited into the bobbin-net trade—the new machinery for which manufacture had just then come into use, and was considered a sure way of making a large fortune—but soon lost his money. His correspondence with me suddenly ceased; and at the end of a few more months, I learned that he had died in London.

My friendship with Whillock had been the means of procuring me an introduction to one whose counsel was of far higher value to me, and whose intelligence was far superior to that of any acquaintanceship I had yet formed in the world. John Hough was a draper, had been married and fixed in business for a year or so when I first knew him, and was eight years older than myself. His father, Vincent Hough, was an old established tradesman in Gainsborough, and was one of the deacons of the Independent church. My new friend, therefore, had been brought up as a dissenter; and he had very decided views and opinions on nonconformity and dissent, while he was a strong partisan of Jonathan Edwards in doctrine. He was, however, a broad general reader, had an excellent library, and made me welcome to the loan of every book in it that I desired to read.

I had come to the knowledge that there was another great supply of old English literature which I could make use of. "Nathaniel Robinson, mercer," many years before, had left his library for the use of the inhabitants of the town; but it had been thrust aside into a corner, and almost forgotten. I was in ecstasies to find the dusty, cobwebbed shelves loaded with Hooker, and Bacon, and Cudworth, and Stillingfleet, and Locke, and Jeremy Taylor, and Tillotson, and Bates, and Bishop Hall, and Samuel Clarke, and Warburton, and Bull, and Waterland, and Bentley, and Boyle, and Ray, and Derham, and a score of other philosophers and divines,—mingled with Stanley's "History of Philosophers," and its large full-length portraits—Ogilvy's "Embassies to Japan and China," with their large curious engravings—Speed's and Rapin's folio histories of England—Collier's "Church History"—Fuller's "Holy War"—Foxe's "Book of Martyrs," the first edition, in black letter, and with its odd, rude plates—and countless other curiosities and valuables.

I must mention another little piece of good fortune that now befell me—although I was indebted for it partly to real kindness, and partly to a little roguery. The dear old lady, Mrs. Trevor, of whom I had purchased my lead pencils and water colours when a child, and from whose tattered and worn Circulating Library I had borrowed so many volumes of tales, novels, and romances, always regarded me as a kind of pet; and I was still her customer for papers and pens, and so on. I noted that a few of the gentry had commenced a "Book Society" at her shop. The subscription of two guineas per annum was above my power to pay; but, as I took the liberty, one day, to handle some of the new volumes and periodicals, she closed the shop door, and, coming close to me, whispered that she thought she could accommodate me with the loan of the books. Suppose I gave her ten shillings for the books of each season, and took care to fetch them in the evening, about the time that shops closed, when it would be certain that none of the genteel subscribers would be in the way?

So the forbidden fruit was secured once more; and I went home all in a glow with delight—for I was taking two numbers of the "London Magazine" with me, and the first volume of Scott's "Kenilworth"!

CHAPTER VI.
STUDENT-LIFE: ITS ENJOYMENTS: 1824—1828.

HOW rich I was, with ten shillings per week, to buy food and clothes—now all this intellectual food was glutting me on every side! And how resolute I was on becoming solitary, and also on becoming a scholar! What though I could not get to Cambridge, like Kirke White, could I not study as hard as he studied, and learn as fast? Friends and acquaintances had left the little old town, one after another; but I would not leave it. I would learn enough in that corner to enable myself to enter on mature life with success; and I would have no friend in addition to my new friend John Hough, with whom I had promised to spend a couple of hours or more, every Saturday night, in intellectual converse.

Yet I would have strengthened my friendship with Thomas Miller, if he would have become a student. We had only seen each other occasionally (although we had ever retained the fond friendship of childhood), for several years. Miller's mother had been compelled to apprentice her boy to a trade; and the person to whom Tom was apprenticed was so vain and ignorant, and tyrannised to such a degree over the strong-willed boy, that Tom one day put him in fear of his life, by throwing an iron instrument at him. So the boy was given up to his mother, who had recently re-married; and her husband taught Tom the trade of a basket-maker. Of course, the lad soon had his own way; and, when working hours were over, passed his time as he pleased. He was strong, handsome, and proud; and was soon a favourite with all the maidens of his own rank in the town. He joined wild company that took to what some people consider to be only the playful tricks of youth; but would sober down a little, now and then, and call upon me, and talk about poetry. Sometimes, he would accompany me in a walk; but, while I wanted to pursue my study, as we walked, he would be venting sallies of fun, or quoting Falstaff, or Bottom the Weaver.

I saw there was unmistakable genius in Miller; and I found he listened to my rehearsals of Coleridge's "Christabel" and Burns'

"Tam o' Shanter" with rapt pleasure; but I could not persuade him to take to real study. He left Gainsborough; and when, a few years afterwards, he sent me his first printed poem, from Nottingham, where he had settled down and married, I felt surprised that he had entered the field of authorship first; and little imagined that I should be such a laggard in entering it myself.

One of the greatest incentives I had to solid study was the reading, in Drew's "Imperial Magazine," an account of the life of Dr. Samuel Lee, Professor of Hebrew in the University of Cambridge, and a scholar, it was said, in more than a dozen languages. He had been apprenticed to a carpenter at eleven years old, had bought Ruddiman's Latin Rudiments on an old book-stall for a trifle, and learnt the whole book by heart; and had stepped on, from Corderius's Colloquies to Cæsar, and from Cæsar to Virgil, and so on; and had learnt to read Greek, Hebrew, and Syriac, all from self-tuition, by the time he was five or six and twenty. Yet he was ignorant of English Grammar and Arithmetic!

I said in my heart, if one man can teach himself a language, another can. But there seemed such a wealth of means of learning now around me, that I felt as if I must attempt to accomplish a broader triumph of self-education than Lee accomplished. I must try if I could not combine the study of languages with that of mathematics; complete a full course of reading in ancient and modern history, and get an accurate and ample acquaintance with the literature of the day, by means of that little convenient opening I mentioned at the close of the last chapter.

I must add, that there was some sadness mingled with these bouyant resolves. The thought of dear Henry Whillock's death would bring serious fears about his spiritual state and my own fitness for death. My new friend Hough carefully reminded me of the true wisdom there was in being prepared to die; and when I told him, without any concealment, of the doubts we had gathered from reading those sceptical books, he solemnly advised me to enter on a course of reading of the Evidences of Christianity. I promised to do so; and I gradually drew up my plans for study and the employment of time into a written form. To this I added written resolves of a very necessary kind: that I would speak grammatically, and pronounce with propriety; and I would do these always.

Some who read this page may scarcely be able to understand the nature of the task I was imposing on myself. Often, for hours, no one would enter the little room where I sat at work in my corner, and my poor mother, at her labour, a little nearer the door. But sometimes troublesome gossips would enter—neighbours to talk about the other neighbours, old friends and acquaintances of my mother's, some of them from the town, and some from the villages, and old playmates and schoolfellows of my own.

Now, to hear a youth in mean clothing, sitting at the shoemaker's stall, pursuing one of the lowliest callings, speak in what seemed to some of them almost a foreign dialect, raised positive anger and scorn in some, and amazement in others. Who was I, that I should sit on the cobbler's stall, and "talk fine"! They could not understand it. With Whillock and my intellectual friends I had conversed in the best and most refined English I could command; but I had used our plain old Lincolnshire dialect in talking to the neighbours. This was all to be laid aside now, and it took some courage to do it. Yet I persevered until the Doric was conquered; and at one time of my life spoke better Attic than, belike, I speak now, in these my days of the yellow leaf—for an old man seems to relapse naturally into the use of his mother tongue.

My written resolves also comprised serious vows that I would lead a strictly moral life; would retire to pray at least once in the day-time, as, well as "say my prayers" at morn and eve; and would inquire diligently into the truth of both natural and revealed religion.

I thought it possible that by the time I reached the age of twenty-four I might be able to master the elements of Latin, Greek, Hebrew, and French; might get well through Euclid, and through a course of Algebra; might commit the entire "Paradise Lost," and seven of the best plays of Shakspeare, to memory; and might read a large and solid course of history, and of religious evidences; and be well acquainted also with the current literature of the day.

I failed considerably, but I sped on joyfully while health and strength lasted. I was between nineteen and twenty when I began to commit Ruddiman's Rudiments to memory—thinking it was better of begin to learn Latin with the book that Lee used—though I found afterwards I might have done better. I committed almost the entire volume to memory—notes and all. Afterwards, I found Israel Lyon's small Hebrew Grammar, on a stall, bought it for a shilling, and practised Hebrew writing as the surest means of beginning to learn, every Sunday evening. I got hold of a Greek Grammar about a year after; but did not master it earnestly, because I thought it better to keep close to the Latin for some time. I also picked up a small French Grammar; but that seemed so easy, that I thought I could master it without care or trouble.

On Sunday mornings, whether I walked, or had to stay indoors on account of the weather, my first task was to commit a portion of the "Paradise Lost " to memory. I usually spent the remainder of Sunday, save the evening, whether I walked or remained at home, in reading something that bore on the Evidences. Thus I not only read through the well-known "Natural Theology" and "Horæ Paulinæ," and "Evidences" of Paley, and the equally popular "Apologies for the Bible and Christianity" of Bishop Watson, Soame Jenyns' "Internal Evidences," Lord Lyttelton's "Conversion of St. Paul," and Sherlock's "Trial of the Witnesses,"—but I diligently read books that required deeper thinking, and some that were filled with profound learning—such as Butler's "Analogy," Bentley's "Folly of Atheism," Dr. Samuel Clarke's "Demonstrations of the Being and Attributes of God," Stillingfleet's "Origines Sacræ," and Warburton's "Divine Legation of Moses."

Historical reading, or the grammar of some language, or translation, was my first employment on week-day mornings, whether I rose at three or four, until seven o'clock, when I sat down to the stall. A book or a periodical in my hand while I breakfasted, gave me another half-hour's reading. I had another half-hour, and sometimes an hour's reading, or study of language, at from one to two o'clock, the time of dinner—usually eating my food with a spoon, after I had cut it in pieces, and having my eyes on a book all the time.

I sat at work till eight, and sometimes nine, at night; and, then, either read, or walked about our little room and committed "Hamlet" to memory, or the rhymes of some modern poet, until compelled to go to bed from sheer exhaustion—for it must be remembered that I was repeating something, audibly, as I sat at work, the greater part of the day—either declensions and conjugations, or rules of syntax, or propositions of Euclid, or the "Paradise Lost," or "Hamlet," or poetry of some modern or living author.

In the spring of 1826, after getting through Valpy's Delectus, and a part of Stewart's "Cornelius Nepos," and also a part of Justin, but somewhat clumsily, with the help of Ainsworth's Dictionary, I commenced Cæsar, and sped on well, so that by the time I had reached the third book, "De Bello Gallico," I found myself able to read page after page, with scarcely more than a glance, now and then, at the dictionary. I remember well my first triumphant feeling of this kind. I sat on Pingle Hill; it was about five in the morning, the sun shone brightly; and as I lifted my eyes from the classic page of the great conqueror of the Gauls and Helvetians, and they fell on the mouldering pile called the "Old Hall"—part of which had been a stronghold of John of Gaunt, and of one of the barons in the reign of Stephen—I said to myself, "I have made a greater conquest, without the aid of a living teacher, than the proudest warrior ever made—for I have conquered and entered into the possession of a new mind." And *that* seems to me the truest expression, when you find you can read a language you could not read before.

When I had finished Cæsar's Commentaries on the Gallic War, I took up the Eneid, and soon grew in love with Virgil: a love which has lasted—for, notwithstanding the protest some people make against the "tameness" of Virgil, as compared with Homer, the graceful Mantuan always affords me high intellectual pleasure.

I was seldom later in bed than three or four in the morning; and when, in the coldness of winter, we could not afford to have a fire till my mother rose, I used to put a lamp on a stool, which I placed on a little round table, and, standing before it, wrapped up in my mother's old red cloak, I read on till seven, or studied a grammar, or my Euclid, and frequently kept my feet moving to secure warmth, or prevent myself from falling asleep.

In the finer seasons of the year I was invariably on the hills, or in the lanes or woods, or by the Trent, by sunrise, or before; and thus often strolled several miles with my book in my hand, before I sat down in the corner to work, at seven o'clock. These long walks in the mornings greatly deepened my love of Nature. I grew increasingly and fondly familiar with the trees, the flowers, the birds, and even with the wild four-footed creatures, and, above all, with the silver windings of the Trent; and often stood to gaze down the vista of a wood, or upon some feature of beauty in a landscape, with a thrill of joyous feeling that I could not have defined to myself, or others. Nothing gave me deeper enjoyment than the grand colouring of the woods in autumn; and when I first saw one of the pictures of Gainsborough, I thought he must have felt, in the woods of Suffolk, similar rapture to that which I had felt in the woods of old Lincolnshire.

My drawing had been given up, and was never resumed; but I occasionally returned to the dear old dulcimer, especially if I felt jaded by overwork, or my dear mother desired the music. Be it remembered, she was now drawing near to sixty, and had declined considerably in strength and energy, so that there was the greater need that I did not neglect to ply the awl. It was little help, indeed, I could render her; but it would have been cruel to have leaned carelessly on her increasing weakness.

My friend Hough's conversation, on the Saturday nights, was both a relief and an inspiration to me. He was not only well read in standard old English literature, more especially divinity, but he was passionately attached to metaphysics,—had read Locke, and Berkeley, and Hobbes, and Dugald Stewart; and during the first year of our acquaintance took to the enthusiastic perusal of Cudworth. The grand expanse of his forehead showed the strength of his reasoning faculties as well as of his ideality; and he kindled into warmth as we entered into debate. With him I discussed questions relating to mind, to religion, to history, and general literature; and these weekly conversations, as I returned to my reading and studies, gave a new impulse to thought and inquiry. He also used to say, "You do me good. You freshen my mind, weekly."

My historical reading was a great delight. I read, thoroughly, Gibbon's "Decline and Fall," and followed it up by reading the Preliminary Discourse to Sale's translation of the Koran, and a translation of Mosheim's Church History. I made written notes, often, as I went along. I analysed Dr. Clarke's "Demonstrations of the Being and Attributes," and it was done so completely that I seemed to know the book by heart. My friend Hough approved it greatly, and showed it to others, till—at last—it was begged, and given away to one who was preparing for the Christian ministry.

In the hurry and whirl of my changeful life, I have lost the journal that I kept so strictly in those years, and all written records of my reading; but I can recall the feeling of pleasure, or profound interest, I experienced in reading many a volume; and the feeling is often associated with some feature of a landscape, or turn of the woods, or appearance of the hills or lanes where I walked. Thus the dear old remembrances often flash upon me, after all these years; and I seem to see the page, and the rural spot where I read it, as clearly as if it had happened only an hour ago. How strange it seems—seeing that I, often, cannot call to mind whether I wrote to such a person last week; and, most commonly, forget the names and features of persons with whom I have but lately become acquainted,—nay, often forget, utterly, some things I saw, or some actions I performed, not a month ago!

Blair's "Lectures on Rhetoric and the Belles Lettres " was another book that I analysed very closely and laboriously, being determined on acquiring a thorough judgment of style and literary excellence. All this practice seemed to destroy the desire of composing poetry of my own. Milton's verse seemed to overawe me, as I committed it to memory, and repeated it daily; and the perfection of his music, as well as the gigantic stature of his intellect, were fully perceived by my mind. The wondrous knowledge of the heart unfolded by Shakspeare, made me shrink into insignificance; while the sweetness, the marvellous power of expression and grandeur of his poetry seemed to transport me, at times, out of the vulgar world of circumstances in which I lived bodily. Besides the two great poets, I made myself familiar with others; and committed to memory thousands of lines by Burns, and Coleridge, and Wordsworth, and Scott, and Byron, and Moore, and Campbell, and Southey, and Keats. And the repetition, daily, of poetry displaying all the harmonies of rhythm—all the opulence of the stores of expressing thought—repressed all desire of composing poetry myself. I said to myself, daily "I am educating my ear and my mind, and I shall be ripe for my true work in time."

The culture I attempted for myself was broad enough, at any rate— for I often diverged into miscellaneous reading, and can remember the pleasure with which I went through the elder Disraeli's "Curiosities of Literature," "Calamities of Authors," and Quarrels of Authors," Warton's "History of Early English Poetry," Johnson's "Lives of the Poets," "Rasselas," etc., Boswell's "Life of Johnson," Landor's "Imaginary Conversations," Southey's "Book of the Church," Lingard's "Anglo-Saxon Antiquities," Colton's "Lacon," Douglas of Cavers on the "Advancement of Society," Bullock's "Mexico," Richardson's "Travels in Egypt and the Holy Land," Head's "Rough Notes of a journey to the Andes," and many other volumes of travels.

The novels of Scott I took care to have from the shelves of the dear old lady's shop, as early after their first appearance as I could come by them,—while I also indulged myself occasionally by reading the new pages of Washington Irving, or such novels as Mrs. Shelley's thrilling creation of "Frankenstein," and Lockhart's sterling stories of "Valerius" and "Reginald Dalton."

The later poetry of Byron, contained in "The Liberal," and that published separately, with the new volumes of Campbell, Moore, Milman, and others, I had also, *by favour*, from those kindly shelves in the little shop I had frequented from a child,—together with each number of the Quarterly and Edinburgh Reviews, and of the European, New Monthly, and Blackwood's Magazines, as duly as they came out. Thus I read the celebrated "Noctes Ambrosianæ" when they were new.

But my great favourite was the London Magazine. Nor have I ever seen a magazine that equalled it, since—at least, to my thinking. A periodical which first set before English readers the Essays of Elia, the Picture Galleries of Hazlitt, De Quincey's "Confessions of an Opium-eater," verses by Keats and sonnets by poor Clare, and tales by Allan Cunningham, and in the later numbers of which Carlyle's "Life of Schiller" first appeared—certainly spread no Barmecide array of dishes before the literary appetite of its readers. The "Monthlies"—there were no "Weeklies" then—have doubled, trebled, nay, quadrupled, in number, since I was a young fellow. One would rather that they were fewer in number; and that the real Men of Genius existing would club their wits to bring out, monthly, a new "London Magazine," as rich as the old one.

CHAPTER VII.
ILLNESS: SCHOOLMASTER-LIFE: IN EARNEST: 1828—1829.

I HAVE taken care not to bedim the brightness of the picture contained in the last chapter. And it would have been untruthful if I had; for its brightness was never dimmed to me. But no one of any experience in life can have read the chapter without suspecting that the strain upon the powers of mind and body described in it could not always be kept up, and that, under such circumstances, there must have been failure, sometimes.

And so it was. I not unfrequently swooned away, and fell along the floor, when I tried to take my cup of oatmeal gruel, at the end of my day's labour. Next morning, of course, I was not able to rise at an early hour; and then, very likely, the next day's study had to be stinted. I needed better food than we could afford to buy; and often had to contend with the sense of faintness, while I still plodded on, with my double task of mind and body.

But it was not till the summer of 1827, when I was about three months over two-and-twenty, that I felt my bodily strength, and, with it, my power of mind, were really giving way. I had, now, "Hamlet" entirely and perfectly by heart, and thought of beginning to commit "Lear" to memory, but dare not; and I felt also compelled to halt at the end of the fourth book of "Paradise Lost." More reluctantly, I had to give up my Hebrew writing, and the book of Hebrew sentences. I must take them up again when I felt stronger. And the Algebra: *that* must also be laid by, for the present. If I relieved myself of some of my labour, it would enable me soon to rally. So I calculated. And so Daddy Briggs said it would be—for he would often call, and talk with his old pupil, and wonder at what I was doing, and talk admiringly and fondly about it.

The autumn came, and I grew weaker. And then, with a sense of mortification I cannot express, I had to lay aside the odd volume of Tacitus, and the neat old copy of Lactantius, "De mortibus Persecutorum," that I had bought from off a stall; and dare not attempt to go on translating them. Greek Grammar and Extracts, and, at last, Greek Testament itself, had all to be given up. I could only read a little light reading—for anything that required thinking brought on pain and nervous torment; and I grew very sad, and often wept, when alone.

All very early rising was now discontinued; for I had to endeavour to preserve strength enough to pursue my bodily labour, or we must come to want. My poor mother's business had grown less and less, as she lost strength and enterprise; and she was often now unable to work at all. Thus, there was every reason why I should fill up the hours with the labour that brought us daily bread; and so, even the rehearsal of grammar and verses had to be discontinued—or be indulged in but seldom.

But I had already ventured too far. The complete failure came. In November of the same year, I had to be carried to bed, having fainted in my chair; and I had to remain in bed several days. For nine successive weeks, I was out of bed only for a short time each day, and my sense of weakness was excessive.

I had the kindly aid of a noble medical man, Dr. Peacock, who is dead, but has left a name memorable for philanthropy in that little town; and food and other helps were rendered me by many—I may say, by all who knew me intimately. If it had not been so, my poor mother must have sunk with the burthen she was not able, now, to bear.

One incident in that illness comes strongly across my mind as I write. I had been brought downstairs, in a somewhat cheerful state of mind, believing that I had got a turn, as we say, and that I should soon be well—when I suddenly fell back, and my appearance alarmed my mother. Her cries brought in two or three of the neighbours, who were passing. One of them took me by the wrist, held it awhile, and told my mother that the pulse had stopped, and I was dead. My eyes were closed, and I could not open them, and I could not speak. The sensation I felt was as if a huge stone lay on my chest. It seems the blood had not ceased circulating at the heart—for it gradually resumed its course through the body; and I opened my eyes, and told the neighbour who had said I was dead that I had heard every word he had spoken! In little more than a year after that time, I saw that neighbour laid in the grave. Such are the unexpected incidents of this our mortal life!

My great burthen of heart and spirit has yet to be approached. I have purposely kept it out of my story for some time, not feeling it congruous to mingle secular and spiritual cares, or the relation of them, familiarly. I was often gently exhorted to seek for the settlement of every doubt by my friend Hough. But doubts arose, as I proceeded with my inquiry into the "Evidences," that I had never felt before. Still I kept up the practice of retiring every day, at noon, for prayer; and it was then, more especially, that I prayed for light. I had analysed Paley's "Evidences," and could repeat to myself the substance of the book. And I had often done this when most troubled with doubt; and it served to enable me to rest on Christ's existence and mission, as facts.

About two months before I was compelled to take to bed, my friend Hough put into my hand the Life of Henry Martyn, the missionary. Its effect, as might be expected, was very powerful upon my mind. The picture of one so perfect as a scholar and a man of refinement, and so fully convinced of the truth of religion—the brilliant short life of intense and devoted missionary labour, crowned with a death that was, almost literally, a martyrdom—took very strong hold of me. I said within myself, "I ought to be ashamed to have a doubt, while Henry Martyn believed; " and resolved I would never dwell on a doubt in future, but pray instead.

In this state of mind, my sickness found me. But now came the sickness of the heart. The good doctor shook his head, as he felt my pulse again and again, and revisited me; and every thought was concentred in the one thought—I might have to meet death very soon! Pray I did, with all my feeble strength, for the conviction of sin was a heavy burthen. Sin of the heart and mind, that is not outward, was my sin; but it was not the less sin for that. Religious people were soon round me. Methodists had a suspicion that I was sceptical, because I had ceased to attend public worship. They did not understand that the chief reason was, that I might gain one whole day for study, weekly. Methodists prayed with me very earnestly, and besought me to give my soul no rest till I had found the pardon of sin; and I assured them that was what I longed to find.

The young curate of the parish church, the pious and laborious Charles Hensley, came also to visit me. He soon discovered that he had found a penitent of a peculiar order; and at once confessed his interest in my studies, and offered to assist me with the loan of Latin and Greek books, should I recover. Mr. Hensley also very seriously urged me to be truly penitent; but was not of opinion that I ought to seek for what Methodists called a "sense of pardon." My friend Hough was on the curate's side; and, amidst these conflicting urgencies, I knew not what to do.

A good constitution and the skill of my kind physician, under the blessing of the Almighty, enabled me at length to leave the sick bed. But I was very weak for some time; and when I attempted a little manual labour, it brought on a peculiar nervous tremor that almost frightened me, and which compelled me to desist, time after time. My friend Hough, and my acquaintance—who afterwards became a dear friend—Charles Kelvey, took counsel together, and proposed to me that I should try the profession of a schoolmaster. I agreed, for I felt I could not work again on the stall; and they sought out a large club-room which was already furnished with forms and boards, that would serve for desks, and made themselves responsible for the rent for the first half year. I issued handbills; and on the tenth of March, 1828, just ten days before I became three-and-twenty, I opened school.

My school was eagerly patronised by the poor; and I had a few of the children of the middle-class. People in the little town had been talking for years about the remarkable youth that was never seen in the streets, and was known to wander miles in the fields and woods, reading. He was believed by some to be a prodigy of learning; and they would send their children to be taught by him. In the course of twelve months I had a hundred scholars on my list, had an average attendance of eighty, and had to think of engaging an assistant.

If it could ever have entered into my nature to set about making money, now was my first "good chance." But it could not, and never will. I have had several "good chances," since that passed away; and I could never make use of them, or suffer such a purpose to enter my mind. We cannot all "make money," although it is necessary that somebody should. I have said, and said it solemnly, that I cannot "make money," and I do not believe that anything which could possibly happen to me in the world could turn my nature into the path of money-getting. But there is something besides that I cannot do. I cannot avoid throwing my whole nature into an undertaking, when I once enter upon it, either from a sense of duty or for self-gratification.

My school was a perfect passion with me for a time. I was in the school-room often at five in the morning until nine at night, taking my meals in a hasty, imperfect way, while the boys were gone home to take theirs. I had quill pens to make in great number, the first work in the morning; and for a time I had early classes each morning. Then again, in the evenings, although other day-schools broke up at five, I drew the elder scholars around the globe, and described the countries upon it, until a late hour, or talked to them on some part of history, or described the structures of animals, or, to keep up their attention, even related a story from the "Arabian Nights."

I spent at least fifty pounds on the walls of the large club-room, by covering them with pictures of every imaginable kind, and filling the corners with large plaster figures and busts. The sill within every window of the school-room was fitted up with small divisions, so that the boys might have a miniature museum of pebbles, coins, etc. I was intent on making their school-room their delight. The pictures fastened themselves on the eyes and brain of one poor boy, John Spicer, the child of a lowly shoemaker. That child did some wondrous things, as beginnings, in art. He was a born genius, and would have gained distinction had he lived.

Four children of an officer of excise were entrusted to my care by their father; and the two elder boys were an important trust. They were highly intelligent, were ripe in arithmetic, and in the school where they had been learning Latin had been put into Horace. But I found the advancement was false. They really did not know what they were about. I did not understand the custom of helping lads out with one half of their translation, and yet never showing them how to translate. I had learned no old teachers' tricks.

So I placed Cæsar's Commentaries before them, and taught them how to select the nominative in each sentence, then the verb, and then the noun governed by the verb, and so on, until they became happy labourers at the book, because they understood it, and felt they were achieving something worth talking about. They also commenced the study of Euclid, daily; and so I had a stimulus, for keeping up my knowledge of Geometry and Latin, in these two pupils.

There was no desire on the part of the parents of any other pupils in my school, that they should learn Latin. But I wished to teach it to all. Soon, I had copies of declensions and conjugations written out on sheets of paper, with lists of the prepositions, and so on; and gave them to a good number of the boys to commit to memory. And to the very last day of my life that I sustained the office of daily schoolmaster, I had the declensions, or conjugations, repeated by the boys, as they stood in class, every morning. The Latin Accidence, I may say, is so firmly fixed in my memory, from hearing these daily repetitions, for about nine years of my life, that I think I could as soon forget my own name as forget any part of it.

A few of the boys to whom I thus taught Latin gratuitously made such promising progress as to enable me to form them into a separate class for the translation of Cornelius Nepos. But the great body of them were never able to construe a Latin sentence. They had no taste for it themselves; and they had no stimulus at home. The stupid listlessness of the parents of my pupils was, indeed, my hindrance from the first; and, in time, it produced disgust.

"I want our Jack to larn to write a good hand. What's the use of his larning Latin? It will nivver be no use to him."

Such were the kind of thanks I had from the poor, when I tried to benefit their children, without any cost to themselves! After the few boys had passed away who had been my first scholars, and I had to begin anew with dull intellects, amid harsh discouragements from their parents, I lost the passion for my profession as a schoolmaster; and I began to feel it, what I fear thousands beside myself have felt it to be—unwelcome drudgery.

But I must go back to the great concern of all—that of religion.

CHAPTER VIII
WESLEYAN METHODIST LIFE: STRUGGLE FOR HOLINESS:
1829—34.

I WENT to the Independent chapel, at the request of my friend Hough, so soon as I was able to attend a place of worship—that is to say, about a month before I opened school. I was thoroughly intent on leading a religious life; but the problem was not solved with me as to what constituted religion, or rather, religious experience. I did not continue for more than about three months to worship with the Independents. The preaching—I forget the name of the preacher—was dry and dull; and it wearied me. Nor was there warmth enough in the worship of the Independents for a nature like mine, while it was so full of the fire which it has taken time and experience to cool.

While attending the Independent chapel on Sunday mornings and evenings I went always to the parish church in the afternoons. The preaching of the young curate, Charles Hensley, gentle as it was, touched chords within me that the Independent minister could not reach. The church service too, was associated with the happy feelings of boyhood, and memories that were wound about the heart; and so I left the chapel, and began to attend the church thrice each Sunday. My friend Hough and the Independent minister rallied me on my "becoming an Episcopalian," as they phrased it. "Nay, nay," said I, "you know I do not believe in Lord Bishops, or Right Reverend Fathers in God; but I want to find peace of mind, and I have not found it yet."

Nor did I find it in attendance on the parish church. I devoutly uttered all the words of the services, and I listened to the sermons. I even partook of the sacrament of the Lord's Supper, because exhorted so to do. But the contest within was becoming sorer and sorer. Now I was exposed to trials of temper among the children, I was often troubled with anger. My new commerce with the world—for I could no longer play the recluse with the care of so many pupils on my hands—my new intercourse with insincere and sinister people, inexperienced as I was, roused disgust and opposition in me, and made me feel I had great pride and a strong will of my own to contend with. Prayer was often neglected, in the throng of occupation, and the heart became less and less devotional. At the close of a long day, when I sank asleep, it was often with a heavy heart, and a sense of increasing sinfulness.

By the end of that year, 1828, I was really wretched on account of my low spiritual state, when I had a few moments for reflection, and was not absorbed in the enthusiastic performance of my school duties. And, at last, I said to myself, "I cannot live in this state. The vows I made to God in sickness are yet unfulfilled. I must either lead a devotedly religious life, or bear about with me a sense of degradation and falseness. Those Methodists, I know from a child, have always professed to have the secret of true piety and true happiness. I will go, and join them; and try if I can find the real cure for this heart-ache."

So, on New Year's Day, 1829, I first went to a Wesleyan Methodist Class Meeting. The leader, Edward Shipham, was a man of no more than ordinary powers of mind. But I thought—to use a Lincolnshire expression—he was of the right breed. I remembered the spiritual glance of his pious father's eyes, and the dear old man's gentleness and love, when I was a child in the Methodist Sunday-school; and, above all, the words I so often heard among the poor, when some one was ill and likely to die—"Go, and fetch Mr. Shipham to pray!" I thought if the father had been in such request as a man of prayer, his son should have learnt something about spiritual religion. These thoughts had determined me in selecting a class-leader.

Four months of deep penitence passed away, amidst warnings against unbelief, and exhortations to faith, from the leader and the members of society; and I readily listened to advice, by whomsoever it was given. I chiefly sought in the writings of Wesley himself— with which I had long been acquainted—an explication of the true mode of seeking the pardon of sin. I was ever in dread of that old spiritual bugbear of my boyhood— *pardoning myself*, instead of receiving the pardon of the Almighty. It was the pardon of the Almighty—"the witness of the Spirit"—so often, so invariably insisted upon in the writings of Wesley, and in all the Methodist sermons of my time—that I thirsted to receive.

But the more I observed the conduct of penitents who were said to "find pardon," or "find peace," in the prayer-meetings, and the more I listened to the language of preachers and leaders who prayed with them, and guided them,—the clearer it became to me that what I had been looking for was ignored.

"Do you feel you can rely on Christ ? Can you confide in Him as your Saviour? Do you believe He really died for *you*?" Such were the questions put at the penitent-form. And if the penitent said "Yes," "Then say, Lord I am Thine!" continued the spiritual director; say, "Lord, Thou hast died for *me*, and I believe Thou *dost* save me!"

And when the mourning one ventured to follow the leader resolutely, in most instances joyous feeling sprang up, and the joyous feeling increased if it were indulged in. But if the mourner only timidly followed the exhorter to believe, his mourning was not turned into joy; and he was told to keep on believing and joy would come.

But no one who took the part of a spiritual director said, "Have you got the witness of the Spirit?" I never heard such a question put to any penitent who professed to "find peace," in all my life; and I have been witness to scores of cases of professed deliverance from the burden of condemnation for sin.

Having thus closely observed how that was ignored which I had been expecting, I was the more inclined to listen to two or three of the oldest and most intelligent members of the Society, who said to me, "You are cheating yourself out of peace by some mistake. What are you expecting? God's word teaches you to believe on the Lord Jesus Christ, and affirms you shall thus be saved. Do as you are directed, and trust God to do His own part, in His own way. Don't bargain with God for anything extraordinary to follow. Do your own part. Believe with all your heart!"

Gradually, I found courage to take their advice. I relied—and was resolved I would rely—on the fact that Christ was any Saviour. And I resolved to rely on it habitually. I would be troubled with none of those absurd "actings of faith" I had learnt when a boy. And peace of mind followed the calm and settled reliance that I practised. I had no direct "witness of the Spirit" such as I had looked for. I had expected a direct impression to be made on my mind by the Holy Spirit—an impression to be clearly distinguished from any act of my own mind. Nothing of the kind followed my act of reliance on the atonement of Christ; and I refused to let myself be disturbed on account of that. I was resolved to hold by the fact that Christ had died for me.

Very soon, some one put into my hand Sigston's "Life of William Bramwell." It proved to be a spark that, for a time, lit my whole soul into flame. I had heard members of the Society talk of holiness of heart, and of "the blessing of sanctification," and of "a clean heart," and of "perfect love," or "the second blessing," as some called it. I read again such of Wesley's own sermons as touched on the nature of holiness. I found that Wesley taught "sanctification," but could never learn that Wesley himself professed to be sanctified. Fletcher's experience was fully described and professed and taught as what all might experience. The experience of Hester Ann Rogers—hers is a well-known book to Wesleyans—also seemed very full and clear.

I had already been reasoning with myself—"What I want is to be holy. I want to cease sinning. The pardon of sin is really of imperfect value, if I continue to sin. I shall need pardoning again. It is entire devotedness to God that I need. I ought to be devoted to Him. It must be right to be so devoted; and it must be wrong to live without rendering God perfect obedience. Does He not ask me for it, in His word? Does He not say 'Be ye holy'? If He commands it, it must be possible to obey. God never mocks man. He would not command it, if it were not possible. But I am mocking God, if I profess to be His, and yet have not given Him my whole heart."

I reasoned, further, that, as I had come out from the world, and joined myself to God's people, I should be acting insincerely if I did not live fully to God. My plans of learning and study? Alas! they had all been suspended. And I reasoned that I must not resume them to kill my spirituality of mind. I must have this holiness of heart. All other acquirements were despicable, compared to it. I had been taken out by a local preacher to begin to preach, and put on the plan as a prayer-leader. And the earnestness of my prayers for holiness soon raised a flame around me. Others began to pray for holiness. And then, in company with a few earnest young men, I began to meet once a week in the house of a female class-leader who for many years had been noted for fervid devotion.

I read Bramwell on my knees by three in the morning. I was swallowed up with the one thought of reaching "perfect love," — of living without sin — of feeling I was always and fully in God's favour. I prayed for it — we all prayed for it — at the weekly meeting we held in the house of the devoted woman I spoke of. One night we had sung "Wrestling Jacob," the hymn which has so often been styled the masterpiece in the Wesleyan Hymn Book, commencing —

"Come, O thou traveller unknown."

We had all sung the hymn with wrapt fervour, but I had sung one verse with an earnestness of feeling, and an agony of resolve, that I think I never sang another verse with in all my life —

"In vain Thou strugglest to get free —
I never will unloose my hold!
Art Thou the Man that died for me?
The secret of Thy love unfold!
Wrestling, I will not let Thee go,
Till I Thy Name, Thy Nature know."

We sang over and over again, on our knees, "Wrestling I will not let Thee go!" — till at last I sprang upon my feet, crying, "I will believe! I do believe!" and the very saying of the words, with all the strength of resolve, seemed to lift me above the earth. And I kept on believing, according to the lesson I had learned in the Life of Bramwell. No thought of consequences that might happen — no fear of the possibility of failure—could prevent me from confessing and professing, with impressive fervour, that God had sanctified my soul. The example was wondrously infectious. Hundreds in the town and circuit began to pray for holiness of heart; and many professed also to obtain it.

How long I maintained the profession of it, I cannot say with exactness. It was for but part of a year, perhaps not more than half a year. But I remember well that I was in a religious state that I have never reached since. For some months I never struck a boy in my school. I felt that I could not strike; and told the children I should strike no more. And the children used to look at me so wistfully, when I spoke to them tenderly and lovingly, if any had done wrong! I instituted prayer four times a day, with singing, in my school; and I have had many testimonies, in afterlife, to the good impressions made on the minds of some of the children.

If, throughout eternity in heaven, I be as happy as I often was for whole days during that short period of my religious life, it will be heaven indeed. Often, for several days together, I felt close to the Almighty—felt I was His own, and His entirely. I felt no wandering of the will—no inclination to yield to sin. And when temptation came, my whole soul wrestled for victory, till the temptation fled.

This was exhausting to the body, as well as to the soul. The perpetual tension of the string of the will seemed, at last, to be more than I could sustain. One day, when I was faint and weak in frame, I lost my temper under great provocation from a disobedient boy in the school, and suddenly seized the cane and struck him. The whole school seemed horror-stricken. The poor children gazed, as if on a fallen angel, with such looks of commiseration on my poor self, as I cannot describe. I wished I was in a corner to weep, for I was choking with tears, and felt heart-broken.

I tried to recover the lost holiness; and sometimes seemed to regain it, or something like it, for a few days; but I was sure to fail again. And similar to my experience was that of scores of our members, in the town, and in the villages of the circuit. And such is the experience in all circuits of the connexion. Often, what is called a "Revival" begins with some one or more striving for holiness. The theme kindles desire in others; and, soon, the theme becomes general, in the meetings of the classes, and the Public Bands, or weekly gatherings for telling of Christian experience. Profession of holiness begins and extends, and sometimes fills a circuit with glowing excitement for many months.

But the decline invariably sets in; and little is said about the doctrine of "sanctification" or "perfect love," it may be, for some years after, save and except when some aged and steady member of the society, or minister, rises to tell his grateful story, perhaps in a quarterly "Lovefeast." Thus, I often heard venerable Henry Anderson, who was ordained by John Wesley, (and whose son and two grandsons are now in the Wesleyan Ministry,) declare his experience when he was eighty years old. "For more than forty years," he used to aver,—and it was doubtless true, "I have not known a feeling contrary to love towards any human being, nor have I ever lost the sense of God's favour!"

But the changes and fluctuations of experience in the circuits is the rule rather than the exception. It was so in the lifetime of John Wesley. He gives many striking relations of it in his "Journal"—the book so well worth reading, and so valuable, as one of the great keys to the knowledge of what was the religious state of England, Scotland, Ireland, and Wales in Wesley's own time. He speaks, sometimes, of the flame of holiness pervading his Societies for a year, and then almost dying out.

That a high degree of religious attainment might be the habitual condition of Methodists, or any other associations for piety, no Christian believer who diligently reads his New Testament can doubt. Perhaps Christian ministers do not preach the doctrine of holiness with sufficient vigour and frequency. I fear, the worldly spirit of professors of religion is the great hindrance to holiness. I mean, more especially, their joining in the world's amusements, and following its fashions. There may be many other reasons why a low standard of religious experience prevails in some societies, and why zeal for holiness, which often reaches intensity during a revival, is so commonly reduced to languor, and even indifference, after a time. I do not feel that I ought to enter on the discussion of such a question here. I barely state the sorrowful fact that great fluctuations in the state of their religious experience prevail in the Methodist societies, with all their manifold means of promoting spiritual growth.

The revival in the Gainsborough circuit that I have spoken of was prolonged by the ministry of John Smith in the adjoining circuit of Lincoln; that ministry so fruitful in sound conversions, and in the quickening of the spirits of those who already professed religion. But from one fearful cause I shall be compelled to relate, the religious feeling of the Gainsborough circuit was well-nigh quenched in the hearts of hundreds; and I became eager to get out of an atmosphere so chilling and mournful.

CHAPTER IX.
LOCAL PREACHER LIFE: SPIRITUAL FALL: 1819—1835.

MY engagement in the office of local preacher was a source of rich delight to me. When I first entered upon it, I was in the full tide of devotional feeling, and used to exhort and teach without any preparation of the thoughts I was to present to the people. This passed off very well for a time; but when the fervour of devotion had somewhat cooled within me, I felt my talk in the village pulpits become vapid. It wearied both myself and the people. I had learned that a few of the local preachers wrote notes of their sermons, before they preached; but the older men did not. I found, however, that the best preacher among them wrote his sermons out in full, and committed them to memory. And I began to reason thus with myself,—"How can I, a comparatively inexperienced person, instruct men of age, some of whom have read their Bibles for threescore years, without I think, and think deeply, on the themes I have to address to them? Am I really showing any respect to their understandings by merely talking thus shallowly to them ? Am I showing respect to Christ, and to Divine Truth, by treating religion as if it were not deserving of serious thought; and as if any raw talker could deal with it worthily?"

Reflection made me ashamed of my rashness, and I set about the preparation of written sermons; and got the greater part of each sermon well fixed in my mind before I ventured to deliver it. The result was more cheering and gratifying than I can easily tell. I had soon larger congregations than any other local preacher in the circuit; and grew into request for anniversary sermons in the surrounding circuits. I threw my whole heart and soul into my preaching; and the effects were often of a rememberable kind. Shouts of praise from believers often overpowered my voice; and I had to pause, and say, "Let us sing a verse, and then go on again." And, not seldom, sobs and tears foreshowed what kind of work there would be for the prayer-leaders when the sermon was over. That many received good by my preaching, I have not the least doubt; and some are living at the present moment, thank God! who declare I was the instrument of their conversion.

I frequently held prolonged meetings in the Sunday evenings, and had to walk home, in all sorts of weather, a distance of from three to six or eight miles at a late hour. When I visited villages or towns in the surrounding circuits, I was usually furnished with a horse; and had to ride back to Gainsborough on the Monday morning to be in time for opening my school at nine o'clock. The rides and journeyings in themselves were often delightful; and I thoroughly enjoyed my outward work as a preacher.

Nor could I continue to take a part in such work without endeavouring to make it serve my own intellectual culture. The writing out of sermons was a noble induction to the art of expressing one's thought. I strove to make my sermons worth listening to. I had become master of a vocabulary of no mean order, by committing Milton and Shakspeare to memory and repeating them so often; and my reading of the old English divines enabled me to acquit myself in the pulpit with more than the ordinary ability of a Methodist local preacher. I possess no copy of any of the sermons I preached in those years; but I know they contained passages of euphony, of pathetic appeal, of picturesque description, and power of argument and declamation, that I should not be ashamed of if I saw them now in print.

Nor did I neglect attendance on any popular living example of eloquence and of the power of preaching that came within my hearing.

The most memorable treat I ever had from the pulpit was in once seeing and hearing Rowland Hill. He was over eighty when I heard him, but still possessed the vigour of ten ordinary preachers. He, of all the preachers I ever heard, occupies the pedestal of veneration in the statue-gallery of my memory. Other popular ministers of the time I also heard from the pulpit of the Independents in Gainsborough; such as Dr. Raffles, who was then young, and in the full exercise of his almost dramatic power in the pulpit; Dr. Bennett of London, "Silver-voiced Bennett" as he was called, than whom I never heard a more instructive preacher; Joseph Gilbert of Nottingham, and Winter Hamilton of Leeds, and Smith of Rotherham, and Dr. Pye Smith, and Ellis the great missionary, and others.

Of all leading Methodist preachers, the wondrous voice and noble form and noble eloquence of Robert Newton were most familiar to me; for he was the favourite, because the most successful, anniversary preacher ever invited to Gainsborough. We were favoured, less frequently with the stately form and high intellectuality of Richard Watson; but no one could ever forget him, who saw and heard him. The poetic power of David McNicol, the spiritual power of Peter McOwan, the manly preaching of Thomas Galland, the stern and relentless scourging of sin by brave Daniel Isaac, the never-ending missionary tales of Joshua Marsden, are all enduringly associated in my memory with that Gainsborough Methodist pulpit. But if I had the power to summon one from the dead, that I might hear him preach again in it—William Dawson of Barnbow should be the man. For originality of conception, richness and variety of imagery, clearness of Scriptural illustration, pathos, humour, power of grappling with the conscience, and mastery in the art of winning a man—William Dawson was the preacher of preachers, in my humble judgment.

If any young lady happens to be intent on the task of reading this Memoir, I imagine she will say, "You seem, sir, to think you have a right to talk about everybody and anything; but you have got into your ninth chapter without making even the slightest allusion to a *certain subject!*"

And, no doubt, the greater number of readers expect a pretty early allusion to the sex and the tender passion, in every biography and autobiography. But I had nothing to communicate, all this time; and therefore could not broach the thought.

And, I suspect, few readers will be surprised that I say so. They will understand that I was too fully absorbed in fervours and passions of one kind or other, to have many moments to think about the tender passion. Indeed, I had never yet spoken a word to a woman, or given her a glance of the eye, that could be called, in our old Lincolnshire speech, "taking notice of her."

But I may now say that I saw the dear one who has now been for thirty-seven years my companion in life, at Christmas of 1829, while on a visit to Lincoln, and conversed with herself and her sister, in the house of her brother. The family were all born Methodists, so to speak, and I went to Lincoln on a Methodist visit, as I may say, for it was to see and hear the revivalist John Smith. Yet although my heart said, "This is the woman I should like for a wife," I spoke not one word about it. And when I saw her brother, in the following year, he told me she had lain months on a sick-bed, and was never expected to recover. In the year following I heard that she was really recovering, and I went over to Lincoln, and, on the 1st of July, 1831, offered my heart and hand, and was accepted.

During that visit to Lincoln, at Christmas of 1829, I also formed a friendship which, next to that of my wife, I deem the most valuable of my whole life. Frederick James Jobson—who is now known as the Rev. Dr. Jobson by the religious world, and as an ex-President of the Wesleyan Methodist Conference—was then but eighteen years old, and had only recently been converted, under the ministry of John Smith; and was "on trial" as a local preacher. He was apprenticed, as an architect, to Edward James Willson, the most learned antiquary in Lincoln, and the best helper Britton could find in drawing up his account of the antiquities of Lincoln Cathedral.

Jobson was full of passion for art, and of admiration for poetry, and had already displayed considerable eloquence as a preacher. His nature was all earnestness; and it was not wonderful that two such earnest natures as his and mine should form a friendship from the moment that we met. We often contrived to meet, even while I remained at Gainsborough—sometimes on a Sunday, that we might preach in the same village, and have time to converse on literary composition, and on our work as preachers. My after-life has often separated me from my dear friend's companionship; but never, in any change of my opinions, or adverse turn of fortune, did he forsake me, or fail to help me in a difficulty. And many a time I have had to rely on him, as my only human help. Our friendship has now lasted, unbroken, for two-and-forty years; and I thank God that ever I had such a true, faithful, and unfailing friend as Frederick James Jobson.

But, to return to my new passion of love. Must I tell it? It awoke my slumbering sense of poetry. I had never attempted verse for, I think, six years. But I wrote verses irresistibly, now; and enclosed them in my love-letters—of which, the reader may take it for granted that I wrote a very great number. Soon, I thought of writing something that might be published. And when I had struck off a number of short pieces, in blank verse and rhyme, the intended volume took a title that I had no thought of. I was persuaded by my friend Charles Kelvey, whom I had brought over from Independency to Methodism, to place *first* in the volume a copy of verses that were only written in a whim, and never intended for publication. "Place that *first*, and call the volume by that name," he insisted, "and it will sell the book!"

Dear Charley! he wished it to be so; but he was mistaken.

Some of my subscribers never paid their subscriptions, and the publication only increased the embarrassment I was experiencing from the cause I shall mention anon. The unfortunate volume was entitled "The Wesleyan Chiefs:" many of the pieces were worthless, and none more so than the one that gave name to the unfortunate little book. But I had one rich pleasure connected with my book, unfortunate as it was. I was favoured with two interviews by James Montgomery of Sheffield—the first literary man of my time that I had ever seen; and he kindly undertook to read the proof-sheets while my volume was being printed. He wrote words on one proof-sheet, at the bottom of the page that contained one little piece of blank verse—they were lines "To Lincoln Cathedral"—"These are very noble lines, and the versification is truly worthy of them."

That consoled me a little for my want of success. And my failure only made the resolve sink the deeper and become the firmer in my mind, that I would, one day, write a poem that should not fail.

Our Gainsborough Circuit, under the two ministers who were stationed in it when I joined the Methodist Society, had an increase of between four and five hundred members in their last year. John Chettle, the superintendent, (whose son, Henry Hulbert Chettle, is now an honoured minister in the same religious body,) was unsurpassed as a theologian by any Wesleyan minister I ever listened to. And his appeals to the understanding, the conscience, and the heart, were often irresistible. William Ash, his colleague, was a man of lowly abilities as a preacher, but greatly beloved for his piety and pastoral qualities; and he was of incalculable value in our prayer-meetings, during the continuance of "the revival." The superintendent who succeeded Mr. Chettle was a heavy man, troubled with liver disease, and died in the circuit. He had, unfortunately, checked rather than encouraged our fondness for devotional and protracted meetings. His colleague, Jonathan J. Bates, was an excellent preacher; but neither did he readily enter into the "revival" spirit. Yet we loved him; and the circuit steadily prospered when he was left at its head, alone.

The coming of a new superintendent, whose name I shall not record here, began to bring disaster on the circuit. He would not work. The members fell off. The monies fell off. And it was resolved, by a very large majority of the official members in the circuit, not to invite him to remain after his first year. He was crafty, as well as idle; and he tricked us. He told us he meant to leave our circuit at the next Conference, and get a circuit in the South of England. And he told us so, openly, in the regular quarterly meeting. We were taken by surprise; but as we did not wish to make any representation in his disfavour to the Conference, we resolved to let him go away quietly.

When the Conference met, and issued the "rough stations," his name was put down for a circuit in the South of England, as we had expected it would be. But when the Conference broke up, he came back upon us, as our superintendent for another year. We learned, by one of the ministers (Mr. Harrison) who was appointed to Doncaster, that the trick had been fixed upon from the first, and that this man had voluntarily lied to us. We wrote, at once, to the President of Conference for the year, 1833, Rev. Richard Treffry; and to the chairman of our district, Rev. John Stephens of Hull. They answered us very promptly and very kindly; but told us there was no remedy, as we had not sent to Conference to say we desired his removal, and they could not remove him: they had not the power to do it, by the laws and constitution of Wesleyan Methodism—which was undoubtedly true.

He persecuted us because of these letters. He suspended myself (who had written the letters, which were signed by forty official persons) and another young local preacher (who had taken the letters round the circuit for signature) from our offices as preachers, without either charge or trial—by a few lines of writing. The society in town and circuit was all discontent, and all discord. The chairman of the district came to Gainsborough, and held a "special district meeting," with the aim of setting all right again; and the two suspended local preachers were restored to the "preachers' plan." But he who had been the cause of the discord maintained the defiant and persecuting spirit still. He prevented us from taking any part in the public prayer-meetings; and he preached at us, in terms that made our skin creep! The misery of remaining in Gainsborough was now so great that I set myself in pursuit of a school in some other town, and prepared for removal.

It was time that I left Gainsborough. I had been foolish enough to leave my school often an hour before the time of proper conclusion in the evening, that I might walk to some part of the circuit, sometimes in the snow, to supply deficiencies of the superintendent, who shirked his work. My school fell off in consequence, and I began to be in difficulties. I grew weary also of the drudgery of teaching, now my first scholars were gone, and the parents of those that remained, or the majority of them, were unwilling for me to follow my own plans in the tuition of the children.

I sought a school in Sheffield and elsewhere; but there seemed no opening, and I was becoming very restless and weary, when a letter suddenly informed me of the death of a schoolmaster in Lincoln—a relative of her to whom I had pledged heart and hand. So I left Gainsborough, took the school at Lincoln, in November, 1833; and on the 16th day of February, 1834, we were married. After a time, my dear mother gave up work, and came to live with us at Lincoln.

When we were married, my beloved wife and I resolved to lead holy and devoted lives. But our resolve was frustrated. The Gainsborough superintendent met the Lincoln superintendent in the house of a Methodist class-leader at Scotton—where the two circuits join—and there gave earnest charge to the Lincoln superintendent to get me out of the Methodist Society as soon as possible. He was bent on stern revenge for the part I had taken in exposing his falseness. I was informed of it, fully, by the person in whose house this revengeful counsel was given—a good devoted man, whose son (Rev. Edward Bramford) is now in the Wesleyan Ministry.

The Lincoln superintendent had no craft or guile about him. But he was a rude, rash man; and was easily impelled to act rashly. He began to talk against me in Methodist houses, before he had spoken one word to me! And soon he began to deal roughly with me, for an omission to preach, when I was too ill to walk to the place. I had also very unexpected unkindness and very unchristian dealing from a leading member of the Society in Lincoln; and the Lincoln superintendent took this person's side. That person has now gone to his account, and I shall not say more about him.

The Lincoln superintendent continued his rough treatment of me, and at last threatened to suspend me from my office as a local preacher. "Nay," I said to him, "I was suspended once; but I will not be hung a second time. Take my name out of the class book,—I am no longer a member of your Society." "That will do!" said he, with a look of satisfaction; "good morning!"

And so they had their will! But the Gainsborough superintendent, who advised this rough man to get me out of the Society, was ejected from the Society (or "left out of the Minutes of Conference") a few years afterwards, himself. He also has gone to his account; and so has the Lincoln superintendent. I trust I pray from the heart, when I cry, "God forgive them all!" But my being thus driven to cut myself off from Methodism was a source of the bitterest agony to my dear wife, for years afterwards; I know it caused bitter grief to the dear friend I have mentioned in this chapter — the best and truest friend, I repeat, that I have ever had in the world; and it soured my own mind against religious professors, and raised within me a wrong, rebellious spirit. My mind grew angry whenever I thought of my ill-treatment; and I soon left off my habit of attendance on public worship. I feel, now, I was very guilty in this: guilty in forsaking God because man had been unkind and unjust to me.

And now, at sixty-six, I see what I did not see, or reflect upon when I was younger: that it is irrational to expect every man to be perfect in a ministerial body composed of a thousand members. I have no doubt, too, that I was often chargeable with a wrong spirit, and most likely uttered tart and provoking observations during the altercations I had with the Gainsborough and Lincoln superintendents. But it must be remembered that I was very inexperienced — ten times more inexperienced at eight-and-twenty, than thousands of lads often are at eighteen; while these Christian ministers were mature men in years, and the Gainsborough minister had not only been long in public life, but was one who had a shrewd knowledge of the world. I cannot help thinking that if I had had to deal with men who had more of "the milk of human kindness" in them, the result and conclusion would have been less disastrous to myself.

I am not yet come to the later period of my life when I fell into an awful alienation of the mind from the faith of Christ; but I cannot help tracing that alienation to its root in these harsh dealings from ministers and professors of religion. I have felt compelled to state the truth, in order that all who read these pages to the end may have some key to unlock what they might otherwise deem very mysterious changes of character in me. And having said so much, I purpose now to leave the entire subject, for the present, in this

Memoir. When the step of separating myself from Methodism was taken, the die was cast anew for my Future—whatever it was to be—and I sought occupation for thought that should not awake tormenting remembrances, and soon found it.

CHAPTER X.
LINCOLN: MECHANICS' INSTITUTE: MUSIC: 1834—1837.

I SOON found myself in a new world at Lincoln; and now, first, may be said to have mingled with the real world, and to have begun to understand that I really belonged to it. The Mechanics' Institute was being formed in the ancient city just at the time that I settled in it. I immediately became a member of the Institute, and was elected on its first Committee: our President being Sir Edward Ffrench Bromhead, and our Secretary the well-known political agent, William Spencer Northhouse. The Institute was started with great enthusiasm. Many young working men in the city had great expectations of learning; and the list of members was very numerous.

The Committee assigned the Curatorship of the Institute to Mr. John Boole, my wife's uncle, who had for many years followed the business of a master shoemaker; but who had, by self-instruction, made considerable progress in mathematics, and who was in high reputation in the city as a man of great intelligence and general information. He opened classes for students in geometry and in algebra; Dr. William Cookson opened a botany class; Mr. W. A. Nicholson a class for drawing; and I opened a class for Latin. A library was formed, lectures commenced; and there were soon very busy doings at the Institute.

My connection with the Institute led to an acquaintanceship with persons of influence to whom I might otherwise have remained unknown; and was the source of some valuable and hearty friendships. But my first most earnest business, when I settled at Lincoln, was to set about the renewal of my studies. What though I was on the verge of twenty-nine years of age? Surely, I thought, I had yet time to make considerable acquirements. I forgot to say that I had been compelled, while at Gainsborough, to attend a little to my Greek,—although absorbed so much in preaching, and entangled with so many other cares,—in order to keep up with, or rather in advance of, my two elder scholars.

When they had finished Cæsar, and gone through a few books of the Eneid, their father wished them to begin Greek. So I, very soon, had to put one into the Anabasis of Xenophon, and the other into the Cyropædia. In Lincoln, I now took up the Memorabilia of Xenophon, ran through the Odes of Anacreon, and then commenced the Iliad. I worked hard at Greek, and also at the Hebrew Genesis, for some time; not suffering my new engagements at the Institute to rob me of the hours I knew I must employ for my own mental advancement, now or never.

But there was no one to teach French in the Mechanics' Institute; and the members of my Latin class, with others, were eager to learn French. I told them I could read it, but could not pronounce it. I very soon learned, however, that I could have a most competent instructor, on terms that I could afford to pay; so I soon secured his aid.

Signor D'Albrione, my new instructor, was a very noble-looking Italian gentleman, a native of Turin, who had been a cavalry officer in the armies of Napoleon, had endured the retreat from Moscow, was at the defeat of Leipzig, and had seen other service under the first Emperor of the French. He was now a refugee in England, on account of his participation in the conspiracy of the Carbonari; and gained his support by teaching languages. Under his instruction— while we read together part of Voltaire's "Charles the Twelfth," and "Le Bourgeois Gentilhomme" of Moliere—I caught such hold of good French pronunciation as would have enabled me soon to converse very pleasantly in the language, could I have found a companion.

As I thought I could easily learn Italian, I took lessons from Signor D'Albrione also in the pronunciation of that language—believing I should not be likely to have so good an opportunity of learning it, perhaps, to the end of life, as I had now. So we read together part of one of the comedies of Goldoni, and then a part of the beautiful "Gerusalemme Liberata," of Tasso, in that most beautiful tongue.

I opened an elementary French Class in the Mechanics' Institute very soon; but it was not until D'Albrione had left Lincoln, and I could have no more instruction from him in French and Italian pronunciation, that I determined to begin German, of which I was very eager to know something. I was soon able to make my way in a volume of tales by Herder, Lessing, and others. My school prospered, for I took care to attend to its duties assiduously; and yet kept firm hold of my studies, rising early in the morning, and, with my book in my hand, as of old, walked from our little home in St. Mary's Street, along the Sincil Dyke, and on to Canwick Common, whenever the weather permitted me to do so.

My attendance on a series of most excellent lectures on Chemistry, by Mr. Murray—a well-known lecturer of the time—at the Institute, opened my way, most unexpectedly, to a new kind of life. I took it into my head to write a paragraph descriptive of the lectures, and sent it to the *Lincoln, Rutland, and Stamford Mercury,* a weekly newspaper of great business character, and understood to be one of the oldest in the kingdom. About a month after the insertion of the paragraph, Richard Newcomb, Esq., of Stamford, proprietor of the paper, called upon me and thanked me for the paragraph; and offered me £20 a year "to collect," as he said, "a few items of market and other news, and send them to him weekly." I accepted the offer, for I understood that it would not occupy much of my time; and I was resolute in keeping hold of my studies, during the first two years that I lived in Lincoln.

But a new attraction arose at last; and all resolves about study, and purposes of intellectual progress, and interests however important, were sacrificed for my new passion. A few young men wished to form a Choral Society, and asked me to allow them the use of my school-room for rehearsals. I consented readily, and became a member of the new society—taking my stand, weekly, as a tenor singer in the choruses. My heart and brain were soon on flame with the worship of Handel's grandeur, and with the love of his sweetness and tenderness. They made me their secretary; and my head went to work to make the music of the Choral Society worth hearing in old cathedralled Lincoln.

I planned, I visited, I wooed, I entreated, till I obtained the aid and
co-operation of the best musicians and the best singers in the ancient
city. Like every true reformer, I had to put down the authority of the
imperfect, and put the authoritative perfect in its place. Over the
company of raw amateurs—de-spite some grumbling—I succeeded
in placing the most perfect "singer at sight," and most thoroughly
experienced person in the music of Handel, to be found in the whole
city, as conductor; the best violinist in the city, as leader; the best alto
and tenor singers in the city, as leaders of their parts in the choruses,
and as principal solo singers; the organist of the cathedral, as leader
on the viola; the best violoncello player in Lincoln, as leader on his
instrument; while I also secured the aid of an experienced
trumpeter. We already had the aid of a good double-bass player,
who was also a sound timist. And I may also say that I had most
valuable aid, by way of counsel and advice, from that most
accomplished musician, the late Rev. George S. Dickson, Incumbent
of St. Swithin's, Lincoln.

The next step was to obtain funds, that professional men might be
remunerated, and the society held together by something more than
mere enthusiasm. I wrote to the nobility, gentry, and clergy of the
county and the city, and to all members of Parliament for
Lincolnshire; and was successful in almost every case. I raised an
income of £200 for the society's first year. Then I besought the Dean,
the Precentor, and Subdean to lend their powers of persuasion; and
the incumbent of the most central church in the city granted us the
use of it for our public concerts of sacred music. Mr. Whall, the most
thoroughly competent organist in Lincoln, presided at the organ;
and, before a crowded audience, the transcendent "Messiah," the
noble "Dettingen Te Deum," the brilliant and warlike "Judas
Maccabæus," the gorgeous "Solomon," the sublime "Israel in
Egypt," and other oratorios of Handel, were performed with an
enthusiasm that had never before been witnessed in Lincoln. The
"Creation" of Haydn, and scattered choral pieces of Mozart and
Beethoven, were also given.

Nor was the solo singing of a mean character. Our conductor,
George Brooke, of the cathedral choir, would have attracted

admiration, as a bass singer of great original powers of expression, and great capability of execution, with the most critical audience in the kingdom. The tenor singing of dear departed Charles Ashton—a universal favourite in Lincoln—was the sweetest I ever heard, except Braham's. Mr. Knowles, our alto solo singer, was not only a very pleasing vocalist, but a competent musician; and is, at the moment I write, a member of the choir in St. George's Chapel, Windsor.

I raised a separate subscription of twenty guineas, for the purchase of concert drums; bought a chromatic slide trumpet at the urgent request of our trumpeter; formed a rich musical library, comprising the forty thick folio volumes of Arnold's complete score of Handel, with German scores of the "Creation," the "Requiem," and the "Mount of Olives"—for the use of the society. I say, I did all this— for, although I met a committee of the performers, that conferred together about the selection of choruses and solos for each concert, as it drew nigh, they took no part in the real business of the society. I had all that to plan and execute for myself.

What mad enthusiasm I felt for music! I often sat up the greater part of a night to transact the writing necessary for the furtherance of the prosperity of that Choral Society. I walked, I ran, I jumped, about the city—I climbed its "steep hill" often half a dozen times in a day— to win subscribers and collect subscriptions, and get performers to be punctual at the rehearsals, and to reconcile their petty animosities and keep them united; and I also spent some little money on the darling project of making music successful in Lincoln. I was ever striving to obtain more subscriptions, that our best performers might be better paid—though I would have scorned to take one farthing myself. The enjoyment—the rapture—I had in listening to the music, was more than a reward for whatever time I gave to the society, or interest I sacrificed for it.

But the check to my enthusiasm came; and the end of all this passionate indulgence of the one sense of hearing—did I say? Nay, if there were not mind in music, it could not master us in this way, and to the degree that it masters many. A passion for music is something far above the mere indulgence of feeling. Oh, how easily

I could again yield to it! But I dare not. Thank God! we shall have music in heaven; and I can wait for it, till I get thither, remembering that the music of heaven will unspeakably transcend all the music of earth.

I say the end came. What no one had thought of trying to do till I did it—and what all acknowledged I had done so well—was deemed, at first, in whispers, an assumption of authority, and, at last, and aloud, and to my face, a most shameful tyranny! I was opposed,—I was thwarted,—I was "called to account,"—I was advised to resign,—I was threatened with dethronement;—and so, eventually, I abdicated, and left the Lincoln Choral Society, which had been my idol and my passion, to conduct itself.

CHAPTER XI.
LINCOLN: BUSY LIFE AS A NEWSPAPER WRITER: 1836—1838.

IT was well that I broke my connection with music, for my passion would have been ruinous to me had I continued to let it sway me in the manner I have described. The proprietor of the newspaper, by whom I had been engaged, at first, at £20 a year, to furnish weekly trifles in the way of news, made larger demands now upon my time and attention. The need of keeping up, in some degree, with the spirit of the age, made him desirous of having reports of the new municipality of Lincoln, and of the various important meetings which took place in the old city—naturally, one may say, as the capital of the shire. He gradually advanced me to £60, and at last to £100 per annum. Of course I ceased to be a schoolmaster; and began now to be regarded by some with strong dislike, and by others with no little fear and dread, as the powerful correspondent of the Lincoln, *Rutland, and Stamford Mercury!*

I wrote paragraphs on abuses that raised up enemies against me; but many of these, when they saw I did not fear them, became my friends. The paper rose in circulation; and the excitement was great every Friday morning, in old Lincoln, to get a sight of their old business paper, which had now become enlivened with such bristling criticisms and startling revelations of abuses. A series of short articles entitled "Lincoln Preachers," was, perhaps, the cause of more excitement than anything beside that I wrote for the *Mercury*.

The Dean, the Precentor, the Chancellor, the Subdean, and the Vicars of the Cathedral, all had their likenesses drawn as preachers and men—according to the presumptuous judgment of him who drew them. Nor were their incomes, their pluralities, and temporalities, any more than their spiritualities, omitted in the brief and summary descriptions given of them. The Dissenting and Wesleyan ministers, as well as the parochial clergy of the city, were also presented with their portraits—very much to their chagrin, vexation, and mortification, in many cases. Some of them made ludicrous attempts, in a secret way, to secure a favourable picture for themselves; and others blustered and threatened.

Let me confess what regret I feel now for much of my newspaper life; for this was by no means the end of it. If I could live over again, and choose the kind of life I would live, it would not be that of a writer for newspapers, although I enjoyed a great part of my employment. I am sure it was the cause to me of real corruption of the heart, and hardening of the feelings. To hear your criticisms quoted with a relish; to know that your sarcasms do really sting and torment people filling important and responsible stations; to know that hundreds like all this, rub their hands with glee, and look eagerly for more of it; to see and hear yourself named as the cleverest fellow in the place, and the man most to be dreaded! There is much that tickles fallen human nature in all this; but I would get out of the way of it, rather than write for it, if I had life to come over again.

Often, it is true, I wrote the sharp criticisms I speak of a thousand times more for mirth than for mischief. But to turn the laugh against a man is often a sorer punishment to him than to whip his back with a cato'-nine-tails. My merriest articles for the general reader were, I doubt not, a real source of grief to the party against whom they were pointed. I had proof of this, more than once. But some new temptation was sure to impel me, very soon, to perpetrate a similar evil joke in another direction.

I resumed the composition of verses in Lincoln. "The Daughter of Plantagenet," and some of the songs in my "Baron's Yule Feast," were written in Lincoln. I also began an historical romance, and wrote about one volume of the three intended volumes; but I did not finish the romance till a later period, that I shall have to speak of. Keeping in my heart of hearts the resolve that I would one day write a poem that should not fail, I used often to ask myself, "What shall the subject be, when the time comes?" But I could not determine, although I mused on many subjects.

The answer came suddenly to my mind, one day, as I sat in one of the recesses of the windows of the old Guildhall, attending a meeting of the town council, in my office of reporter to the *Stamford Mercury*, I conceived, as it seemed in a moment, the creation of either a drama, or an epic, wherein the spirits of suicidal kings, and other remarkable personages, should be interlocutors on some high theme, or themes; and resolved to call it "The Purgatory of Suicides." I wrote down, on one of the leaves of my reporting book, the names of Demosthenes, and Hannibal, and Brutus, and Cassius, and Cato, and Nero, and Achitophel, and Judas Iscariot, and Castlereagh, and others, at the time, and preserved the leaf. I also kept the title before me, and never thought of changing it for one moment.

I have said that I felt as if really entering the world and beginning to belong to it, in Lincoln. And how utterly new a great deal of the life I saw and joined in Lincoln, was to me! My office on the newspaper brought me into the world of politics. It will have been seen, already, that I had been a Radical from boyhood; and, now, of course, I belonged in Lincoln to the Lytton-Bulwer party. For the great novelist, dramatist, and so on,—the present *Conservative* Lord Lytton, was then the *Liberal* Sir Edward Lytton Bulwer. And when I asked him, one day, at the table of one of his principal supporters, what government he would prefer for England, if we could choose the kind of government, now?—he replied, without hesitation "A Republican Government."

Sir Edward Lytton Bulwer was at one time in great favour in Lincoln; and, so far as I was able, I helped his cause by upholding it in the *Mercury*, and endeavouring to strengthen his interest with the Lincoln electors. I had often to report his speeches, and have a most vivid remembrance of their eloquence, and of the remarkable energy with which, very often, they were delivered.

Attendance at political meetings, public dinners, and concerts of music, involved the consumption of time, the consumption of wine, and late hours. I became a social man, a "lover of good company," as men call it. The religious seriousness was gone. Yet my new friendships were all of the intellectual cast.

There was one with whom I ought to have been better acquainted. I lament, greatly, that I did not try to draw him nearer to me. But sometimes the slender ties of half-relationship create family likes and dislikes that prevent the formation of what might otherwise be really valuable friendships. I allude to one whose memory is already honoured by the very foremost mathematicians and deepest thinkers, but whose name will become truly illustrious in the wiser future, the late Dr. George Boole, professor of Mathematics in Queen's College, Cork (Ed - *prophetic words indeed, for in the 20th Century Boole's algebra of logic—known now as "Boolean Algebra"—was to become an essential tool in the design of digital computers*).

My wife's mother was a Boole, and was sister to Dr. Boole's father— the curator of the Mechanics' Institute, whom I have already mentioned. Young George came to see his cousins, one day, in that Christmas week of 1829, when I first went to Lincoln as a visitor. He was then a boy of fourteen; had mastered Leslie's Geometry, under his father's teaching; was learning Latin, and thinking of Greek; and almost overwhelmed me with inquiries about the contents of books he had not read.

I heard often of his intellectual progress during our courtship; but never saw him again until, in the first year of our marriage, he came to Lincoln, and read an encomium on Sir Isaac Newton, before a crowded audience, in the Mechanics' Institute. The first Earl of Yarborough, who was present, had given a marble bust of the immortal one to the Institute; and it was unveiled before George began to read his paper. The writing showed how his mind had expanded; but I drew a far larger conclusion, as to the growth of his intelligence, when he called to see his cousins (my wife and her sister), and I could converse with him.

Some time afterwards, he settled in Lincoln, and opened a school. I saw him now and then; but he was shy and formal. I ,think I could have brushed away all his shyness, if I had set myself to do it. But I, proudly, let the shyness grow between us, till it reached estrangement. In after years, he called on me in London, and talked friendlily and freely; and I then felt that he had distanced me so far in his reach of mathematical science, and in his knowledge of languages—in fact, in all knowledge—that I was but a dwarf in his presence. My acquaintance with some facts of his private life, and knowledge of his tenderness towards his parents and care of them in their age, warrant me in saying that he was as good as he was great. I shall increasingly regret, to my life's close, that I did not strive to draw him towards me as a near and intimate friend. I might have done it, if I had set about it aright.

Gilbert Collins became my most frequent companion and closest friend in Lincoln. He was, at first, a clerk in the Old Bank, and afterwards manager of the Hull Branch Bank, at Lincoln. We were nearly of an age; had been attached to the same religious denomination, and had left it; and had an equally strong attachment to the study of languages. Collins had learned Latin at school, and had taught himself Greek, and had translated for himself the entire Iliad and Odyssey. Of the Greek Testament, he had a more perfect knowledge than any one I ever knew. He was laboriously constructing a Harmony of the Four Gospels, in Greek, when I knew him; and you could not mention a Greek text in the Gospels, but he would give you the context, in a moment. He was also a chess-player; and we sometimes spent an hour at the game; but I was never a proficient in it.

Collins one day bought an old quarto Arabic Grammar which had been tumbled about for years in an old book shop. There was a considerable vocabulary of Arabic words at the end; and the whim seized us both to set on and learn Arabic. I copied the words from the vocabulary, in what we thought very pretty Arabic writing; and we were much taken with our project, when, one evening, George Boole suddenly stepped in, and found us earnestly bent over our new toy. He examined the quarto book with interest; but seemed to have difficulty in restraining his laughter when he saw our Arabic writing, and heard us gravely say we were determined to learn the language.

"But where will you get your Arabic books?" asked George; "and how can you read them without a dictionary? You could not get a copy of Richardson's dictionary, I should think, under some twelve or fifteen pounds." We felt ashamed of our thoughtlessness, and laid the project aside.

It would please one's self, very much, to put the names of all one's friends in print: at any rate, such is my own feeling. Yet the general reader might question, not only the propriety, but the sanity, of such an act. Ergo, I shall leave many kind and hearty friendships that I formed in Lincoln uncommemorated. I shall, for the present, mention one only, and then pass on to my more active history. The most important friendship I formed in Lincoln, and, perhaps, the most influential on my own mind, at the time, was that with Charles Seely.

He was then a rising young merchant; but has now for many years been M.P. for Lincoln; while his son—the little Charley whom I used to take on my knee—is M.P. for Nottingham. Charles Seely selected me as an intellectual companion simply from the fact that he thought my company was worth having. For when our friendship was first formed I was but a poor schoolmaster, and had no newspaper influence, or influence of any kind, in the city. He would have me, almost every Sunday, at his table; and often we sauntered by the Witham, or along the Canwick fields, or by the venerable Minster, in the dusk of evening; and sometimes I rode with him, in his mercantile journeys, to Boston or Sleaford. Our conversations were on politics, on human character and society, or on general literature; but how often, during the years that have passed since I left Lincoln, have I thought of the one strong, deep impression I caught of my friend's character—"This is the man whose purpose is formed, and he will accomplish it,"—and how completely that impression has been realised!

My changeful life has separated me from my friend; but I have watched his patriotic course in Parliament, and out of it, with intense gratification. I have seldom seen him during all these years, and our correspondence has necessarily been very limited; yet let me gratefully say that, in my season of sickness and helplessness, a very few years ago, I had substantial proof that my friend had not lost the remembrance of those dear old times in Lincoln.

But my Lincoln chapters must come to an end. In September, 1838, I asked leave of my patron, Mr. Richard Newcomb, to take a week's holiday, and go to see London. He granted leave; but took alarm, and wrote to me, before I had been two days in the capital, desiring me not to look out for a better situation; but to call at Stamford on my way home, as he had something to offer me worth my acceptance. I called; and he at once said, "Cooper, I want you to come and live at Stamford. I mean to retire, and give the management of the paper up to yourself, after I have put you in the way of it a little. You will live here, in this house, so as to be near to your business. I mean to live at Rock Cottage. So go and dispose of your things at Lincoln; and bring Mrs. Cooper with you, to live at Stamford"

I took him at his word, and asked for no "terms," but assured him I would do what he wished me to do, for I felt really attached to him, and strongly desirous of serving him. And as soon as I could accomplish it, I disposed of our little furniture, but not of my books; and my dear wife and I left Lincoln for Stamford. My poor mother preferred to go back to Gainsborough. We went and lived in the house in High Street, Stamford; but Mr. Newcomb did not go out of it. He simply assigned us two apartments in it. And I soon saw that he could not bring his mind to give up the management of his paper to another: it had become, as it were, a part of his existence. He grew angry if I asked to take a larger share in the management; and, at last, kept me in the counting-house as his clerk, and would not let me write even one line for the Mercury! He was giving me £250 a year, with coals and the two rooms rent-free, and I had other privileges which made my situation worth £300 per annum; but he shut me out of his company, and I had no society. I wish I had cheerfully accepted the solitude, as of old, and worked hard to produce a book. But I rashly gave notice to leave; and so, on the 1st of June, 1839, we got on the stage-coach, with our boxes of books, at Stamford,—and away I went to make my first venture in London.

CHAPTER XII.
FIRST LONDON LIFE: VICISSITUDES: 1839—1840.

I THOUGHT I might very fairly expect a little introductory help, in London, from the literary baronet and Liberal M.P. whom I had humbly striven to serve in Lincoln. So I took the manuscript of my unfinished romance, and called upon him, at his house in Hertford Street, Mayfair. He received me, smoking, with a thousand smiles; and assured me he would show the manuscript to his publishers. I called at his door, once or twice, during the seven weeks that elapsed before I saw him again; and then wrote to tell him that I would wait upon him on such a day. He came, hastily, into the room where I waited, put the manuscript into my hand, and said, "I regret to say that although Messrs. Saunders and Otley consider it a work of merit, they have so many other things in hand, that they cannot receive it at present. Good morning, Mr. Cooper!"—and he bowed and disappeared through folding-doors into another room, in an instant. His servant opened the door behind me, as I stood staring, and showed me the way into the street.

I wish the literary baronet had either kindly told me one truth, that my writing was too faulty to offer for publication, and I had better try to achieve a more perfect work before I sought a publisher; or that he had honestly told me another truth, that he had never shown my poor manuscript to Messrs. S. and O., and did not choose to take any trouble on my behalf. I speedily learned the truth; and it gave me poor hope of making my way by the help of friends in London.

We lodged in St. George's Road, Southwark, that I might be near Thomas Miller, who then lived in Elliott's Row, in the same road. He was writing "Lady Jane Grey," when I reached London. It was the third romance he had written for Colburn, the publisher; but I found he only received small sums for his labour, and had to work hard to bring up his young family. He declared himself to have no power whatever to help me to literary employ; but we again became companions, and he took me over his favourite walks to Sydenham, Dulwich, Greenwich, and other parts of Surrey and Kent, and we talked of old times. At the very time I write, I learn that he is ill, and needs help. He has written forty books, in his time—all tending to improve working men's minds. Is it right that this industrious hard-worker should be left to want in his old age ?

Before I left Lincolnshire I had corresponded with Sir Culling Eardley Smith, while he was sheriff of the county; and when he learned that I was in London and wanted employment, he wrote to request me to go over to Bedwell Park, Herts. He thought I could assist the *Herts Reformer*, a Liberal paper in which he took an interest. I went to Hertford, and saw the proprietor, but found that he really had no need of my services, although he was willing to oblige Sir Culling; but I would not impose myself upon him.

Sir Culling also gave me an introduction to Josiah Conder, who was then editor of the *Patriot* newspaper. Mr. Conder was sure that he could make no room for me—they were quite full-handed; but he would give me a note to Alaric Watts. I called on Alaric Watts, who was busy editing, I think, three or four papers, at that time—in one of the courts in Fleet Street. He laid down his pen, and asked me a few questions, said he had no office vacant, in his own gift, and he did not know of anything—would I call again? The interview did not last more than three minutes; and though I called again, several times, I was always told he was not in. Mr. Conder next gave me a note to Mr. Southgate, a small publisher in the Strand, who issued the *Sunbeam* and the *Probe*; and I earned of him perhaps five pounds, by contributing reviews and prose sketches, till the two ephemeral papers ended.

I had many other ventures and adventures, in a small way; but it would weary any mortal man to recite them; and the recital would only be an old story which has been often told already, by poor literary adventurers. The very little money I could bring to London was soon gone; and then I had to sell my books. I, happily, turned into Chancery Lane, and asked Mr. Lumley to buy my beautifully bound Tasso, which I had bought of D'Albrione, and "Don Bellianis of Greece," a small quarto blackletter romance, which I had bought from an auctioneer in Gainsborough, who knew nothing of its value.

Mr. Lumley gave me liberal prices, wished I could bring him more such books, and conversed with me very kindly.

I had to visit him again and again, on the same needy errand; and, seeing my need, he asked if I would copy for him, at the British Museum, the oldest printed book in the Library—Caxton on Chess. I undertook to do so; Miller procured for me William Jerdan's note of recommendation to Sir Henry Ellis, the librarian, and I was soon free of the Reading Room—a privilege I have always taken care to retain by getting my ticket renewed whenever I revisit London. How I loved that old reading-room—so humble, when compared with the incomparable magnificent one erected by Panizzi!—and how well acquainted I grew with the varied contents of its shelves!

When I had copied Caxton, Mr. Lumley told me, if I could not find more remunerative employ, he would get me to assist him in making catalogues of the old books he was sending to America—of which he despatched thousands of volumes, at that time. Then he began to issue a Bibliographical journal, or monthly book advertiser, and I helped in some manner with that. All this was very subordinate labour, and but little money could be afforded for it; but I was treated with such respectful kindness by Mr. Lumley, that I retain a very grateful remembrance of him.

We were often at "low-water mark," now, in our fortunes; but my dear wife and I never suffered ourselves to sink into low spirits. Our experience, we cheerily said, was a part of "London adventure;" and who did not know that adventurers in London often underwent great trials before success was reached? We strolled out together in the evenings, all over London, making ourselves acquainted with its highways and byways, and always finding something to interest us in its streets and shop windows.

I must not pass by a remarkable reminiscence of two Sundays in the year 1839. I had gone with my dear wife to hear Thomas Binney, at the Weigh House Chapel; and Robert Montgomery, at St. Dunstan's in the West—(when I also heard Adams on the organ); and Caleb Morris, in Fetter Lane; and Melville, (afterwards the "Golden

Lecturer") at Camberwell; and Dr. Leifchild, at Craven Chapel; Thomas Dale, at St. Bride's Church; and other preacher-notabilities of the time; but one Sunday, being alone in the street near Charing Cross, I met a literary man whom I had known in Lincoln—John Saunders, then employed on Charles Knight's Penny Magazine, and afterwards the author of "Abel Drake's Wife," and other novels; and he invited me to go with him to hear the celebrated Robert Owen open a new institution in John Street, Tottenham Court Road. I went, and heard Mr. Owen deliver the opening address in that lecture-hall, little imagining that I should lecture there so often in the after-time.

Seeing an advertisement in the *Times* the next day, that W. J. Fox would lecture, the following Sunday, at South Place, Finsbury Square, on the System of Robert Owen, I resolved to go thither. As I came in sight of the chapel, I saw Robert Owen, walked close behind him, paid my shilling, like him, to sit in the strangers' gallery, and sat close by his side to listen to the lecture—little imagining that the lecturer would become my friend in the future, and I should often occupy his pulpit. Such are the remarkable incidents in human life!

I began a new story, during these months of unfruitfulness: a story which was intended to be autobiographical, in some degree. But from the dissipating necessity of going hither and thither to seek employ, and the need of doing some kind of work, however humble, to earn part of a crust, I made but little progress with the sketch. The fragment will be found at the end of two volumes of tales that were published for me some years afterwards, and were named "Wise Saws and Modern Instances." During these months of London vicissitude I also tried to keep up my fragmentary reading of Latin, Greek, French, Italian, and German—until, at length, I had no grammar or dictionary left! Every book I brought from Lincolnshire—and I had about five hundred volumes, great and small—had been sold, by degrees; and, at last, I was compelled to enter a pawnshop. Spare articles of clothing, and my father's old silver watch, "went up the spout," as the expression goes of those who, most sorrowfully, know what it means. Travelling cloak, large box, hat-box, and every box or movable that could be spared in any possible way, had "gone to our uncle's"—and we saw ourselves on the very verge of being reduced to threadbare suits—when deliverance came!

I had, like thousands of poor creatures who follow the practice daily, in London, frequently answered advertisements in the daily newspapers, about editor-ships and reporterships, and contributing of leading or other articles to periodicals—but had no response: no, not one syllable! I had been in London from the evening of the 1st of June, 1839, until near the end of March, 1840—when I answered an advertisement respecting the editorship of a country paper printed in London. I went to the printing-office of Mr. Dougal Macgowan, in Great Windmill Street, Haymarket; and, after some conversation, was engaged, at a salary of three pounds per week, as editor of *The Kentish Mercury, Gravesend Journal, and Greenwich Gazette,*—a weekly newspaper which was printed in Great Windmill Street, but which must be published in Kent, to render it a Kentish paper, it was thought.

So we gave up our London lodging, and went to live at Greenwich, in order that I might publish the paper there. I remained in my new post only till the end of November in the same year; but I saw a great deal of the delightful county of Kent during that year 1840, having to visit all the towns of any size worth visiting, and some of them many times over, on errands connected with the business of the paper. Our delectable walks in Greenwich Park, too, can never be forgotten by my dear wife or myself. Every week-day that I was not journeying over Kent, I had to be in London, to get up the paper for the printer. Do not let me fail to record that I had to perform my work on classic ground. Mr. Macgowan's printing-office had formerly been the Anatomical Museum of the immortal John Hunter; and I did the work of my editorship, daily, in what had once been his study, or private sitting-room!

I only twice or thrice saw the proprietor of the Kentish Mercury— Mr. Wm. Dougal Christie, then a young barrister in chambers, in the Temple—but who has since been distinguished as an M.P., *Charge d'affaires* at Rio Janeiro; and as the excellent editor of Dryden and

Shaftesbury. We did not agree in our notions respecting the management of the paper; and so I, again, "gave notice to leave."

"Another act of rashness!" cries out the reader; but I say otherwise, this time. In the course of fourteen days I had a letter from the Rev. S. B. Bergne, Independent minister of Lincoln, enclosing a letter from the manager of a Leicester newspaper, inquiring, "Can you inform us of the whereabouts of Thomas Cooper, who wrote the articles entitled 'Lincoln Preachers' in the *Stamford Mercury*?"

I dropped the letter from my hands; and my wife remembers well my excited look, as I exclaimed, "The message has come at last!—*the message of Destiny!* We are going to live at Leicester!"

Don't say "Pooh! stuff and nonsense!" good reader. Is there any one thing you can truly say you comprehend? "No," you reply; "I can only apprehend things." Just so. And it is because I am deeply conscious of the same truth, that I have learned to be slower in crying out—"Superstition!" than I used to be. I find there are *mysteries* in our existence that I cannot fathom; and I am compelled to leave them unfathomed, and go on with the duties of active and useful life.

I left Leicester, my birthplace, when a year old, as I have told you, and had never seen the place again to the time I am now speaking of, although I was now thirty-five years old. Yet I tell you, reader, that I had a peculiar impression on my mind, for many years, that I had something to do of a stirring and important nature in Leicester. I did not wish to go to Leicester, for all my aspirations, during many years, had centred in London. And I had no presentation to the mind of the exact work I had to do in Leicester, nor anything resembling that. When there was nothing in the employment of my thoughts, at the time, to lead to such an impression, it would frequently visit me—resting on my mind with a force that amazed me—until something summoned away my attention elsewhere.

Instead of writing to tell the person who inquired for my "whereabouts," I went over to Leicester at once, by the railway. The person who was entrusted with the management of the paper told me that it had but a limited circulation, and they could not afford me much money. However, I took the situation at two pounds per week, and agreed to go and live at Leicester. I remember that, as I had closed accounts at Great Windmill Street, had paid my last visit thither to say "good-bye" to Mr. Macgowan, on the Saturday afternoon, and was passing through the Strand on my way to take the steam-boat for Greenwich, I saw a large placard outside the office of the *Sun* newspaper, proclaiming, "Birth of the Princess Royal!" So that it was on the 21st November. On Monday, the 23rd, 1840, my dear wife and I left Greenwich and London, and took up our lodging in Leicester.

CHAPTER XIII.
LEICESTER: WRETCHEDNESS OF STOCKINGERS: 1840—1841.

I FOUND a dear old friend in Leicester: that same energetic Joseph Foulkes Winks who had instituted our Mutual Improvement Society and adult school at Gainsborough. I soon learned that he had not grown rich, except in the number of his children; but he was as merry-hearted as ever, and as full of energy; for, in addition to his business as printer and bookseller, he was a busy politician, Baptist preacher, and editor of three or four small religious periodicals. My employment on the *Leicestershire Mercury* seemed to me very trifling. I was simply expected to attend the petty sessions, or weekly magistrates' meeting, at Leicester and Loughborough, and to make paragraphs concerning lectures and occasional meetings. I saw plainly that the manager of the paper did not wish me to do overmuch. I expressed my discontent and impatience to my friend Winks; and he told me to wait, for something was about to be done with the paper that would effect a change favourable to myself. But I was soon sent on the errand which led to the fulfilment of my "destiny."

"There is a Chartist lecture to be delivered at All Saints' Open, to-night. As there is nothing else for you to attend to, you may as well go and bring us an account of it. We do not want a full report."— Such was the fiat of the manager of the *Leicestershire Mercury*, that sent me to hear the first words I ever heard spoken by a Chartist lecturer.

Before I left Lincolnshire, and during the year and half I spent in London, I had read in the papers of the day, what everybody read, about the meetings of Chartists—from the great assemblage in Palace Yard, on the 17th September, 1838, when the high-bailiff of Westminster presided,—where the immortal Corn Law Rhymer advocated the political rights of the working classes, and where so many bold speeches were made by men of rank and station, as well as by working men—to the assembling of the "general Convention," and the breaking up of that political body; and the Monmouthshire riots and consequent banishment of Frost, Williams, and Jones, in February 1840. I say I had read about these transactions in the newspapers; and of the fierce agitation against the cruel enactments of the new Poor Law, under Oastler and Stephens. And I had seen mention of the Bull Ring meetings at Birmingham; and of the seizure and imprisonment of many of the Chartist leaders; and then of the release of some of them. But I had never attended a Chartist meeting, or met with any one who maintained Chartist opinions.

Doubtless, the necessity I was under of finding some employment that I might have bread, prevented me from feeling much curiosity about public meetings, during the earlier part of the time that I was in London. And then, when I became editor of the Kentish paper, I was eager to get back to Greenwich every evening, when my work was done in London, and glad to take up some favourite book, or walk with my wife in the beautiful park, rather than seek out political meetings.

The Chartist meeting, in Leicester, that I was now sent to report, gave very small promise of importance. I discovered the small room in "All Saints' Open," after some inquiry, and found, at first, some twenty ragged men collected. The place was filled in the course of about a quarter of an hour, with women as well as men; and all were, apparently, of the necessitous class, save, perhaps, half a dozen who were more decently dressed than the crowd.

The lecturer entered, and, amidst eager clapping of hands, made his way to the small platform. A working man told me his name was John Mason, and he was a Birmingham shoemaker. The lecture was delivered with great energy; but it was sober and argumentative, and often eloquent. The political doctrines advocated were not new to me. I had imbibed a belief in the justice of Universal Suffrage when a boy from the papers lent me by the Radical brushmakers. I heard from John Mason simply the recital of the old political programme of the Duke of Richmond, and his friends, at the close of the last century; of noble, honest Major John Cartwright; of Hunt and later Radicals. I had never had any doubt of the equity that demanded a redistribution of Electoral Districts, short Parliaments, the abolition of the property qualification for members of Parliament, and the payment of members. Of all the "Six Points" of "the People's Charter," there was but one I did not like: the Ballot. And I do not like it now.

It will be seen that there was nothing to startle me in the lecturer's political doctrines. And I discerned no tendency to violence in his address. He was, indeed, as I thought, exceedingly temperate in his language; and it was only when he came to the wind-up that he struck the note that roused strong feeling. He earnestly exhorted his hearers not to be led away from their adherence to the People's Charter by the Corn Law Repealers.

"Not that Corn Law Repeal is wrong," said he; when we get the Charter, we will repeal the Corn Laws and all the other bad laws. But if you give up your agitation for the Charter to help the Free Traders, they will not help you to get the Charter. Don't be deceived by the middle classes again. You helped them to get their votes— you swelled their cry of 'The bill, the whole bill, and nothing but the bill!' But where are the fine promises they made you? Gone to the winds! They said when they had gotten their votes, they would help you to get yours. But they and the rotten Whigs have never remembered you. Municipal Reform has been for their benefit—not for yours. All other reforms the Whigs boast to have effected have been for the benefit of the middle classes—not for yours. And now they want to get the Corn Laws repealed—not for your benefit—but for their own. 'Cheap Bread!' they cry. But they mean 'Low Wages.' Do not listen to their cant and humbug. Stick to your Charter. You are veritable slaves without your votes!"

Such was the strain of the peroration. The speech was received with frequent cries of "Hear, hear," and "That's right!" and sometimes with clapping of hands and drumming of feet.

Two or three of the better-dressed men, who sat on the platform, spoke, at the end, of the sufferings of those who were yet in prison for the People's Charter and then they gave three cheers for Feargus O'Connor, who was at that time a prisoner in York Castle; and three cheers for Frost, Williams, and Jones, whom they said they would have back again; and it was nearly eleven o'clock when the meeting broke up.

As we passed out into the street, I was surprised to see the long upper windows of the meaner houses fully lighted, and to hear the loud creak of the stocking-frame.

"Do your stocking weavers often work so late as this?" I asked of some of the men who were leaving the meeting.

"No, not often: work's over scarce for that," they answered; "but we're glad to work any hour, when we can get work to do."

"Then your hosiery trade is not good in Leicester?" I observed.

"Good! It's been good for nought this many a year," said one of the men; "We've a bit of a spurt now and then. But we soon go back again to starvation!"

"And what may be the average earning of a stocking weaver?" I asked,—"I mean when a man is fully employed."

"About four and sixpence," was the reply.

That was the exact answer; but I had no right conception of its meaning. I remembered that my own earnings as a handicraft had been low, because I was not allowed to work for the best shops. And I knew that working men in full employ, in the towns of Lincolnshire, were understood to be paid tolerably well. I had never, till now, had any experience of the condition of a great part of the manufacturing population of England, and so my rejoinder was natural. The reply it evoked was the first utterance that revealed to me the real state of suffering in which thousands in England were living.

"Four and sixpence," I said; "well, six fours are twenty-four, and six sixpences are three shillings: that's seven-and-twenty shillings a week. The wages are not so bad when you are in work."

"What are you talking about?" said they. "You mean four and sixpence a day; but we mean four and sixpence a week."

"Four and sixpence a week!" I exclaimed. "You don't mean that men have to work in those stocking frames that I hear going now, a whole week for four and sixpence. How can they maintain their wives and children?"

"Ay, you may well ask that," said one of them, sadly.

We walked on in silence, for some moments, for they said no more, and I felt as if I could scarcely believe what I heard. I knew that in Lincolnshire, where I had passed so great a part of my life, the farmers' labourers had wages which amounted to double the earnings these stockingers said were theirs. I had heard of the suffering of handloom weavers and other operatives in the manufacturing districts, but had never witnessed it. What I heard now seemed incredible; yet these spirit-stricken men seemed to mean what they said. I felt, therefore, that I must know something more about the real meaning of what they had told me. I began to learn more of the sorrowful truth from them; and I learned it day by day more fully, as I made inquiry.

A cotton manufacturer builds a mill, and puts machinery into it; and then gives so much per week, or so much per piece of work, to the men and women and boys and girls he employs. But I found that the arrangement in the hosiery trade was very different. The stocking and glove manufacturers did not build mills, but were the owners of the 'frames' in which the stockings and gloves were woven. These frames they let out to the 'masters,' or middlemen, at a certain rent, covenanting to give all the employ in their power to the said 'masters.' The Messrs. Biggs, in my time, owned twelve hundred frames, it was said. Perhaps, fifty of these would be let out to William Cummins, thirty to Joseph Underwood, and so on to other 'masters' or middlemen. The 'masters' employed the working-hands, giving so much per dozen for the weaving of the stockings or gloves, and charging the man a weekly frame-rent—which was, of course, at a profit above the rent the 'master' paid the owner of the 'frame.'

But it was by a number of petty and vexatious grindings, in addition to the obnoxious 'frame-rent,' that the poor framework-knitter was worn down, till you might have known him by his peculiar air of misery and dejection, if you had met him a hundred miles from Leicester. He had to pay, not only 'frame-rent,' but so much per week for the 'standing' of the frame in the shop of the 'master,' for the frames were grouped together in the shops, generally, though you would often find a single frame in a weaver's cottage. The man had also to pay threepence per dozen to the 'master' for 'giving out' of the work. He had also to pay so much per dozen to the female 'seamer' of the hose. And he had also oil to buy for his machine, and lights to pay for in the darker half of the year. All the deductions brought the average earnings of the stocking-weaver to four and sixpence per week. I found this to be a truth confirmed on every hand.

And when he was 'in work,' the man was evermore experiencing some new attempt at grinding him down to a lower sum per dozen for the weaving, or at 'docking' him so much per dozen for alleged faults in his work; while sometimes—and even for several weeks together—he experienced the most grievous wrong of all. The 'master' not being able to obtain full employment for all the frames he rented of the manufacturer, but perhaps only half employ for them—distributed, or 'spread' the work over all the frames.

"Well," the reader will very likely say, "surely, it was better to give all the men half-work, than no work to some, and half-work to others." But the foul grievance was this: each man had to pay a whole week's frame-rent, although he had only half a week's work! Thus while the poor miserable weaver knew that his half-week's work, after all the deductions, would produce him such a mere pittance that he could only secure a scant share of the meanest food, he remembered that the owner of the frame had the full rent per week, and the middleman or 'master' had also his weekly pickings secured to him.

Again: a kind of hose would be demanded for which the frame needed a deal of troublesome and tedious altering. But the poor weaver was expected to make all the alterations himself. And sometimes he could not begin his week's weaving until a day, or a day and a half, had been spent in making the necessary alterations. Delay was also a custom on Monday mornings. The working man must call again. He was too early. And, finally, all the work was ended. The warehouses were glutted, and the hosiery firms had no orders. This came again and again, in Leicester and Loughborough and Hinckley, and the framework-knitting villages of the county, until, when a little prosperity returned, no one expected it to continue.

How different is the condition of Leicester now thirty years have gone over! All who enter it for the first time are pleased with the air of thrift the town wears, and the moving population of the streets. I saw lounging groups of ragged men in my time. I hope what I saw will never be seen again. And I heard words of misery and discontent from the poor that, I hope, are not heard now. I should not like to hear them again, for I know not what they might again impel me to say or do.

CHAPTER XIV.
LEICESTER: MY CHARTIST-LIFE BEGUN: 1841.

I SAID in an earlier chapter that I found myself in a new world at Lincoln; but Leicester was a new world indeed to me, although I had been born in it, nearly thirty-six years before. How unlike it was to the life I had just seen in London: that medley of experience of everything great and little which a man can scarcely have anywhere but in the capital. How unlike it was to the life I knew in Lincoln, where I had mingled a good deal with the well-to-do circles of society, and shared in their enjoyments. But how utterly unlike it was to the earlier old Lincolnshire life that I had known, wherein I mingled with the poor and saw a deal of their suffering,—yet witnessed, not merely the respect usually subsisting between master and servant, but in many instances the strong attachment of the peasantry to the farmers, and of the farmers to their landlords.

Here, in Leicester, in my office of reporter, I soon was witness to what seemed to me an appalling fact: the fierce and open opposition, in public meetings, of working men to employers, manifested in derisive cries, hissing and hooting, and shouts of scorn. The more I learned of the condition of the people, the more comprehensible this sad state of things seemed to me—but what was to be the remedy? My old friend Winks believed in the justice of universal suffrage, with myself; but as he belonged to the party of the old political leaders, and they had decided to ask for the repeal of the Corn Laws, he kept aloof from the Chartists. I got into talk with a few of the lesser employers, and they seemed at their wit's end for a remedy.

The working men, I found, were divided. One party believed in the justice of the demands made by the Chartists, but held that the repeal of the Corn Laws, would benefit them—and these supported the manufacturers at the public meetings. The other party demanded the People's Charter as a first measure and they were the majority at public meetings.

I often wished that some influential person—some one who had a character in the town for real goodness—would offer a compromise. The three brothers, John, William, and Joseph Biggs, who were large employers, had such a character, in my time, and deserved it, too. The compromise that I wished for was a proposal to demand both Charter and Corn Law Repeal, and take anything that could be got first. But there was no spirit of compromise. The manufacturers, to a man, stuck to one side, and would have no union for the Charter.

As I considered the Chartist side to be the side of the poor and the suffering, I held up my hand for the Charter at public meetings. Of course, I might have taken neither side—the custom which is most usual with reporters; but I was made of mettle that *must* take a side, and I could only take the side I did take.

I soon learned that this was an offence in their eyes who supported the *Leicestershire Mercury*; and I speedily added to the offence. The Chartists had started a penny weekly paper to which they gave the high-sounding title of *The Midland Counties Illuminator*. It was mean in appearance, and the fine, intellectual old man, George Bown, who edited the paper, lacked assistance. I wrote him a few articles under promise of secrecy; but soon found that everybody knew what I did. I was, therefore, not surprised when the manager of the *Leicestershire Mercury* told me that I must seek a new situation, for that the paper had no sale sufficient to enable the proprietors to pay my salary.

"Never mind, Tom," said my old friend Winks, when I told him that I had received notice to leave the *Mercury* in a month's time; "don't you leave Leicester. There will be something for you to do soon."

"Don't leave Leicester!" said a group of Chartists, whom I met in the street, and who had heard of my dismissal; "stay and conduct our paper; George Bown wants to give it up."

And in a day or two a deputation from the Chartist committee came to offer me thirty shillings a week, if I would stay in Leicester to conduct their little paper. My friend Winks shook his head at it.

"Have nothing to do with them, Tom," said he; "you cannot depend on 'em. You'll not get the thirty shillings a week they have promised you."

"I don't expect it," I replied; "but I think I can make the paper into something better, if they will give it into my hands; and I think I can do some good among these poor men, if I join them."

My friend argued against me strongly, and at last angrily, declaring that I should ruin myself. But my resolution was taken. I felt I could not leave these suffering stockingers. During the earlier weeks after I entered Leicester, I had so little to fill my mind, or even to occupy my time, that I purposed returning, in right earnest, to my studies, so soon as I could repossess myself of the requisite books. But the more I learned of the state of the poor, the less inclined I felt to settle down to study. The accounts of wretchedness, and of petty oppressions, and the fierce defiances of their employers uttered by working men at public meetings, kept me in perpetual uneasiness, and set me thinking what I ought to do. The issue was that I resolved to become the champion of the poor. "What is the acquirement of languages — what is the obtaining of all knowledge," I said to myself, "compared to the real honour, whatever seeming disgrace it may bring, of struggling to win the social and political rights of millions?"

The day after they had sent to ask me to conduct their paper, I said to one of the Chartist Committee, "Cannot I have a meeting in your little room at All Saints' Open, next Sunday evening, that I may address your members?"

"I am sure we shall be all glad to hear you," said he.

And so, having respect to the day, I spoke to them for an hour, partly on a religious theme, and partly on their suffering and wrongs, and on the question of their political rights. I offered a prayer — it was the prayer of my heart — at the beginning and close of the meeting. This was in March, and I held these Sunday night meetings in the little room till the stirring events of the spring and summer of that year, 1841, compelled us to seek a much larger arena for our enterprise.

The working men paid me thirty shillings for the first week; but could only raise half the sum the second week. I found they were also in debt for paper. So I proposed that they gave up their periodical to me entirely, and I would father their little debt. I obtained twenty pounds of a friend whom I must not name, and made an engagement with Albert Cockshaw, the printer, to print the *Midland Counties Illuminator* on larger and better paper, and with better type. And I also took a front room in the High Street, as an office for my paper. The Chartists soon elected me their secretary; and a great number of them urged me to make my new place in the High Street a shop for the sale of newspapers—saying they would take their weekly *Northern Star* of me. So I sold not only the Chartist *Northern Star*, but papers and pamphlets of various kinds, and my little shop became the daily *rendezvous* of working men. The paper rose in sale—for some of the men, who had no work, took it into the villages, and thus added to its circulation.

As soon as the weather permitted, I began to get the people together for meetings in the open air. On Sunday mornings, I usually went to one of the neighbouring villages; but in the evening we held our meetings in some part of Leicester.

The events of 1841 soon grew very exciting. The death of Sir Ronald Ferguson, M.P. for Nottingham, reduced the Whig majority to one on great questions. And the cry became loud through the land for a general election. Notwithstanding that the Whig governments of Earl Grey and Lord Melbourne had won Parliamentary Reform, Municipal Reform, put the Church Revenues into the hands of Commissioners, and, above all, given a cheap postage to the people, every body said, "Let us have a change!" But the wildest advice was given by some who professed the most ultra-democratic doctrines. "Let us end the power of the Whigs—vote for Tories in preference to Whigs, the authors of the accursed Poor Law!" became the cry. Colonel Perronet Thompson, the veteran advocate for Corn Law Repeal, kindly wrote me "Letters" for my paper. But he advocated such measures! That old and steady advocates of freedom should have recommended us to help the Tories, sounds very strange to me now. But the poor took up the cry readily. They remarked that the Whigs had banished John Frost and his companions, and had thrown four hundred and thirty Chartists into prison; and therefore the Whigs were their worst enemies. "We will be revenged upon the Whigs," became the cry of Chartists.

Mr. Walter, the well-known proprietor of the powerful *Times*, so long a determined foe of the New Poor Law, offered himself for Nottingham. The Nottingham Chartists determined to support him, and wished some of us to go over from Leicester, to give what help we could. I and John Markham went over, and spoke at a few meetings. But I said to Mr. Walter, as we met him in the street, "Sir, don't have a wrong idea of the reason why you are to have Chartist support. We mean to use your party to cut the throats of the Whigs, and then we mean to cut your throats also!" I said it with a jocular air, and Mr. Walter laughed; but he understood that the joke was an earnest one.

Mr. Walter was returned for Nottingham; but, in the course of a few weeks, the general election came on. And, before it, came Sir John Easthope and Wynn Ellis, the members for Leicester, and a great meeting for Corn Law Repeal was held in Leicester market-place; and John Collins of Birmingham, and Markham and I, had to have our waggons for a platform opposed to the grand stand of the respectables; and the war was now fairly begun. Meetings in the open air were kept up nightly—unless the weather forced us into the little room at All Saints' Open—until the day of nomination for members of parliament.

John Swain, the person with whom I lodged, was very savagely opposed to the New Poor Law, and he proposed to me to meet, secretly, one of the influentials of the Tory party who had something to say to me concerning the approaching election.

"I cannot advise any of our Chartists to vote for the Tories," I said to him.

"The Chartists have not twenty votes among them all," said he; and no one is going to ask you to get the Chartists to vote for a Tory."

I consented to see the Tory gentleman, and his proposal was that I should get the Chartists to hold up their hands, at the nomination, for the Tory candidate.

"I believe," said I, "that the greater number of Chartists will do that for the sake of revenge on the Whigs, without my asking them."

"I shall want to see you again," said he, "on the night before the nomination. I shall have to ask a favour of you, and I hope you will not refuse me."

The next step taken by our Leicester Chartists was a very flattering one to myself. They proposed that I should be nominated by two Chartist "freemen" as the Universal Suffrage candidate for the parliamentary representation of my native town!

But, behold! there was a sudden stoppage to the seemingly prosperous current of my new fortunes. Mr. Cockshaw, the printer, told me he could not print another number of my paper. I owed him a few pounds; but I did not believe—nor did he say—that this was his reason for discontinuing the printing of my paper. "I am not at liberty to tell the reason," were his words. There was but one interpretation put upon his conduct by our Chartists. Mr. Cockshaw was printer for the Corporation, and I had written in what was deemed an unmannerly style of some of its members, and, doubtless, I had; and they wanted to end my paper, and also get me out of the town.

I defeated the Whiggish stratagem, however. There was not a printer in the whole town of Leicester who dared to print my paper, for fear of offending the Corporation dignitaries, or dignitaries of somekind—except Thomas Warwick, an honest, lowly man, although he voted for the Tories, who had a small quantity of type, and that but of a mean kind. I bargained with him, however; and as I could no longer issue my smart-looking paper at three-halfpence,

The Midland Counties Illuminator—we kindled a smaller refulgence, *The Chartist Rushlight*, at one halfpenny. The fun of the thing pleased everybody but the Whigs; and the Tories bought our *Rushlights* as fast as the printer could throw them off, and our Chartists were very merry over it.

The night before the nomination, the Tory gentleman sent for me.

"All I ask of you," he said, "is that you will secure us as many resolute men of your party as possible, to keep a firm stand in the centre and immediately *before the hustings*. They shall be paid for their work."

"You think that will enable your party to get the show of hands?"

"Exactly. We feel sure that the Mayor will pretend that the Whigs have the show of hands—especially if he can say,—I could not see how the people voted who were not in front."

"I do not see that it will be wrong to do what you ask," said I; "for even if they do really enable you to get the show of hands, *that* will not determine the election; and your money will do our poor fellows good."

"There will be no polling," said he; "but keep that secret, please."

The "Captain Forester" who had been announced as the Tory candidate had not yet made his appearance; and I knew, now, that he was only a dummy and so felt no hesitation whatever in promising the Tory gentleman that I would do what he wished. And, accordingly, I summoned a few determined men, and they soon brought up scores of others; and I took care they were all paid before they went and took up their stand in front of the hustings. Three small linen bags were given to me, on the nomination morning, each containing ten pounds in silver; and I paid away every coin to the poor ragged men, and wished I had ten times as much to give them. The Tory gentleman did not give me the bags, nor was he present when I received them. A Tory tradesman, who bore the highest character in Leicester for uprightness and kindness to the poor, handed me the bags—but I do not tell his name.

CHAPTER XV.
ELECTIONS: CHARTIST LIFE: 1841.

THEY are about to abolish our old-fashioned Nomination Days—and not before due time. But I must confess I enjoyed the old days. I used to enjoy them in the old Guildhall at Lincoln, when Bulwer was proposed by a leading Liberal, and old Dean Gordon used to propose Colonel Sibthorpe. Poor dear old Sibby! I can see his odd grimaces, and hear him swear so funnily in his speeches, as if it were but yesterday! And the joke when old Ben Bromhead had got his written speech in his hat, and young Charley Fardell stole it out! To see how old Ben twisted his hat round to find the stolen speech, while the people were laughing. Ah, some of those Lincoln days were naughty days,—and one must not tell the history of them, to the full.

I must confess I enjoyed the nomination day in Leicester market-place. Our Chartists kept their stand well, in the centre, before the hustings. As I faced them, the Tories with their blue flags were on my right, and the Whigs with their orange and green flags were on my left. I, as the universal suffrage candidate for the representation of Leicester, had the largest show of hands, for only a part of our Chartist crowd held up their hands for "Colonel Forester" who was not to be found—while all the working-men who were on the Tory side held up their hands for me, to spite the Whigs. But the Mayor said Sir John Easthope and Wynn Ellis had the show of hands—at which there was much shouting on the Whig side—much shouting for joy—but the scene was soon changed.

One of our Chartist flag-bearers *happened*, intentionally, to droop his flag on one side, till it touched the heads of some of the Whigs who were shouting. The gudgeons caught the bait! They seized the poor little calico flag and tore it in pieces!

"Now, lads, go it! " shouted some strong voices in the Chartist ranks, and the rush was instant upon the Whig flags. A few escaped; but his own supporters declared that the orange and green flags which were "limbed," or torn up in the course of perhaps ten minutes, had cost Sir John Easthope seventy pounds—for they were all of silk.

A more gentle joke was played something earlier. Samuel Deacon, a well-known native of Leicester, had made a large tin extinguisher, and fastened it to a pole. With this he approached the hustings, and before I could be aware of what he meant to do—placed it on my head, while the Whigs cried out, "There! he has extinguished the Rushlight!"

The election for the borough was over; but then came the elections for the north and south of the county. I and Bairstow were proposed at Loughborough, for the Northern Division of the county; but we had no great number of hands held up for us. On the nomination day for the Southern Division of the county, which was held in Leicester Castle yard, I thought I had the show of hands again; but the Sheriff decided for the Tories.

I was also present at the Nottingham election—where the Chartists suddenly reversed their policy, and voted against Walter, and in favour of the noble philanthropist, Joseph Sturge. Feargus O'Connor, while in York Castle, had advocated the policy of voting for the Tories in preference to the Whigs but he now came down to Nottingham, and by his speeches encouraged the Chartists to support Joseph-Sturge. With the thought of rendering help in some form or other, McDouall, Clark, and other Chartist leaders, also came to Nottingham. The Tories, on the other side, secured the presence of the redoubtable Joseph Raynor Stephens.

The night before the day of nomination the Tories drew a waggon into the market-place, and Stephens mounted it to address the crowd. The Liberals had already scented the intent of their opponents, and drew up a waggon facing the other, and at about twenty yards from it. Joseph Sturge, Henry Vincent, Arthur O'Neill, and other friends of Mr. Sturge, were in the waggon when O'Connor and the other leaders of our Chartist party reached it. We climbed up into the waggon; but soon found there could be no speaking. The crowd were assailing Stephens with the vilest epithets, and tearing up his portrait which had formerly been issued with the *Northern Star*, arid throwing the torn fragments at his face.

Stephens, meanwhile, with his spectacles on, and with folded arms, stood silently and majestically defying the crowd.

The Tory lambs—the reader has heard of the "lambs of Nottingham!"—the roughs who do all the work of blackguards, either on the Whig or the Tory side—the Tory lambs began to lose patience because the crowd would not hear Stephens; and the leaders of them—chiefly butchers in blue linen coats—were seen to form themselves into a body and soon charged upon the Chartist crowd with their fists. The battle was fierce, and the Tory lambs were forcing their way towards our waggon.

Mr. Sturge, with Vincent, and the rest of Mr. S.'s friends, quitted the waggon; and it was wise of them to do so. It was not our part, however, to retreat. Feargus waited until the Tory lambs got nearer, and then, throwing his hat into the waggon, he cried out "Now, my side charge!" and down he went among the crowd; and along with him went McDouall and Tom Clark—and gallantly they fought and faced the Tory butchers. It was no trifle to receive a blow from O'Connor's fists; and he "floored them like nine-pins," as he said himself. Once, the Tory lambs fought off all who surrounded him, and got him down, and my heart quaked,—for I thought they would kill him. But, in a very few moments, his red head emerged, again from the rough human billows, and he was fighting his way as before.

I did not quit the waggon. Neither did another of the so-called Chartist leaders of the time, who, it was said, had been in the Navy several years, and was usually called "The old Commodore," or "Commodore Mead."

"Cooper," said he, "I think we had better not quit the waggon."

"No," said I; "you stick by me, Commodore, and I'll play the Admiral; and we'll keep the ship."

So we remained, and looked upon the battle. Suddenly, I saw Stephens unfold his arms, and pull off his spectacles to see who was drawing near to him. It was McDouall, who had long had a sore private grudge against him. Stephens did not stay another moment; but turned his back, jumped off the other side of the waggon, and made his way out of the crowd into a friendly shop in the Long Row forthwith.

O'Connor and his party finally put the Tories to flight, and sprang upon the Tory waggon, when three lusty cheers were given; and after Feargus and McDouall had addressed the crowd it dispersed.

The nomination day was a very signal day in Nottingham. O'Connor and Vincent were proposed and seconded as candidates, as well as Mr. Sturge; but it was merely to give them the right of addressing the people. And their speeches were noble. O'Connor displayed greater knowledge of the science of politics, if I may so speak, than I ever heard him display at any time; and Vincent's oratory was charmingly ornamental, and drew forth bursts of cheering. But when Joseph Sturge spoke, and, in the course of his speech, turned to look upon the aged Tory, Walter, who was sitting near his feet, you might have heard a pin fall in that vast audience. Joseph solemnly entreated his opponent to remember that death was at hand, and the great account must be given for our life-course, before the throne of the Eternal Judge. I saw Walter's lower jaw fall, and a conscience-stricken look pass over his face as he listened to Sturge's words; and I did not wonder at the silence of the crowd, and the awe I saw depicted on all their faces.

Mr. Sturge's committee were very confident that he would win the election. McDouall and Clark and I accompanied O'Connor to the committee-room that evening. Thomas Beggs and others said they were sure of Mr. Sturge's return, for they had received so many pledges in his favour. It was agreed that it would be well to watch during the night whether any of the Tory agents were slily creeping about to try to bribe voters. O'Connor said he would not sleep.

"We will parade the town, Cooper," said he; "and you shall lead the singing. We shall be ready then to secure the polling-booths in the morning, so that the first votes may be for Mr. Sturge: *that* is always the surest step towards winning an election."

And parade the town we did, singing "The lion of freedom is come from his den" (a song attributed to me, but I never wrote a line of it: it was the composition of a Welsh Chartist woman) and

> "We won't go home till morning—till Walter runs away!
> We won't go home till morning—till Sturge has won the day!"

So foolish are the ways of men at election times! I have seen the gravest and soberest men do the wildest and silliest things, at such times; and therefore cannot wonder that I have done them myself.

We called Joseph Sturge out of bed, about two o'clock in the morning; and he stood, in his shirt, at the chamber window, while we gave three cheers for his success, and three groans for Walter, and then bade him "Good morning." About three o'clock, O'Connor said "How d'ye feel, Cooper—pretty well?" I told him I was well enough. "Then," said he, "I'll go and have a sleep, for I'm drowsy; but take care that you keep the people together, Cooper, and I'll be with you before the polling-booths are open."

But he did not return; and the men began to drop off, till I had but a paltry few to lead, and they were chiefly half-starved, lean stockingers, several of them from Sutton-in-Ashfield. We took care to be in the neighbourhood of the polling-booths by five o'clock; but by six the Tory voters began to crowd into the booths under the fierce protection of the "Lambs the butchers, armed with stout sticks.

"Shall we have a fight, and drive 'em out?" said one of the poor stockingers to me; "we'll do it—if you'll speak the word."

"No," said I, "they would soon break some of your poor heads or limbs. You have not the strength to cope with these men. You had better go home and go to bed; and I'll go to the Sturge committee."

I went and told Thomas Beggs, and others, that the Tories would have all the first votes.

"Never mind that," said one of the committee; "we are sure of the election."

"But if Walter keeps at the head of the poll till noon, the waverers will then go in and vote for him, instead of Mr. Sturge," said I.

I found it was in vain to talk to them, so I left them to seek O'Connor; but found he had gone back to London. Nor could I find any other of our men. It turned out as I said it would. Walter kept at the head of the poll till noon, and then the waverers hastened to vote for him. Joseph Sturge failed. That he might have won that election had the polling booths been filled with his friends in the morning, I feel the greatest certainty. Mr. Walter lost his seat for bribery; but Joseph Sturge was not returned in his stead.

To return to Leicester. I was put out of the little shop in High Street; but Mr. Oldfield let me a house in Church Street. So I had now a good shop and several rooms of considerable size. Two large rooms were set apart as coffee-rooms, and they were the resort of workingmen, daily; but on Saturday evenings they were crowded. All meetings of committees were also held in these rooms. In the shop below, I also commenced the sale of bread. During the remaining part of the year 1841, I had a really good business, — there being a little prosperity in the staple trade of the town until some weeks after Christmas.

Instead of the halfpenny *Rushlight*, I started the penny *Extinguisher* — taking the name from the playful fact that occurred at the election. I continued to address the people on Sundays, in the evenings, and began now to take my stand in the market-place for that purpose. We always commenced with worship, and I always took a text from the Scriptures, and mingled religious teaching with politics. When autumn came, we felt uncertain as to where our Sunday meetings were to be held during the dark evenings. There was a very large building in the town, which had originally been built for Ducrow, called "the Amphitheatre." It held 3,000 people. I had hired it for O'Connor to speak in, and for other extraordinary meetings; but could not think of paying three pounds for the use of it every Sunday night. In front of it was a large first-floor room, which had been used also by Ducrow's "horse-riders," as a dressing-room, and which was called the "Shaksperean Room." I got the use of it, for all or any kind of meetings, at so much per week; and so now I held my Sunday night meetings invariably in the " Shaksperean Room."

I shall not dwell on one recital. John Markham, a shoemaker, who had been a Methodist local preacher, was considered their "leader" by the Chartists, when I entered Leicester. We continued friendly for some time. But himself and a few others began to show signs of coldness in the course of the autumn, and went back to the little old room at All Saints' Open, and constituted themselves a separate Chartist Association. So I proposed that we should take a new name; and, as we now held our meetings in the "Shaksperean Room," we styled ourselves "The Shaksperean Association of Leicester Chartists."

I shall conclude this chapter with the solemn record that my dear mother died on the 1st of August (her birthday) in this year, being seventy-one years of age. I went over to Gainsborough to bury her, in the churchyard so well known to me from the days of childhood.

> "I laid her near the dust
> Of her oppressor; but no gilded verse
> Tells how she toiled to win her child a crust,
> And, fasting, still toiled on: no rhymes rehearse
> How tenderly she strove to be the nurse
> Of truth and nobleness in her loved boy,
> Spite of his rags."

CHAPTER XVI.
CHARTIST POETS: CHARTIST LIFE, CONTINUED: 1842.

I HAD not joined the ranks of the poor and the oppressed with the expectation of having those rough election scenes to pass through. And now I had passed through them, I began to turn my thoughts to something far more worthy of a man's earnestness. As soon as the Shaksperean Room was secured, I formed an adult Sunday-school, for men and boys who were at work on the week days. All the more intelligent in our ranks gladly assisted as teachers; and we soon had the room filled on Sunday mornings and afternoons. The Old and New Testaments, Channing's "Self-culture," and other tracts, of which I do not remember the names, formed our class-books. And we, fancifully, named our classes, not first, second, third, etc., but the 'Algernon Sydney Class,' 'Andrew Marvel Class,' 'John Hampden Class,' 'John Milton Class,' 'William Tell Class,' 'George Washington Class,' 'Major Cartwright Class,' 'William Cobbett Class,' and so on.

I began also to teach Temperance more strongly than before. I became a teetotaler when I entered Leicester, and I kept my pledge, rigidly, for four years. We devised a new form of pledge,—"I hereby promise to abstain, etc., until the People's Charter becomes the law of the land;" and I administered this pledge to several hundreds. I fear the majority of them kept their pledge but for a brief period, yet some persevered.

Next, I drew up a body of rules for our Chartist Association; and, as we so often indulged in singing, I proposed to two of our members who had occasionally shown me their rhymes, that they should compose hymns for our Sunday meetings. John Bramwich, the elder of these persons, was a stocking-weaver, and was now about fifty years old. He had been a soldier, and had seen service in the West Indies and America. He was a grave, serious man, the very heart of truth and sincerity. He died of sheer exhaustion, from hard labour and want, in the year 1846. William Jones, the other composer of rhymes I referred to, was a much younger man, of very pleasing manners and appearance. He was what is called a "glove-hand," and therefore earned better wages than a stockinger. He had been a hard worker, but had acquired some knowledge of music. He published a small volume of very excellent poetry, at Leicester, in 1853, and died in 1855, being held in very high respect by a large circle of friends.

The contributions of Bramwich and Jones to our hymnology, were published in my weekly *Extinguisher*, until we collected them in our "Shaksperean Chartist Hymn Book." The following is the most favourite hymn composed by Bramwich.—We sang it to the hymn tune "New Crucifixion."

> Britannia's sons, though slaves ye be,
> God, your Creator, made you free;
> He life and thought and being gave,
> But never, never made a slave!
>
> His works are wonderful to see,
> All, all proclaim the Deity;
> He made the earth, and formed the wave,
> But never, never made a slave!
>
> He made the sky with spangles bright,
> The moon to shine by silent night;
> The sun—and spread the vast concave,
> But never, never made a slave!
>
> The verdant earth, on which we tread,
> Was by His hand all carpeted;
> Enough for all He freely gave,
> But never, never made a slave!
>
> All men are equal in His sight,
> The bond, the free, the black, the white:
> He made them all,—them freedom gave;
> God made the man—Man made the slave!

Fourteen hymns were contributed by Bramwich to our "Shaksperean Chartist Hymn Book," and sixteen by William Jones. The following

was our favourite hymn of those composed by Jones, and we usually
sang it to the hymn tune called "Calcutta."

> Sons of poverty assemble,
> Ye whose hearts with woe are riven,
> Let the guilty tyrants tremble,
> Who your hearts such pain have given.
> We will never
> From the shrine of truth be driven.
>
> Must ye faint—ah! how much longer?
> Better by the sword to die
> Than to die of want and hunger:
> They heed not your feeble cry:
> Lift your voices—
> Lift your voices to the sky!
>
> Rouse them from their silken slumbers,
> Trouble them amidst their pride:
> Swell your ranks, augment your numbers,
> Spread the Charter, far and wide!
> Truth is with us:
> God Himself is on our side.
>
> See the brave, ye spirit broken,
> That uphold your righteous cause;
> Who against them hath not spoken?
> They are, just as Jesus was,
> Persecuted
> By bad men and wicked laws.
>
> Dire oppression, Heaven decrees it,
> From our land shall soon be hurled;
> Mark the coming time and seize it—
> Every banner be unfurled!
> Spread the Charter!
> Spread the Charter through the world.

I venture to add one of the only two hymns that I contributed to our Hymn Book: we sang it in the noble air of the "Old Hundredth."

God of the earth, and sea, and sky,
To Thee Thy mournful children cry:
Didst Thou the blue that bends o'er all
Spread for a general funeral pall?

Sadness and gloom pervade the land;
Death—famine—glare on either hand;
Didst Thou plant earth upon the wave
Only to form one general grave?

Father, why didst Thou form the flowers?
They blossom not for us, or ours:
Why didst Thou clothe the fields with corn?
Robbers from us our share have torn.

The ancients of our wretched race
Told of Thy sovereign power and grace,
That in the sea their foes o'erthrew—
Great Father!—is the record true?

Art Thou the same who, from all time,
O'er every sea, through every clime,
The stained oppressor's guilty head
Hast visited with vengeance dread?

To us,—the wretched and the poor,
Whom rich men drive from door to door,—
To us, then, make Thy goodness known,
And we Thy lofty name will own.

Father, our frames are sinking fast:
Hast Thou our names behind Thee cast?
Our sinless babes with hunger die:
Our hearts are hardening!—Hear our cry!

Appear, as in the ancient days!
Deliver us from our foes, and praise
Shall from our hearts to Thee ascend —
To God our Father, and our Friend!

We now usually held one or two meetings in the Shaksperean Room on week nights, as well as on the Sunday night. Unless there were some stirring local or political topic, I lectured on Milton, and repeated portions of the "Paradise Lost," or on Shakspeare, and repeated portions of "Hamlet," or on Burns, and repeated "Tam o' Shanter;" or I recited the history of England, and set the portraits of great Englishmen before young Chartists, who listened with intense interest; or I took up Geology, or even Phrenology, and made the young men acquainted, elementally, with the knowledge of the time.

Often, since the days of which I am speaking, some seeming stranger has stepped up to me, in one part of England or another — usually at the close of a lecture — and has said, "You will not remember me. I was very young when I used to hear you in Leicester; but I consider that I owe a good deal to you. You gave me a direction of mind that I have followed," — and so on. If events had not broken up the system I was forming, how much real good I might have effected in Leicester!

These thoughts have just brought to mind a pleasing incident which I ought to have mentioned earlier. I had been appealing strongly, one evening, to the patriotic feelings of young Englishmen, mentioning the names of Hampden and Sydney and Marvel; and eulogizing the grand spirit of disinterestedness and self-sacrifice which characterised so many of our brave forerunners, when a handsome young man sprung upon our little platform and declared himself on the people's side, and desired to be enrolled as a Chartist. He did not belong to the poorest ranks; and it was the consciousness that he was acting in the spirit of self-sacrifice, as well as his fervid eloquence, that caused a thrilling cheer from the ranks of working men. He could not be more than fifteen at that time; he passed away from us too soon, with his father, who left Leicester, and I have never seen him but once, all these years. But the men of Sheffield have signalized their confidence in his patriotism by returning him to the House of Commons; and all England knows if there be a man of energy as well as uprightness in that house, it is Anthony John Mundella.

Our meetings were well attended, the number of our members increased greatly, and all went well until January, 1842, when the great hosiery houses announced that orders had ceased, and the greater number of the stocking and glove frames must stand still. The sale, not only of the *Northern Star*, but of my own *Extinguisher*, declined fearfully. Some of the working men began to ask me to let them have bread on credit; and I ventured to do it, trusting that all would be better in time. Our coffee-room was still filled, but not half the coffee was sold.

One afternoon, without counselling me, some five hundred of the men who were out of work formed a procession and marched through the town at a slow step, singing, and begging all the way they went. It wrung my heart to see a sight like that in England. They got but little, and I advised them never to repeat it.

While difficulties increased, I gave up both the sale of bread and the publication of my *Extinguisher* for a few weeks. But several of the most necessitous men declared they must perish if I did not let them have bread. So I returned to the sale of bread—but had to give it to some to prevent them from starving. Of course I contracted debt by so doing; and I did it very foolishly. I would not do it again; at least, I hope I should not do it. I found also that our cause could not be held together without a paper. We had no organ for the exposure of wrongs—such as the attempts of some of the grinding 'masters' to establish the Truck System, extraordinary acts of 'docking' men's wages, and so on.

So I now issued another paper, and called it the *Commonwealthsman*, and inserted in it the lives of the illustrious Hampden, Pym, Sir John Eliot, Selden, Algernon Sydney, and others of their fellow-strugglers for freedom. I had a good sale for the earlier numbers—for they were sold for me by agents at Manchester, Sheffield, Birmingham,

Wednesbury, Bilston, Stafford, and the Potteries. But trade grew bad in other towns; and the sale soon fell off.

In Leicester everything looked more hopeless. We closed the adult school—partly because the fine weather drew the men into the fields, and partly because they were too despairing to care about learning to read. Let some who read this mark what I am recording. We had not many profane men in our ranks, but we had a few; and when I urged them not to forsake school their reply was, "What the hell do we care about reading, if we can get nought to eat?"

A poor framework-knitter, whom I knew to be as true as steel, concealed the fact of his deep suffering from me for several weeks, though I saw the change in his dress, and knew that he must have pawned all but the mere rags he was wearing. He was frequently with me in the shop, rendering kindly help. I spoke to him, one night, about his case; but some one came into the shop and interrupted me, and he suddenly retired. At eleven o'clock, just before we were about to close the shop, he came in hastily, laid a bit of paper on my desk, and ran out.

On the bit of paper he revealed his utter destitution, and the starvation and suffering of his young wife and child. On the previous morning, the note informed me, his wife awoke, saying, "Sunday come again, and nothing to eat!"—and as the babe sought the breast there was no milk!

About the same time—I think it was in the same week-another poor stockinger rushed into my house, and, throwing himself wildly on a chair, exclaimed, with an execration,—"I wish they would hang me! I have lived on cold potatoes that were given me these two days; and this morning I've eaten a raw potato for sheer hunger! Give me a bit of bread, and a cup of coffee, or I shall drop!" I should not like again to see a human face with the look of half insane despair which that poor man's countenance wore.

How fierce my discourses became now, in the market-place, on Sunday evenings! I wonder that I restrained myself at all. My heart often burned with indignation I knew not how to express. Nay— there was something worse. I began—from sheer sympathy—to feel a tendency to glide into the depraved thinkings of some of the stronger, but coarser spirits among the men. It is horrible to me to tell such a truth. But I must tell it. For if I be untruthful now, I had better not have begun my Life-story.

The real feeling of this class of men was fully expressed one day in the market-place when we were holding a meeting in the week. A poor religious stockinger said,—"Let us be patient a little longer, lads. Surely, God Almighty will help us soon."

"Talk no more about thy Goddle Mighty!" was the sneering rejoinder. "There isn't one. If there was one, He wouldn't let us suffer as we do."

Such was the feeling and language of the stronger and coarser spirits; and it was shared by such of the Socialists as we had among us. Not that there was ever any union of the Socialists with us, as a body. They had a room of their own in Leicester, and their leading men kept at a distance from us, and even protested against the reasonableness of our hopes. Indeed, to show us that we were wrong, they brought Alexander Campbell and Robert Buchanan (the father of Robert Buchanan the poet) to Leicester, to lecture on their scheme of "Home Colonisation" and challenged us to answer them. I sustained the challenge myself, as the champion for the People's Charter.

During the summer of 1842, I often led the poor stockingers out into the villages,—sometimes on Sunday mornings, and sometimes on week day evenings,—and thus we collected the villagers of Anstey, and Wigston, and Glenn, and Countesthorpe, and Earl Shilton, and Hinckley, and Syston, and Mount Sorrel, and inducted them into some knowledge of Chartist principles. One Sunday we devoted entirely to Mount Sorrel, and I and Beedham stood on a pulpit of syenite, and addressed the hundreds that sat around and above us on the stones of a large quarry. It was a *Gwennap*—Wesley's grand Cornish preaching-place—on a small scale.

Our singing was enthusiastic; and the exhilaration of that Chartist "camp-meeting" was often spoken of afterwards. Now and then, I preached Chartist sermons on Nottingham Forest,—where at that time there was another natural pulpit of rock; but it was seldom I had meetings there, though I liked the place, the open air, and the people, who were proud of their unenclosed "Forest,"—unenclosed, now, no longer—but thickly built upon.

As the poor Leicester stockingers had so little work, they used to crowd the street, around my shop door, early in the evenings; and I had to devise some way of occupying them. Sometimes I would deliver them a speech; but more generally, on the fine evenings, we used to form a procession of four or five in a rank, and troop through the streets, singing the following triplet to the air of the chorus "Rule Britannia."

> "Spread—spread the Charter—
> Spread the Charter through the Land!
> Let Britons bold and brave join heart and hand!"

Or chanting the "Lion of Freedom," which I have already alluded to,—the words of which were as follows:

> The Lion of Freedom is come from his den;
> We'll rally around him, again and again:
> We'll crown him with laurel, our champion to be:
> O'Connor the patriot: for sweet Liberty!
>
> The pride of the people—He's noble and brave—
> A terror to tyrants—a friend to the slave :
> The bright star of Freedom—the noblest of men:
> We'll rally around him, again and again.
>
> Who strove for the patriots—was up night and day—
> To save them from falling to tyrants a prey?

'Twas fearless O'Connor was diligent then:
We'll rally around him, again and again.

Though proud daring tyrants his body confined,
They never could conquer his generous mind:
We'll hail our caged lion, now freed from his den:
We'll rally around him, again and again.

The popularity of this song may serve to show how firmly O'Connor was fixed in the regard of a portion of the manufacturing operatives, as the incorruptible advocate of freedom. As a consequence, they immediately suspected the honesty of any local leader who did not rank himself under the banner of Feargus, the leader-in-chief.

CHAPTER XVII.
CHARTIST LIFE, CONTINUED: CORN-LAW REPEALERS: 1842.

OUR singing through the streets, in the fine evenings, often accompanied with shouts for the Charter, had no harm in it, although many of the shop-keepers would shut up their shops in real, or affected, terror. This only caused our men to laugh, since all knew there was no thought of injuring anybody.

"But why did you sing 'Spread the Charter,' and and why did you keep up your Chartist Association?" the thinking reader will say. Had you any hope of success? You yourself, and the men you led, must have had some real or imaginary expectation of a change."

If the reader be little acquainted with the political, industrial, and social history of this country, I recommend him to turn to an article entitled "Anti-CornLaw Agitation," which he will find in No. 141 of the *Quarterly Review*, published Dec. 1842. The article is, of course, filled with the strongest spirit of antagonism to the celebrated "Anti-Corn-Law League;" but it will present the inquirer with a truthful and most thrilling epitome of the state of things in the manufacturing districts at that period.

It was not simply a few poor ragged Chartists in Leicester who were expecting a change. It was expected in all our industrial regions. Agitation, under the influence of the powerful League, was rife all over the Midlands and the Northern Counties. Manufacturers declared things could not go on much longer as they were. They began to threaten that they would close their mills, or, as the Tories interpreted the threats, to try to precipitate a revolution! The speeches of Richard Cobden, John Bright, Joseph Sturge, George Thompson, James Acland, and a host of less powerful agitators—had not only stirred up a strong feeling of discontent, but had excited a confident expectation of relief.

Now thirty years have passed away, I see how much poor Chartists resembled the fly on the wheel during that period of political agitation. But men far more experienced than my poor self thought that Chartism would succeed before Corn Law Repeal; that a great change was at hand, and that the change would not be Free Trade, but a great enlargement of the franchise, and the accompanying political demands embodied in the People's Charter.

We petitioned Parliament twice during the time that I was in Leicester, and two petty Conventions were held in London; to the first of which one of the members of the old Convention, Thomas Rayner Smart, was sent as our delegate from Leicester; and young Bairstow to the second. Duncombe and Wakley supported the prayer of these Chartist petitions very boldly and bravely. But there was nothing in the behaviour of the vast majority of the House of Commons that indicated any enlargement of the franchise to be at hand. Yet we still held by the People's Charter, and fondly believed we should succeed.

Feargus O'Connor, by his speeches in various parts of the country, and by his letters in the *Northern Star*, chiefly helped to keep up these expectations. The immense majority of Chartists in Leicester, as well as in many other towns, regarded him as the only really disinterested and incorruptible leader. I adopted this belief, because it was the belief of the people; and I opposed James Bronterre O'Brien, and Henry Vincent, and all who opposed O'Connor, or refused to act with him.

Common sense taught me that no cause can be gained by disunion. And as I knew no reason for doubting the political honesty and disinterestedness which O'Connor ever asserted for himself, and in which the people believed, I stuck by O'Connor, and would have gone through fire and water for him. There was much that was attractive in him when I first knew him. His fine manly form and his powerful baritone voice gave him great advantages as a popular leader. His conversation was rich in Irish humour, and often evinced a shrewd knowledge of character. The fact of his having been in the House of Commons, and among the upper classes, also lent him influence. I do not think half a dozen Chartists cared a fig about his boasted descent from "Roderick O'Connor, the king of

Connaught, and last king of all Ireland;" but the connection of his family with the "United Irishmen" and patriotic sufferers of the last century, rendered him a natural represenstive of the cause of political liberty.

I saw no honest reason for deserting him, and getting up a "Complete Suffrage Association," if the people who got it up veritably meant politically what we meant as Chartists. The working men said there was deceit behind their cry of "Complete Suffrage;" and I maintained their saying. For the demagogue, or popular "leader," is rather the people's instrument than their director. He keeps the lead, and is the people's mouthpiece, hand and arm, either for good or evil, because his quick sympathies are with the people; while his temperament, nature, and energetic will fit him for the very post which the people's voice assigns him.

Besides, we could not think of giving up our demand for the People's Charter, to adopt the new cry for "Complete Suffrage," when we remembered what had occurred in Leicester before that cry was heard. I can never forget the stirring shout that went up from the voices of working men in one of our Chartist meetings in the New Hall, when the eloquent successor of the great Robert Hall, the Rev. J. P. Mursell, uttered the words,

"Men of Leicester, stick to your Charter! When the time comes, my arm is bared for Universal Suffrage!

It is true that Mr. Mursell never attended another Chartist meeting, although he was eagerly enough looked for, and his presence hoped for by our poor fellows.

"Where's Parson Barearm?" shouted one of the merriest of them, on one of our meeting nights, while the room rang with laughter.

Nor was it the Rev. Mr. Mursell alone, of the middle-classes, who was known to sympathise with us in our political creed. The Messrs. Biggs, Baines, Viccars, Hull, Slade, and others, were understood to regard the People's Charter as a fair embodiment of popular rights, although they acted and voted with the League.

I maintained union—but no mere factiousness. I never suffered any meeting to be held by Chartists, while I was leader in Leicester, to oppose the repeal of the Corn Laws. It was a part of Chartist policy, in many towns, to disturb Corn Law Repeal meetings. I never disturbed one; and never suffered my party to do it. The Leicester Whigs *said we did*. But it was a falsehood. We were called disturbers as soon as we entered a meeting, and before we had spoken! Of course, there was a policy in that; but it was a dirty policy.

When we were fairly permitted to take our part, they saw what we meant. There was one large meeting of the Corn Law Repealers, in the market-place, that I remember well, where I and a few of my Chartist friends were allowed to be on the platform. I interrupted no speaker, nor did a single Chartist utter a word of disapproval. They finished their speeches, and put their proposition to the vote. I held up my hand, and cried to my own party who composed a large part of the crowd, "Now, Chartists!" and every man of them held up his hand for Corn Law Repeal. I then told the chairman that I should beg leave to make another proposition, and I would not take up much time in doing it. I then proposed a resolution in favour of the People's Charter; and the chairman put it formally to the vote. Mr. Wm. Baines, Mr. Slade, Mr. Hull, Mr. Joseph Biggs, and three or four others on the platform, held up their hands with the great body of working men. "On the contrary!" said the chairman; and there was a solitary hand held up. It was that of Mr. Tertius Paget. I have no doubt he remembers it well—but never mind! He was a young man then.

To resume the broken thread of my narrative. The decrease of work, and the absolute destitution of an immense number of the working classes in Leicester, led to alarming symptoms, in the summer of 1842. The Union Poor House, or 'Bastile,' as it was always called by the working men, was crowded to excess; and the throngs who asked for outdoor relief for a time seemed to paralyse the authorities. A mill was at length set up at the workhouse, and it had to be turned by the applicants for relief. The working of the wheel they declared to be beyond their strength; and no doubt some of the poor feeble stockingers among them spoke the truth. They complained of it also as degrading, and it kindled a spirit of strong indignation among the great body of working men in Leicester.

Meetings were held in the market-place to protest against the measures of the Poor Law Guardians, and against the support afforded to them in their harsh measures by the magistrates. And at these meetings I and my Chartist friends were often speakers. The labourers at the mill were only allowed a few pence per day; and about forty of them used to go round the town in a body, and beg for additional pence at the shops. At length they resisted one of the officials set to watch them at the wheel, and this led to a riot, in which the windows of the Union Poor House were broken. Police, however, were soon on the spot: the disorder was quelled, and the ringleaders taken into custody.

The whole affair was utterly unconnected with our Chartist Association. None of the men who were in custody were on our books as members and: they might have been tried and dismissed, or imprisoned, as the case might be, had it not been for the proposal made to me by a man who had generally passed for a Tory, but who suddenly came and offered his name and his subscription, as a member of the Shaksperean Chartist Association.

This was Joseph Wood, an attorney of low practice, but well known in the town. He offered to conduct the cases of the men who had been placed in custody for the "Bastile Riot," as it was called, and who had to be brought before the magistrates. Their relatives and friends had no sooner accepted his offer, than he sought a private interview with me, and proposed a scheme which too well accorded with my excited imagination and feelings. It was, that I should, in a formal way, by the drawing up of an agreement and signing it, become his clerk, that he might empower me to conduct the poor rioters' cases before the magistrates, myself. And I did this, bullying and confounding the witnesses, and angering the magistrates, by my bold defence of the offenders, for two whole days. The market-place was thronged with crowds who could not get into the over-filled magistrate's room to hear the trials. And at last the magistrates did—what, if they had been possessed of the brains and courage of men, they would have done, at first—put an end to my pleading, by declaring that I was not a properly qualified representative of any attorney. By their foolish cowardice and incompetence, the town of Leicester was in more danger of a real "riot," than it had ever been, by our harmless singing of the " Lion of Freedom" through its streets. A troop of horse was sent for from Nottingham to overawe the working men; and the convicted "rioters" were sentenced and sent to gaol.

For myself, the "destiny" was in progress. I was elected as delegate from Leicester to the Chartist Conference, or Convention, which it had been resolved should be held in Manchester, on the 16th of August. As I had some small accounts owing to me for my *Commonwealthsman*, in Birmingham, Bilston, Wolverhampton, Stafford, and the Staffordshire Potteries, I thought I would take that route to Manchester. We had learned in Leicester that some of the colliers were on strike in the Potteries, and that the whole body of them had struck, in South Staffordshire, or the "Black Country," and were holding meetings in the open air, almost daily; but I had no foresight of danger in going among them.

CHAPTER XVIII.
CHARTIST LIFE, CONTINUED: THE RIOT IN THE
STAFFORDSHIRE POTTERIES: 1842.

I LEFT Leicester on Tuesday, the 9th of August, 1842, and lectured that night, in the Odd Fellows Hall, Birmingham. The next morning I was taken on to Wednesbury, to assist in holding a meeting of the colliers on strike, at which, it was thought, 30,000 men were present. Arthur G. O'Neill, Linney, Pearson, and others addressed the colliers, counselling them to persevere with their strike; and, above all things, to avoid breaking the law or acting disorderly. I addressed them on the necessity of uniting to win the People's Charter. On Thursday night, I spoke on the same subject to another meeting of colliers at Bilston. On Friday morning, I addressed another meeting, in the open air, at Wolverhampton; and the same evening, addressed two meetings at Stafford, one in the market-place, and the other on the Freemen's Common.

The people, everywhere, seemed perfectly orderly. A policeman, stimulated by the Tory party at Stafford, tried to create disorder; but I drew the people away from the market-place to the common, and defeated their purpose. And all seemed perfectly quiet when I reached Hanley, the principal town of the Potteries, on the Saturday. I saw nothing of the colliers who were on strike; and companied with the Teetotal Chartists, whom I had known when I paid a few days' visit to Hanley, in April preceding.

On Sunday morning, in company with these Chartist friends, I went and spoke in the open air at Fenton, and in the afternoon at Longton. In the evening I addressed an immense crowd at Hanley, standing on a chair in front of the Crown Inn: such ground being called "the Crown Bank," by the natives. I took for a text the sixth commandment: "Thou shalt do no murder"—after we had sung Bramwich's hymn "Britannia's sons, though slaves ye be," and I had offered a short prayer.

I showed how kings, in all ages, had enslaved the people, and spilt their blood in wars of conquest, thus violating the precept, "Thou shalt do no murder."

I named conquerors, from Sesostris to Alexander, from Caesar to Napoleon, who had become famous in history by shedding the blood of millions: thus violating the precept, "Thou shalt do no murder."

I described how the conquerors of America had nearly exterminated the native races, and thus violated the precept, "Thou shalt do no murder."

I recounted how English and French and Spanish and German wars, in modern history, had swollen the list of the slaughtered, and had violated the precept, "Thou shalt do no murder."

I rehearsed the plunder of the Church by Henry the Eighth, and the burning of men and women for religion, by himself and his daughter, Mary—who thus fearfully violated the precept, "Thou shalt do no murder."

I described our own guilty Colonial rule, and still guiltier rule of Ireland; and asserted that British rulers had most awfully violated the precept, "Thou shalt do no murder."

I showed how the immense taxation we were forced to endure, to enable our rulers to maintain the long and ruinous war with France and Napoleon, had entailed indescribable suffering on millions; and that thus had been violated the precept, "Thou shalt do no murder."

I asserted that the imposition of the Bread Tax was a violation of the same precept; and that such was the enactment of the Game Laws; that such was the custom of primogeniture and keeping of the land in the possession of the privileged classes; and that such was the enactment of the infamous new Poor Law.

The general murmur of applause now began to swell into loud cries; and these were mingled with execrations of the authors of the Poor Law.—I went on.

I showed that low wages for wretched agricultural labourers, and the brutal ignorance in which generation after generation they were left by the landlords, was a violation of the precept, "Thou shalt do no murder."

I asserted that the attempt to lessen the wages of toilers under ground, who were in hourly and momentary danger of their lives, and to disable them from getting the necessary food for themselves and families, were violations of the precept, "Thou shalt do no murder."

I declared that all who were instrumental in maintaining the system of labour which reduced poor stockingers to the starvation I had witnessed in Leicester,—and which was witnessed among the poor handloom weavers of Lancashire, and poor nail-makers of the Black Country—were violating the precept, "Thou shalt do no murder."

And now the multitude shouted; and their looks told of vengeance— but I went on, for I felt as if I could die on the spot in fulfilling a great duty—the exposure of human wrong and consequent human suffering. My strength was great at that time, and my voice could be heard, like the peal of a trumpet, even to the verge of a crowd composed of thousands. How sincere I was, God knows! and it seemed impossible for me, with my belief of wrong, to act otherwise.

I fear I spent so much time in describing the wrong, and raising the spirit of vengeance in those who heard me, that the little time I spent in conclusion, and in showing that those who heard me were not to violate the precept, "Thou shalt do no murder," either literally, or in its spirit, but that they were to practise the Saviour's commandment, and to forgive their enemies, produced little effect in the way of lowering the flame of desire for vengeance, or raising the spirit of gentleness and forgiveness.

Before the conclusion of the meeting, which was prolonged till dusk, I was desired to address the colliers on strike, on the same spot,— "the Crown Bank"—the next morning at nine o'clock. I agreed, and instantly announced the meeting.

I was lodging at honest and devoted Jeremiah Yates'; but often went across the road to the George and Dragon, an inn to which a large room was attached, in which Chartist meetings were usually held. When I reached the inn that night, the Chartist Committee told me they had received instruction from the Chartist Committee in Manchester to bring out the people from labour, and to persuade them to work no more till the Charter became law—for that that resolution had been passed in public meetings in Manchester and Stockport, and Staleybridge, and Ashton-under-Lyne, and Oldham, and Rochdale, and Bacup, and Burnley, and Blackburn, and Preston, and other Lancashire towns, and they meant to spread the resolution all over England.

"The Plug Plot," of 1842, as it is still called in Lancashire, began in reductions of wages by the Anti Corn-Law manufacturers, who did not conceal their purpose of driving the people to desperation, in order to paralyse the Government. The people advanced at last, to a wild general strike, and drew the plugs so as to stop the works at the mills, and thus render labour impossible. Some wanted the men who spoke at the meetings held at the beginning of the strike to propose resolutions in favour of Corn Law Repeal; but they refused. The first meeting where the resolution was passed, "that all labour should cease until the People's Charter became the law of the land," was held on the 7th of August, on Mottram Moor. In the course of a week, the resolution had been passed in nearly all the great towns of Lancashire, and tens of thousands had held up their hands in favour of it.

I constituted myself chairman of the meeting on the Crown Bank, at Hanley, on Monday morning, the 15th of August, 1842, a day to be remembered to my life's end. I resolved to take the chief responsibility on myself, for what was about to be done. I told the people so. I suppose there would be eight or ten thousand present. I showed them that if they carried out the resolution which was about to be proposed, no government on earth could resist their demand. But I told them that "Peace, Law, and Order" must be their motto; and that, while they took peaceable means to secure a general turn-out, and kept from violence, no law could touch them.

John Richards, who was seventy years of age and had been a member of the First Convention,—the oldest Chartist leader in the Potteries,—proposed the Resolution, "That all labour cease until the People's Charter becomes the law of the land."

A Hanley Chartist, whose name I forget, seconded it, and when I put the resolution to the crowd all hands seemed to be held up for it; and not one hand was held up when I said "On the contrary." Three cheers were given for success, and the meeting broke up.

I went to my lodging at the George and Dragon, to remain till the evening, when I should lecture in the room, according to printed announcement. But I had not been many minutes in the inn, before a man came in with a wild air of joy, and said they had got the hands out at such and such an employer's; others followed; and then one said the crowd had gone to Squire Allen's, to seize a stand of arms that had be longed to the Militia. And then another came, and said the arms were at Bailey Rose's; and they had gone thither for them; and then another said they had done neither.

I strolled out and saw the shopkeepers shutting all their shops up, and some putting day-books and ledgers into their gigs, and driving off! I stepped into the Royal Oak, a small public-house kept by Preston Barker, whom I had known in Lincoln. A man came in there whom I stared to see. It was my old Italian instructor, Signor D'Albrione! He had been settled in the Potteries for a short time, as a teacher,—a fact I had no knowledge of. Men soon came in with more reports of what the crowd were doing—but the reports were contradictory.

I went out into the street, and had not gone many yards before I saw a company of infantry, marching, with fixed bayonets, and two magistrates on horseback accompanying their officers, apparently in the direction of Longton. Women and children came out and gazed, but there was scarcely a male person to be seen looking at the soldiers. I met a man soon, however, who told me that the crowd, after visiting Bailey Rose's, had gone to Longton, and no doubt the soldiers were going thither also.

I passed to and fro, and from and to my inn, and into the streets, viewing the town of Hanley as having become a human desert. Scarcely a person could be seen in the streets; all the works were closed, and the shops shut. I went again to my inn and wrote a letter to Leicester, telling our committee that they must get the people into the market-place and propose the Resolution to work no more till the Charter became the law of the land. Then there was the sudden thought that I must not send such a letter through the post-office. A Chartist came into the inn whom the landlord said I might trust; and he offered to start and walk to Leicester with the letter at once. I wrote another letter for my dear wife, gave the man five shillings, and committed the two letters to his care. He delivered them safely, the next morning, in Leicester.

The day wore on, wearily, and very anxiously, till about five in the afternoon, when parties of men began to pass along the streets. Some came into my inn, and began to relate the history of the doings at Longton, which had been violent indeed. Yet the accounts they gave were confused, and I had still no clear understanding of what had been done.

By six o'clock, thousands crowded into the large open space about the Crown Inn, and instead of lecturing at eight o'clock in the room, the committee thought I had better go out at once, and lecture on the Crown Bank. So I went at seven o'clock to the place where I had stood in the morning. Before I began, some of the men who were drunk, and who, it seems, had been in the riot at Longton, came round me and wanted to shake hands with me. But I shook them off, and told them I was ashamed to see them. I began by telling the immense crowd—for its numbers were soon countless—that I had heard there had been destruction of property that day, and I warned all who had participated in that act, that they were not the friends, but the enemies of freedom—that ruin to themselves and others must attend this strike for the Charter, if they who pretended to be its advocates broke the law.

"I proclaim Peace, Law, and Order!" I cried at the highest pitch of my voice. "You all hear me; and I warn you of the folly and wrong you are committing, if you do not preserve Peace, Law, and Order!"

At dusk, I closed the meeting; but I saw the people did not disperse; and two pistols were fired off in the crowd. No policeman had I seen the whole lay! And what had become of the soldiers I could not learn. I went back to my inn; but I began to apprehend that mischief had begun which it would not be easy to quell.

Samuel Bevington was the strongest-minded man among the Chartists of the Potteries; and he said to me, "You had better get off to Manchester. You can do no more good here." I agreed that he was right; and two Chartist friends went out to hire a gig to enable me to get to the Whitmore station, that I might get to Manchester: there was no railway through the Potteries, at that time. But they tried in several places, and all in vain. No one would lend a gig, for it was reported that soldiers and policemen and special constables had formed a kind of cordon round the Potteries, and were stopping up every outlet.

Midnight came, and then it was proposed that I should walk to Macclesfield, and take the coach there at seven the next morning, for Manchester. Two young men, Green and Moore, kindly agreed to accompany me; and I promised them half-a-crown each.

"But first," said I, "lend me a hat and a greatcoat. You say violence is going on now. Do not let me be mixed up with it. I shall be known, as I pass through the streets, by my cap and cloak; and some who see me may be vile enough to say I have shared in the outbreak."

So Miss Hall, the daughter of Mr. Hall, the landlord of the George and Dragon, lent me a hat and great-coat. I put them on, and putting my travelling cap into my bag, gave the bag to one of the young men, and my cloak to the other; and, accompanied by Bevington and other friends, we started. They took me through dark streets to Upper Hanley; and then Bevington and the rest bade us farewell, and the two young men and I went on.

CHAPTER XIX.
CHARTIST LIFE CONTINUED: REMARKABLE NIGHT JOURNEY:
1842.

MY friends had purposely conducted me through dark streets, and led me out of Hanley in such a way that I saw neither spark, smoke, or flame. Yet the rioters were burning the houses of the Rev. Mr. Aitken and Mr. Parker, local magistrates, and the house of Mr. Forrester, agent of Lord Granville (principal owner of the collieries in the Potteries) during that night. Scenes were being enacted in Hanley, the possibility of which had never entered my mind, when I so earnestly urged those excited thousands to work no more till the People's Charter became the law of the land. Now thirty years have gone over my head, I see how rash and uncalculating my conduct was. But, as I have already said, the demagogue is ever the instrument rather than the leader of the mob. I had caught the spirit of the oppressed and discontented thousands, and, by virtue of my nature and constitution, struck the spark which kindled all into combustion.

Nor did the outbreak end with that night. Next morning thousands were again in the streets of Hanley and began to pour into the other Pottery towns from the surrounding districts. A troop of cavalry, under Major Beresford, entered the district, and the daring colliers strove to unhorse the soldiers. Their commander reluctantly gave the order to fire; one man was killed at Burslem. The mob dispersed; but quiet was not restored until the day after this had been done, and scores had been apprehended and taken to prison.

Many days passed before I learned all this. I must now call the reader's close attention to a few facts which very closely concern myself, and show that, amidst the fulfilment of the "destiny," an Everpresent and All-beneficent Hand was guiding events, and preventing a *fatal* conclusion to my error. My friend Bevington, and those who were with him, charged the two young men, Green and Moore, who accompanied me, not to go through Burslem, because the special constables were reported to be in the streets, keeping watch during the night; but to go through the village of Chell, and avoid Burslem altogether.

I think we must have proceeded about a mile in our night journey when we came to a point where there were two roads; and Moore took the road to the right while Green took that to the left.

"Holloa!" I cried out, being a short distance behind them, "what are you about? what is the meaning of this?"

"Jem, thou fool, where art thou going to?" cried Moore to the other.

"Why, to Chell, to be sure!" answered Green.

"Chell! thou fool, that's not the way to Chell: it's the way to Burslem," cried Moore.

"Dost thou think I'm such a fool that I don't know the way to Chell, where I've been scores o' times?" said Green.

"So have I been scores o' times," said Moore ; "but I tell thee that isn't the way to Chell."

"I tell thee that I'm right," said the one.

"I tell thee thou art wrong," said the other.

And so the altercation went on, and they grew so angry with each other that I thought they would fight about it.

"This is an awkward fix for me," said I, at length. You both say you have been scores of times to Chell, and yet you cannot agree about the way. You know we have no time to lose. I cannot stand here listening to your quarrel. I must be moving some way. You cannot decide for me. So I shall decide for myself. I go this way," —and off I dashed along the road to the left, Moore still protesting it led to Burslem, and Green contending as stoutly that it led to Chell.

They both followed me, however, and both soon recognised the entrance of the town of Burslem, and wished to go back.

"Nay," said I, "we will not go back. You seem to know the other way so imperfectly, that, if we attempt to find it, we shall very likely get lost altogether. I suppose this is the highroad to Macclesfield, and perhaps it is only a tale about the specials."

In the course of a few minutes we proved that it was no tale. We entered the market-place of Burslem, and there, in full array, with the lamp-lights shining upon them, were the Special Constables! The two young men were struck with alarm; and, without speaking a word, began to stride on, at a great pace. I called to them, in a strong whisper, not to walk fast—for I knew that would draw observation upon us. But neither of them heeded. Two persons, who seemed to be officers over the specials, now came to us. Their names, I afterwards learned, were Wood and Alcock, and they were leading manufacturers in Burslem.

"Where are you going to, sir?" said Mr. Wood to me. "Why are you travelling at this time of the night, or morning rather? And why are those two men gone on so fast?"

"I am on the way to Macclesfield, to take the early coach for Manchester," said I; "and those two young men have agreed to walk with me."

"And where have you come from?" asked Mr. Wood; and I answered, "From Hanley."

"But why could you not remain there till the morning?"

"I wanted to get away because there are fires and disorder in the town—at least, I was told so, for I have seen nothing of it."

Meanwhile, Mr. Alcock had stopped the two young men.

"Who is this man?" he demanded; "and how happen you to be with him, and where is he going to?"

"We don't know who he is," answered the young men, being unwilling to bring me into danger; "he has given us half-a-crown a piece, to go with him to Macclesfield. He's going to take the coach there for Manchester, to-morrow morning."

"Come, come," said Mr. Alcock, "you must tell us who he is. I am sure you know."

The young men doggedly protested that they did not know.

"I think," said Mr. Wood, "the gentleman had better come with us into the Legs of Man" (the principal inn, which has the arms of the Isle of Man for its sign), "and let us have some talk with him."

So we went into the inn, and we were soon joined by a tart-looking consequential man.

"What are you, sir?" asked this ill-tempered-looking person.

"A commercial traveller," said I, resolving not to tell a lie, but feeling that I was not bound to tell the whole truth. And then the same person put other silly questions to me, until he alighted on the right one, "What is your name?"

I had no sooner told it, than I saw Mr. Alcock write something on a bit of paper, and hand it to Mr. Wood. As it passed the candle I saw what he had written,—"He is a Chartist lecturer."

"Yes, gentlemen," I said, instantly, "I am a Chartist lecturer; and now I will answer any question you may put to me."

"That is very candid on your part, Mr. Cooper," said Mr. Alcock.

"But why did you tell a lie, and say you were a commercial traveller?" asked the tart-looking man.

"I have not told a lie," said I; "for I am a commercial traveller, and I have been collecting accounts and taking orders for stationery that I sell, and a periodical that I publish, in Leicester."

"Well, sir," said Mr. Wood, "now we know who you are, we must take you before a magistrate. We shall have to rouse him from bed; but it must be done."

Mr. Parker was a Hanley magistrate, but had taken alarm when the mob began to surround his house, before they set it on fire, and had escaped to Burslem. He had not been more than an hour in bed, when they roused him with the not very agreeable information that he must immediately examine a suspicious-seeming Chartist, who had been stopped in the street. I was led into his bedroom, as he sat in bed, with his night-cap on. He looked so terrified at the sight of me—and bade me stand farther off, and nearer the door! In spite of my dangerous circumstances, I was near bursting into laughter. He put the most stupid questions to me; and at his request I turned out the contents of my carpet-bag, which I had taken from the young men, with the thought that I might be separated from them. But he could make nothing of the contents,—either of my night-cap and stockings, or the letters and papers it held. Mr. Wood at last said,—

"Well, Mr. Parker, you seem to make nothing out in your examination of Mr. Cooper. You have no witnesses, and no charges against him. He has told us frankly that he has been speaking in Hanley; but we have no proof that he has broken the peace. I think you had better discharge him, and let him go on his journey."

Mr. Parker thought the same, and discharged me. His house was being burnt at Hanley while I was in his bedroom at Burslem. I was afterwards charged with sharing the vile act. But I could have put Mr. Parker himself into the witness-box to prove that I was three miles from the scene of riot, if the witnesses *against* me had not proved it themselves. The young men, by the wondrous Providence which watched over me, were prevented going by way of Chell. If we had not gone to Burslem, false witnesses might have procured me transportation for life!

Were these young men true to me? Had they deserted me, and gone back to Hanley? No: they were true to me, and were waiting in the street; and now cheerily took the bag and cloak, and we sped on again, faster. We had been detained so long, however, that by the time we reached the "Red Bull," a well-known inn on the highroad between Burslem and the more northern towns of Macclesfield, Leek, and Congleton, one of the young men, observed by his watch that it was now too late for us to be able to reach Macclesfield in time for the early coach. The other young man agreed; and they both advised that we should strike down the road, at the next turning off to the left, and get to Crewe—where I could take the railway for Manchester. We did so; and had time for breakfast at Crewe, before the Manchester train came up, when the young men returned.

A second special Providence was thus displayed in my behalf. If we had proceeded in the direction of Macclesfield, in the course of some quarter of an hour we should have met a crowd of working men, armed with sticks, coming from Leek and Congleton to join the riot in the Potteries. That I should have gone back with them, I feel certain; and then I might have been shot in the street, as the leader of the outbreak; or, if taken prisoner, I might have forfeited my life.

Do not feel surprised, reader, when I say I feel certain I should have gone back with that crowd. How rapid are our changes of mind and the succession of our impulses and resolves, when we are under high excitement, none can know, except by dread experience. As we journeyed along that night, I was compelled to keep behind the young men, in order to do battle with my own thoughts. If truth did not demand it, I would hardly tell what tumultuous thoughts passed through me.

"Was it not sneaking cowardice to quit the scene of danger? Ought I not to have remained, and again, on the following morning, have summoned the people to hear me, and proclaimed 'Peace, Law, and Order'?

"Or, what if like scenes should be transacting in Lancashire and elsewhere, and this be really an incipient Revolution—ought I not to have remained, and displayed the spirit of a leader, instead of shunning the danger?

"Could I expect the people to take the advice I had given them in the morning, and expect all to be as quiet as lambs, when labour was given up? Had I not better turn back, and direct the struggle for freedom?

"No: it was better to go on to the Manchester convention, and learn the truth about Lancashire, and know the spirit of the leaders with whom I had to act. O'Connor would be there; and surely he would not be deficient in courage, if he saw any real opportunity of leading the people to win a victory for the People's Charter.

"But, whatever others might do, if the report given in respecting the spirit of the people, by members of the Convention, showed that there was a strong resolve to work no more till Right was done—I would fight if the people had to fight. Why not end the Wrong, at once, if it could be ended?"

When I entered the railway carriage at Crewe, some who were going to the Convention recognised me,—and, among the rest, Campbell, secretary of the "National Charter Association." He had left London on purpose to join the Conference; and, like myself, was anxious to know the real state of Manchester. So soon as the City of Long Chimneys came in sight, and every chimney was beheld smokeless, Campbell's face changed, and with an oath he said, "Not a single mill at work! something must come out of this, and something serious too!"

CHAPTER XX.
CHARTIST LIFE CONTINUED: MY FIRST TRIAL AND ACQUITTAL: 1842.

IN Manchester, I soon found McDouall, Leach, and Bairstow, who, together with Campbell, formed what was called "The Executive Council of the National Charter Association." They said O'Connor was in Manchester, and they hoped he would be at a meeting to be held that afternoon, at a public-house. He came to the place, but said it was not advisable to hold the Conference there: some better place must be had for the evening; and we had better separate. We all thought he seemed frightened.

In the streets, there were unmistakable signs of alarm on the part of the authorities. Troops of cavalry were going up and down the principal thoroughfares, accompanied by pieces of artillery, drawn by horses. In the evening, we held a meeting in the Reverend Mr. Schofield's chapel, where O'Connor, the Executive, and a considerable number of delegates were present; and it was agreed to open the Conference, or Convention, in form, the next morning, at nine o'clock. We met at that hour, the next morning, Wednesday, the 17th of August, when James Arthur of Carlisle was elected President. There were nearly sixty delegates present; and as they rose, in quick succession, to describe the state of their districts, it was evident they were, each and all, filled with the desire of keeping the people from returning to their labour. They believed the time had come for trying, successfully, to paralyse the Government. I caught their spirit—for the working of my mind had prepared me for it.

McDouall rose, after a while, and in the name of the Executive proposed, in form, that the Conference recommends the universal adoption of the resolution already passed at numerous meetings in Lancashire,—that all labour shall cease till the People's Charter becomes the law of the land. When the Executive, and a few others, had spoken, all in favour of the universal strike, I told the Conference I should vote for the resolution because it meant fighting, and I saw it must come to that. The spread of the strike would and must be followed by a general outbreak. The authorities of the land would try to quell it; but we must resist them. There was nothing now but a physical force struggle to be looked for. We must get the people out to fight; and they must be irresistible, if they were united.

There were shouts of applause from a few, and loud murmurs from others,—and up rose O'Connor.

"I do not believe," said he, "that there is a braver man in this Conference than Mr. Cooper; and I have no doubt that he would do what he proposes others should do. But we are not met here to talk about fighting. We must have no mention of anything of the kind here. We are met to consider what can be done to make the Charter the law of the land; and the general extension of the strike which has been begun is proposed as the means to be used. Let us keep to the resolution before the meeting."

In spite of O'Connor's protest, Mooney of Colne, Christopher Doyle, and one or two other delegates, stood up, and in a fiery style told the Convention they were for the strike because they were for fighting; and they were glad I had spoken out—for the strike really meant fighting.

But now uprose William Hill, who had been a Swedenborgian minister, and so was often termed "Reverend"—but who had for some years been O'Connor's servant, as editor of the *Northern Star*. He admired, he said, the clear intelligence which had led me to proclaim in so decided a manner that the strike meant fighting; but he wondered that so clear an intellect should dream of fighting. Fighting!—the people had nothing to fight with, and would be mown down by artillery if they attempted to fight. The strike had originated with the Anti Corn-Law League, and we should simply be their tools if we helped to extend or prolong the strike. It could only spread disaster and suffering. He denounced the strike as a great folly and a mistake; and he moved a resolution that the Conference entirely disapproved of it.

Richard Otley of Sheffield followed on the same side. He was astonished, he said, to hear his friend Cooper talk of fighting. How could I expect poor starving weavers to fight? and what had they to fight with? Had I calculated that if we endeavoured to form battalions for fighting, the people would need food and clothing—they would need arms and powder and shot; they would, very likely, have to bivouac in the fields-anyhow, could I expect poor weavers to do that? It would kill them in a few days.

Nothing caused so much amazement in the Conference as the speech of George Julian Harney. He supported Editor Hill—even he, Julian, the renowned invoker of the spirits of Marat, Danton, and Robespierre, in the old Convention times!—Julian, the notorious advocate of physical force, at all times!

"What! Julian turned 'moral-force humbug!' what will happen next?" was said by the advocates of the strike. And yet, Julian had supported Editor Hill in a very sensible manner; and a more sincere or honest man than Julian, perhaps, never existed.

There were only six votes in favour of Editor Hill's amendment. O'Connor spoke late—evidently waiting to gather the spirit of the meeting before he voted with the majority, which he meant to do from the first. Yet he meant to do nothing in support of the strike, although he voted for it!

McDouall was a different kind of spirit. He hastily drew up an exciting and fiercely worded address to the working men of England, appealing to the God of Battles for the issue, and urging a universal strike. He got Leach to print this before the Convention broke up in the evening. The address was brought into the Convention, and McDouall read the placard; but Editor Hill defiantly protested against it; and O'Connor moved that instead of its being sent out in the name of the Convention, the Executive should send it out in their own name. McDouall said the Executive would do so—and the Conference broke up.

The publication of the address, with the names of the Executive appended to it, caused the police to look after them very sharply. Campbell got off to London, McDouall got away into Yorkshire, and only Leach was left at his own home in Manchester, where the police soon found him. Bairstow, I took back with me to Leicester. We walked through Derbyshire, as far as Belper, and then took the railway.

I found Leicester in a state of terror and discouragement. Before my letter from Hanley reached them, the working men had taken their own resolution, and held a meeting in the market-place, declaring their adherence to the strike which had commenced in Lancashire. They then withdrew to an elevation in the neighbourhood of Leicester, which bears the singular name of "Momecker Hill." Here they were charged by the county police, and dispersed. It often causes a laugh in Leicester, to the present time, when old Chartist days are mentioned, and some one says, "Were you at the Battle of Momecker Hill?"

Laughter was not perceptible in Leicester, when I re-entered it. The police, I was told, had charged the people in the streets, as well as upon Momecker Hill, and smitten and injured several with their staves. I called Chartist friends together, with great difficulty; and endeavoured to reassure them. And then I issued a printed address to the magistrates of Leicester, boldly reprehending them for dispersing the people; and assuring them that I should still contend for the People's Charter.

I had not been one week at home, before the Leicester police came and handcuffed me, and took me to the Town Hall, where—in presence of Stokes, the Mayor, who looked as white as a sheet, and never spoke a word!—I was handed over to the constable of Hanley, who had come to apprehend me. We reached Hanley at night, and I was taken to a "lockup," where a large, coarse fellow, who was set to watch over me, put huge iron bolts on my ancles, so that I could not sleep as I lay in my clothes on a board. The next day I was taken to Newcastle-under-Lyme, and brought before Mr. Mainwaring and Mr. Ayshford Wyse, magistrates. Several witnesses appeared against me; and I saw what I must expect when the real trial came. I had to complain of the "leading questions" put to the witnesses, eliciting replies which were damaging to myself.

"He proclaimed 'Peace, Law, and Order,' and shouted it aloud," said one of the meanest of the witnesses, with a laugh.

"But *how* did he say it?" asked Mr. Mainwaring; " did he say it as if he meant it?"

"Oh, no!" cried Dirty Neck, as the fellow was called in the Potteries; "it was only *innuendo*."

"Is there any particular statute against *inuendo*?" I asked the magistrate; "would it not be strange, if I were convicted of the crime of *inuendo*? Do you think it right, sir, to put answers into men's mouths in this way?"

They committed me to Stafford Gaol, on the charge of aiding in a riot at Hanley, etc. But I was kept at Newcastle-under-Lyme until next day, Sunday—when, to my amazement, I was borne away in an open carriage drawn by four horses, with a troop of cavalry, having drawn swords, escorting me, to the Whitmore station, on what was then called the "Grand Junction Line," there being no railway through the Potteries at that time, as I said before. At the Whitmore station, the constable of Newcastle-under-Lyme handcuffed me to his wrist, and took me in the train to Stafford; and so on Sunday evening, the 28th of August, 1842, I first became a prisoner in Stafford Gaol.

From that time till the commencement of the Special Assizes, in October, eight hundred persons were brought to Stafford Gaol, as participators in the riot of the 15th August. I was surrounded with a score, and sometimes more, of these men, in the prison ward, in the daytime; but I slept alone. During these six weeks, before I was brought up for my first trial, and while surrounded with the colliers and potters who were charged with sharing in the riots, I composed several of the simple tales which will be found in "Wise Saws and

Modern Instances," published in 1845. I also commenced my intended "Purgatory of Suicides," in blank verse, and struck off one hundred lines. But these were afterwards abandoned.

The day of trial came, the 11th of October, before Sir Nicholas Conyngham Tindal, Lord Chief Justice of the Common Pleas: Sir William Follett, the Solicitor-General, and Mr. Waddington, being the two prosecuting barristers. I had engaged Mr. Williams, an honest Radical of the Potteries, as my attorney; and he engaged Mr. Lee, as the barrister to assist me on law points only—as I had determined to conduct my own case. William Prowting Roberts, the "Chartist Attorney-General," as he was often called, also kindly promised to assist me with advice.

I felt stunned, as if a person had given me a blow on the head, when Roberts came to have a private interview with me in the prison, but a week before the trial, and he told me I was to be tried for the alleged crime of "arson," or aiding and abetting the burning of justice Parker's house.

"They are about to arraign you," he also said, on the morning before the trial, "in company with seventeen other prisoners. Now, if you permit that, you are a lost man. Mind what I say: you have a chance of a fair trial, if you do two things—first, you must demand 'to sever,' that is, to be tried alone. If you persist in your demand, you will gain it. Secondly, you must 'challenge the jury,' that is, you must ask every Juryman, before he is sworn, whether he has served on any trial during this Special Assize—and then object to him, if he has so served,—for all who have hitherto served are prejudiced men. Refuse to plead either 'guilty' or 'not guilty,' before the court grants you leave to sever and to challenge the jury."

I refused to plead until both demands were granted me, although I was resisted, very sternly, by Sir William Follett. Two or three witnesses swore that they saw me arm-in-arm with William Ellis (whom I had never known or seen in my life) walking to the fire at justice Parker's house. One witness, Mr Macbean, surgeon of Hanley, gave his evidence in a clear, honest, and intelligent manner;

but no one else did. The Solicitor-General, both in addressing the jury and in cross-examining my witnesses, used great unfairness, as I thought. Once he made me spring up and contradict him.

"My lord, and gentlemen of the jury," he said, in his very deep voice, "the prisoner at the bar is declared by several witnesses to have said, while addressing the crowd that had just returned to Hanley, after burning the house of the Reverend Mr. Vale, at Longton, 'My lads, you have done your work well, to-day!' What work, gentlemen? Why the destruction of property, to be sure—"

"Sir William!" I cried out, " you are slaughtering me! You know it is false to say I meant they had done their work well in destroying property. You know that your most intelligent witness, Mr. Macbean, declared the words were, 'You have done your work well in turning out the hands!' And those were the words: wrong or right, I shall not deny them."

Moore, Green, Worthington, Sylvester, and others of my own witnesses, not only proved my *alibi*, but the later witnesses *against* me showed that I was at Burslem, in Justice Parker's bedroom, at the time that the earlier witnesses swore they saw me, arm in arm, with William Ellis, in the streets of Hanley! I occupied some two hours of the time of the Court in delivering my own address. I dealt, first, with the evidence of the witnesses and their contradictions; secondly, I told the truth about my *alibi* on the night of the riots; and thirdly, I sketched my own life, and asked the jury if they could believe any intent of urging men to the destruction of property could dwell in the mind of one who had spent so much of his life in mental and moral cultivation?

The judge, it was observed by Roberts, who was his kinsman, and knew him well, was much affected with my address; and some of the ladies who sat near him shed tears. In summing up, the judge told the jury, most positively, that they could not convict me of the crime of arson; that I certainly was at Burslem, and not at Hanley, during the time that Mr. Parker's house was on fire. The jury retired; and, after twenty minutes of agonizing suspense for myself, gave in their verdict of "*Not* Guilty."

I was taken down into the " glory-hole," as the felons call the filthy place under the Courts of Assize in Stafford; and there I first saw William Ellis, who had just been sentenced to twenty-one years' transportation, although, he assured me, most solemnly, he was not at the fires. I was taken back to the prison, and two days afterwards I was again taken, in the prison-van to the Court, and arraigned again before Sir Nicholas Conyngham Tindal—first for the crime of conspiracy with William Ellis, Joseph Capper, and John Richards; and secondly, for the crime of sedition.

Again, kindly instructed by Roberts, I asked "to traverse:" that is, to have my trial adjourned to the next Assizes. Sir William Follett smiled with gladness when he heard my request. The ambitious, hard-working, highly intelligent man was dying; and the fortnight's terrible work at Stafford, though he was paid several thousands for it, hastened his end. He readily consented, and Daddy Richards, as he was always called in the Potteries, was also allowed to traverse. But Capper would not traverse.

"I want to go whooam," said the obstinate old man ; "try me and get done wi' me I've done nowt amiss."

So they arraigned him, separately, on the charge of sedition, and soon brought him in guilty, and sentenced him to two years' imprisonment. I knew when they had done that, that I should receive a sentence of imprisonment also for two years, at some future day. Daddy Richards and I were taken back to prison till we could find bail. Daddy found good bail in the Potteries. Mr. Robert Haimes, of Oundle, in Northamptonshire, a beneficent gentleman of eighty years of age, went, first, by mistake, to Lancaster, and then to London, that—with my friend and benefactor, Mr. Samuel Mullen— he might give bail for myself, although I was utterly unknown to him, except by mere report, as a poor Chartist in trouble. Although we thus readily found friends—substantial friends—who offered bail for us, the Staffordshire magistrates threw all kinds of impediment in our way—evidently desiring to keep us in prison. After five more weeks had passed we were liberated. My first imprisonment had thus lasted eleven weeks.

CHAPTER XXI.
CHARTIST LIFE, CONTINUED: STURGE CONFERENCE: SECOND TRIAL: 1842—1843.

I HAD a public entry into Leicester—a procession round the town, with flags,—and all that sort of thing; but I saw, before the day was over, that all had been going wrong in my absence. Duffy, an excitable Irishman, who had suffered a long imprisonment for Chartism, and had so suffered that he had become sad and soured, had formed a party with a few turbulent men; and two or three other petty parties were opposed to these: in brief, all was discord and jealousy. My poor wife, too, who had sustained her burden of trouble most heroically, had gradually declined, till she was obliged to tenant her bedroom only.

The election of Mr. Thomas Gisborne for Nottingham drew me away from home for a few days. It was determined to give Thomas Slingsby Duncombe, M.P., a public entry into Nottingham,—as the political patron or advocate under whose persuasion Mr. Gisborne was to be accepted by the Nottingham electors. O'Connor wished me to meet him at Nottingham, to do honour to Duncombe ; and so I went over. Our Chartists joined the procession with their flags, mingling friendlily with the other shades of Liberals ; and O'Connor and I, adorned with rosettes, led the horses of the open carriage in which Mr. Duncombe entered Nottingham. He was in the very prime of life, and I never saw a handsomer man in form and figure; nor could aught surpass, in attractiveness, the winning smile he wore, and the graceful way in which he acknowledged the hearty and almost tumultuous welcome he received.

During Christmastide, at Leicester, Chartist divisions were hushed, that we might make provision for taking our part in what was afterwards called the 'Great Birmingham Conference,' and by some the 'Great Sturge Conference.' Since it was composed of more than 400 persons, it might well bear a designation of importance. The leaders of the Complete Suffrage party had met Lovett, Collins, O'Brien, and other old Chartists who were not of O'Connor's party, at Birmingham, in an earlier part of the year; and it had then been determined to hold a Conference on a large scale of representation.

Leicester was privileged to return four delegates. The Complete Suffrage party wished two of the delegates to be chosen in a meeting composed of parliamentary electors only; and to leave the unrepresented to elect the two other delegates. But this did not meet the views either of Chartists or of working men generally. They forced their way into the meetings called by the respectables; and the respectables disappeared. It was of their own respectable good pleasure that they withdrew. If they had remained, working-men would have voted for the Rev. J. P. Mursell and Mr. William Baines, to be delegates with Duffy and myself. But respectables held our characters to be defective, and they would not act with us. So we acted by ourselves. I and Duffy and two other Chartists were voted delegates for Leicester, and we went to Birmingham: no respectables went.

Our Chartist delegates were the most numerous party in the Birmingham Conference; but my expectation rose when I saw so many persons present belonging to the middle class. I thought that if such persons would assemble with us to confer about presenting a petition to Parliament for making a law whereby all mature men should have the franchise, it showed we were really advancing. If the strike for the Charter had ended almost as soon as it begun, and had ended disastrously,—if neither we nor the Anti Corn-Law League had succeeded in paralysing the government, it looked as if there were a party in the country who were determined yet to let the Government understand that there was real cause for discontent, and it was time the wrong should be righted.

The truly illustrious Joseph Sturge was elected chairman of the Conference, by acclamation—for not a single working-man delegate in the meeting wished for any other chairman. And now, if Mr. Sturge himself, or Edward Miall, or the Rev. Thomas Spencer, or the Rev. Patrick Brewster of Paisley, or Mr. Lawrence Heyworth of Liverpool, or any other leading member of the Complete Suffrage party present, had risen in that assembly, and spoken words of real kindness and hearty conciliation, I am persuaded that not even O'Connor himself, if he had desired it, could have prevented the great body of working-men delegates from uttering shouts of joy.

But there was no attempt to bring about a union—no effort for conciliation—no generous offer of the right hand of friendship. We soon found that it was determined to keep poor Chartists "at arm's length." We were not to come between the wind and *their* nobility. Thomas Beggs of Nottingham, a mere secondary member of the Complete Suffrage party, was put up to propose their first resolution, to the effect,—That the "People's Bill of Rights" form the basis from which the petition should be drawn that this Conference would present to Parliament.

But what was the "People's Bill of Rights"? A document which had been drawn up by a barrister, it was said, at the request of the Complete Suffrage party, in which the six points of our Charter were embodied, and some definite propositions were made for distributing the country into equal electoral districts. But Chartists knew nothing of all this. And it was preposterous to ask us to vote for what we knew nothing of. Copies of the new bill were laid on the tables. But who could be expected to read and digest a mass of print amounting to many pages, in the lapse of a few hours, or while listening to exciting speeches, and then give a judgment on it? Murmurs of discontent, and soon of indignation, began to arise— when up rose William Lovett, throwing up his tall form to its full height, and, with a glance of haughty defiance towards the Complete Suffrage leaders, to our utter amazement he led the attack upon them!

If they had made up their minds, he said, to force their Bill of Rights upon the Conference, he would move that the People's Charter be the basis from whence the petition should be drawn for presentation to Parliament. He also openly charged the Complete Suffrage party with unmanly secrecy, "You have not kept faith with me," he said; when I and my friends met you, in this town, some months ago, we were given to understand that no measures contrary to our views would be taken without our being informed of it; and now this resolution is proposed—so contrary to fairness. If you will withdraw your motion, I will withdraw mine; and then we will endeavour to come to a fair agreement. If you refuse to withdraw your resolution, I stand by mine as an amendment."

Lovett's conduct won the hearts of all who were O'Connor Chartists, and, apparently, of O'Connor himself—for he followed with a highly-spiced eulogium on Lovett. But Lovett evidently did not accept his flattery. He was irreconcilably opposed to O'Connor, as a mere trader on political agitation; and he was, constitutionally, too proud to bear the thought of being under another's leadership. But so far as parties could be distinguished in that Conference, there were now but two. We had looked on Lovett and his friends as a doubtful party when the Conference was opened. All thought of that was now gone; and the debate soon began to be very stormy— for the Complete Suffrage party stuck by their "People's Bill of Rights," and we stuck by our "People's Charter."

The best orator in the Conference was a friend of Lovett's, utterly unknown to the great majority of delegates. He was then a subordinate in the British Museum, but has now, for many years, been known to all England as the highly successful barrister, Serjeant Parry. The Reverend Patrick Brewster of Paisley distinguished himself by the length of his speech; and Mr. Lawrence Heyworth by his offensiveness.

"We will espouse your principles, but we will not have your leaders," he cried; and when the outcry against him grew strong, he grew still more offensive—"I say again," he shouted, "we'll not have you—you tyrants!"

The good chairman now interposed, and begged of him not to proceed in that style; or I think George White, and Beesley, and a few others, who were heard swearing roughly, would have been disposed to try another and more conclusive way of arguing than mere speech.

The Rev. Mr. Spencer, a clergyman of the Complete Suffrage party, was heard with kindly patience, for he addressed us respectfully, though he did not convince us. We had a clergyman on our side also—a very great contrast, every way, to Mr. Spencer—but well known for many years, among London Radicals, as a very determined politician: the famous, fat "Parson Wade," as he was always called.

"What is this 'Bill of Rights'?" he asked; "this mysterious something which we are expected to swallow—this thing begotten in darkness, and brought forth in a coal-hole—this

'Monstrum horrendum, informe, ingens, cui lumen ademptum.'

This pig in a poke?—What is it? I say. We know nothing about it. And I wonder at the effrontery—nay, sir, I tell you plainly I wonder at the impudence of any party who can call together a Conference like this, and mock us with such a proposition."

"I am a Chartist," he cried, in conclusion; "I am a whole hog! and I don't care who knows it."

During the time that some prosy speaker was occupying the Conference, or rather consuming their time, I fell into conversation with James Williams of Sunderland. He expressed to me his regret that something had not been done—even if the attempt were unsuccessful—to bring back the Conference to fairness. I told him it was too late—for it was now far on, on the second day;—but it would be well to propose a resolution even if none voted with us. It would be a protest for fairness, if it were no more. So he moved, and I seconded, a proposition that both People's Charter and People's Bill of Rights be laid on the table, that they might form the basis of the petition to be sent to Parliament by the Conference. I do not think we had half a dozen supporters. It was, as I said, too late. Chartists were not likely to give way under such circumstances. To abandon their Charter, for which so many of them had suffered imprisonment, and for which all had endured scorn and persecution—in order to accept a proposition so offensively advocated by some, and so irrational in its suddenness—could not be expected of them.

When the decisive vote was taken, we were apparently as three to one; and Joseph Sturge, after a little hesitation, rose and told us that he and his friends had come to the determination to leave us: they would withdraw, and hold a Conference by themselves. All was tumult for a time. An independent Quaker, from the Isle of Wight, protested, and said he would not withdraw. The Rev. H. Solly, of Yeovil, also refused to withdraw. And Arthur O'Neill, though no O'Connorite, stuck by us, like a true-hearted partisan of the side of the poor, as he has always been. Henry Vincent withdrew with the Complete Suffrage party. We blamed him; but, during the last thirty years, he has done more to liberalize the middle classes, in politics, than any other man.

What a wretched look did the face of good Joseph Sturge weal as he uttered his last words to us, and stepped down from the chair!

"Cooper," said O'Connor to me, "that man is not happy. He does not want to leave us." And I thought so too.

Mr. Patrick O'Higgins of Dublin, an old associate of Feargus—(there was a rumour, once, that he was to marry O'Connor's sister)—was proposed by O'Connor as our chairman, and Lovett as our secretary; and we prepared to continue the Conference; but we felt wearied, although there was a deal of talk.

I asked Lovett, openly, if we might expect him to join us heartily in our effort to get the Charter; but he told us, unhesitatingly, that he meant to abide by his own plans; and unless we accepted them he could not join us. Not a man of the O'Connorite party felt disposed to do this; so my attempt to conciliate Lovett failed. He and Parry, and his other friends, left us before the Conference was formally concluded; and we retired to a smaller room, where I proposed a plan of organisation, with a view of strengthening our members; but the Executive opened a quarrel with O'Connor; and soon it was all quarrel and confusion, and we came to a conclusion without any form at all.

When my plan of organisation was published, Editor Hill proposed his. Letters followed in the *Northern Star*; and a fuss was made about "Organisation " for a time; but no real and effective organisation ever took place. That Birmingham Conference ruined the prospects of Chartists; and the Complete Suffrage party never made any headway in the country. The middle and working classes could form no union for winning the broad franchise; and so the expectation of winning it grew faint and fainter.

The months of January and February, 1843, passed away very drearily. I was in debt to John Cleave for copies of the *Northern Star* and other periodicals; I was in debt to Warwick, my printer; I was in debt to my baker, for bread given away to the poor; I was in debt to the lawyer who had prepared my case for defence and perfected my bail. And the divisions which had sprung up rendered it difficult for me to keep the Chartist party together—although Markham, the old leader, now, in the time of my trouble, showed himself friendly.

It was proposed to raise money for the law expenses by the performance of a play. So we hired the Amphitheatre, and I took the part of Hamlet—as I knew the whole play by heart. We performed the play twice; but I found it useless to proceed further in that direction: the amphitheatre, which, as I have already said, held 3,000 people, was crowded to excess, each night; but the people who went on the stage as actors and actresses, all demanded payment, both for the cost of their dresses and their time, and so the income hardly covered expenses.

I was glad when we reached the month of March, 1843, and the Spring Assizes at Stafford drew near. The judge, this time, was the Hon. Sir Thomas Erskine; and the Counsel arrayed against myself, and Daddy Richards, and Capper (for Ellis was already across the sea), were, Serjeant Talfourd, M.P., Mr. Godson, M.P. for Kidderminster, Mr. Richards, an elderly barrister, and young Mr. Alexander.

My second trial commenced on my birthday, March 20th, 1843. I was angered greatly when I found that the Hanley lawyers and magistrates had resolved, in this my second trial, to revive the old, vilely false charge of "arson,"—although I had been acquitted of the charge after a full trial, where I had the most powerful pleader at the bar against me, and the best lawyer on the Bench for my judge!

I would have no counsel; nor had I the slightest legal assistance this time. I was sole lawyer and sole counsel for myself and also for my companions in trouble. The trial began on Monday morning, and I exerted all my strength up to Saturday at noon in cross-examining the witnesses brought against us, and making them contradict themselves—for some of them were the very scum of the Potteries for bad character, and would have sworn away any man's life for a few shillings. Major Beresford was the last witness brought up against us; and I was surprised when they told me there were no more witnesses to appear, as the list they gave me before the trial contained several other names.

The Court broke up for an hour, and then I had to begin my defence. I had only half finished when the usual time came for closing the Court; and so I had to resume on Monday morning—making about ten hours altogether for my defence. I do not think that I ever spoke so powerfully in my life as during the last hour of that defence. The peroration, the Stafford papers said, would never be forgotten; and I remember, as I sat down, panting for breath and utterly exhausted, how Talfourd and Erskine and the jury sat transfixed, gazing at me in silence; and the whole crowded place was breathless, as it seemed, or a minute.

The witnesses on our side were not subjected to much cross-examination, except my friend Bevington; but his intelligence and perfect self-possession brought him easily through. The Judge and Counsel and jury were all wearied, and hastened to come to an end. Judge Erskine took nearly the whole of Tuesday to sum up; and first told the jury that he should not read to them that part of his notes which recorded the evidence that I was present at the fires—unless they wished it to be read—but should write *Mistake* on all the pages, instead. The jury conferred together a few moments, and desired him to write *Mistake*. I felt this to be a great triumph—for God had delivered me from the snare of those who still hoped they should get me sent over the sea; and I was declared innocent of the charge of felony!

We were, of course, declared Guilty of the crimes of Sedition and Conspiracy; but the good, kind-hearted Erskine said, that, since our case had been removed by "Writ of Certiorari " to the Court of Queen's Bench when we traversed, he should not pronounce sentence, but leave that to the Chief justice and judges of that Court. So again John Richards and I went back to our homes, by virtue of our bail.

CHAPTER XXII.
PLEADING IN THE COURT OF QUEEN'S BENCH:
CHARTIST PRISONER LIFE: 1843.

AND now the most heartrending trial I had ever to meet in my life was at hand. My poor dear wife was in a very dangerous state, worn almost to a skeleton, always in bed, and incapable of helping herself; and I had to leave her in that state on the 2nd of May—for we were summoned to appear in London to receive sentence on the 4th. I had told her that I expected two years' imprisonment, because they had given Capper that sentence. One of her sisters, with other women, who stood around her bed, as I stooped to give her, as I expected, the last token of love in this life, burst into an exclamation of amazement, as they saw her glance upwards and smile, with an expression that meant, "We shall meet in heaven!"

I spoke in the market-square of Northampton on the evening of the 2nd of May, and in the John Street room, in London, on the evening of the 3rd. On the morning of the 4th, in the court of Queen's Bench, O'Connor, Harney, Doyle, Leach, Bairstow, Hill, Parkes, Arran, Railton, Brooks, James Arthur, and several other members of the Manchester Convention, and I with them, were first arraigned, and bound in £100 each to keep the peace, and appear again when summoned, and then dismissed. Next, Daddy Richards and I (for Capper was safe in Stafford Gaol, and Ellis was sent across the sea) were re-arraigned, as convicted of sedition and conspiracy, before Lord Denman (the Lord Chief Justice of the Queen's bench), Sir John Patteson, and Sir John Williams; and we were directed to plead "in mitigation of judgment, or sentence."

Sir Frederick Pollock and Serjeant Talfourd were in court all day; but Sir William Follett was only called in, from the House of Commons, just at the close. O'Connor, Wheeler, Skevington of Loughborough, and a great band of Chartists, were also in court, all day, and witnessed all the proceedings. Judge Patteson and Judge Williams read judge Erskine's notes of our trial; and again, it was read out that "*Mistake*" was written on the evidence for felony, by the judge, at the request of the jury. When they had finished the reading of judge Erskine's notes, I began to plead, and referred to printed proofs that the outbreak originated with the Anti-Corn-Law League; but was interrupted by Lord Denman, who told me that I had said all that at Stafford, and need not repeat it now. I recommenced; but again he interrupted me, saying, very angrily,—

"We cannot have the time of this court taken up with mere repetitions of what you said at Stafford. You are here simply to plead in mitigation of judgment—and so, go on, sir!"

The last words were spoken with such haughty harshness, that I burst into tears. I had been taught to worship this man, all my life. He was Brougham's coadjutor in the defence of poor Queen Caroline, and bore so high a name for patriotism, liberality, and uprightness, that my sensitive nature felt his words as if my mother had chidden me.

"My lord," I said in a broken voice, "is that worthy of yourself—of the name of Denman? I cannot address the Court, if your lordship speaks to me in that manner. Will you allow John Richards to go on, and let me address the Court when he has done?"

"If you like!" said the Lord Chief Justice, in the same haughty tone.

So I sat down, and Daddy Richards went on, and very admirably, too—for the old man had fine native powers, and spoke with a little stateliness that was very becoming to a white-headed, large-foreheaded man of threescore and ten. He told the Court that he learnt his first lessons in patriotism and politics from "the Right Honourable Charles James Fox, and the Right Honourable William Pitt." He gave a really clever sketch of the progress of opinion in politics during his own time—strongly set forth the broken promises of the Whig Ministry and its supporters—and argued well for the People's Charter; in conclusion, telling the Lord Chief justice, to his face, that his lordship's doings in the past had greatly helped the progress of Chartism.

"My lords," said the fine old man, "I have spent my life in the good old cause of freedom, and I believe still that it will prevail. I am seventy years old; but I shall live to see the People's Charter become the law of the land yet!"

The judges smiled, and O'Connor and the Chartists looked as if they could have liked to give the old Daddy three cheers. I resumed when the old man concluded—I think about one o'clock; and I went on till five, and then asked if I might conclude my plea on the morrow.

Lord Denman eyed me with cruel archness this time, and, with a grim mocking smile, said,—"We mean to hear you out to-night"

So he beat me out of my naughty design of making them sit two days; and in another hour and a half I concluded.

Sir William Follett was now summoned from the House of Commons to address the Court.

"My lords," said he, "I entreat you to pass a severe sentence on the prisoner Cooper: you will probably have some consideration for the advanced age of the prisoner Richards."

Sir John Patteson, the large dark-eyed, and large-horned judge—for he was deaf, and wore huge hearing horns—had to pronounce sentence; and he spoke to us with admirable courtesy—but sentenced me to two years', and John Richards to one year's, imprisonment in Stafford Gaol.

I sprang up immediately, and begged, before the Court was broken up that the judges would allow me literary privileges during my imprisonment—as the chaplain of Stafford Gaol had forewarned me that if I came there again as a convicted offender, I could have nothing but the Bible and Prayer Book to read, and could not be allowed to write or receive a letter, or make use of pen, ink, and paper; since all that was contrary to the rules of the prison.

"We have no control over the rules of any gaol in the kingdom," replied the Lord Chief justice, as haughtily as ever; "at present you are committed to the custody of the Marshal of the Marshalsea—so get down, sir!"

We remained only one week in the Queen's Prison "Queen's Bench Prison" as it used to be called. Richard Oastler then occupied what the prisoners called " the state-room"; and I and Daddy Richards dined with him on the Sunday. Mr. Oastler wrote to Lord Kenyon to intercede with Lord Denman, and get him to express his wish to the Stafford magistrates that I should be allowed the literary privileges I had asked for; but Denman sternly refused.

We were suddenly told, at ten o'clock on the night before we left the Queen's Prison, that we were to be taken to Stafford at six the next morning. I neither took off my clothes, nor slept, that night; but passed it in busily revolving the events of the last two years of my life, and resolving that I would turn the two years' imprisonment into a fresh start for an honourable life, or die. I vowed that I would break down the system of restraint in Stafford Gaol, and win the privilege of reading and writing, or end my life in the struggle. I thought I should never see my dear wife again: she would die before I left the prison, and so I need not be careful of my life on her account. And if I could not write the poem on which I believed my whole future on earth depended—if it were to be honourable—it was not worth enduring two years' dismal and unrelieved imprisonment, to come out in rags and with a ruined constitution.

My resolution was at once put to the test when we reached Stafford Gaol again. My box, in which I had a considerable number of books, was taken from me, and one of the turnkeys demanded the key to it. I refused to give it him; and he said he must take it from my pocket.

"Do, if you dare," said I ; "if you attempt it, I'll knock your teeth down your throat!"—and I said it in such a way that he slunk aside, and said no more.

We were put into the same day-room with Capper; and for the first few weeks we all three slept in one room. Very soon, we were placed in separate sleeping cells. Each cell had a stone floor; was simply long enough to hold a bed, and broad enough for one to walk by the side of it. An immense slab of cast iron formed the bedstead, and it rested on two large stones. A bag stuffed so hard with straw that you could scarcely make an impression on it with your heel formed the bed. Two blankets and a rug completed the furniture. There was no pillow; but remembering that, from my former imprisonment, I had brought in with me a small Mackintosh pillow, which I could blow up and put under my head. The best thing I had was a very large and very heavy camlet travelling cloak. If I had not brought this with me, I could not have slept in that cell during the winter without becoming a cripple for life, or losing my life.

The prison-bell rang at half-past five, and we were expected to rise and be ready to descend into the day-yard at six. At eight, they brought us a brown porringer, full of "skilly"—for it was such bad unpalatable oatmeal gruel, that it deserved the name— and a loaf of coarse, dark-coloured bread. At twelve at noon, they unlocked the door of our day-room, and threw upon the deal table a netful of boiled potatoes, in their skins, and a paper of salt—for dinner. At five in the evening, they brought us half a porringerful of "skilly;" but no bread. At six, we were trooped off, and locked up in our sleeping cells for the next twelve hours.

I demanded better food; and was told I could not have it. I asked to write to my wife, and receive a letter from her; but still they refused. One day I slipped past one of the turnkeys, as he unlocked our day-room door, ran along the passages, and got to the door of the governor's room, and thundered at it till he came out in alarm.

"Give me food that I can eat," I said; "or some of you shall pay for it."

"Go back—get away to your day-room," cried the governor.

"I will, if you will give me something to eat," I said.

"Here—come here, and take him away!" cried the governor to two of the turnkeys who had just then appeared, but who looked sorely affrighted.

"I'll knock the first man down who dares to touch me," said I; and the turnkeys stood still.

The governor burst into laughter, for he saw they were plainly in a fix.

"What d'ye want to eat, Cooper?" said he, in a gentle tone ; "tell me, and I'll give it you."

"All I want of you, at present," said I, "is a cup of good coffee, and a hearty slice of bread and butter. When I can speak to the magistrates, I shall ask for something more."

And I did ask the magistrates; but they would not yield. So I led the officers of the prison a sorely harassing life, poor fellows! I was ever knocking at the door, or shattering the windows, or asking for the surgeon or governor, or troubling them in one way or other. I had not gone to the gaol chapel since my return to Stafford. I refused to do so; because when I was in the gaol during those eleven weeks, we Chartist prisoners had to be locked up in a close box while we were in the chapel, and look at the chaplain through iron bars. I said I would not be treated in that degrading way, and refused to go. But when we had been about a month in the gaol, the second time, Capper said to me one day as they returned from the chapel,—"You should go to the chapel now; they have taken us out of the lock-ups, and we sit in the open chapel, along with the short-timers, now."

I made no reply to Capper; but what he said raised a resolve in my mind at once. He told me this on a Wednesday; but Friday was also a chapel day. So when the Friday came, I took one of the prayer-books in my hand, and placed myself next the door, to be ready to step out in a moment, when the turnkey opened it, and said, "Chapel!"

He unlocked the door; and, before he could say "Chapel," he stammered, in surprise, "Are *you* going, to-day?"

"Yes," said I, and stepped past him in a moment. Capper and Richards took their seats in the open part of the chapel, facing the pulpit, and I sat down beside them, keeping my eyes strictly fixed on the open door, where the chaplain must enter. I no sooner caught sight of his white surplice, than I bounded forward, and seizing him by the arm, just as he was about to step up into the pulpit, I cried,—

"Are you a minister of Christ? If you be, see me righted. They are starving me, on skilly and bad potatoes; and they neither let me write to my wife, or receive a letter from her—if she be alive!"

The poor chaplain shook like an aspen leaf, and stared at me with open mouth, but could not speak!

"D'ye hear, man?" I cried, shaking him by the arm—"Will you see me righted, I say?"

"He's mad!—he's mad!" gasped the poor chaplain; "take him off! take him away!"

Four of the turnkeys seized me by the legs and arms, and bore me away, while I made the chapel and vaulted passages ring with my shouts of "Murder! murder!"

This violence exhausted me greatly; and the surgeon prescribed some extra food. I think it was two boiled eggs, with coffee and bread and butter. But as all went on as usual the next day, I continued to tease the keepers, and to send messages to the governor, and to ask for the magistrates; but nothing was yielded to me. So about eight or ten days after my adventure in the chapel, I said to Capper and old Daddy Richards,—

"Go out into the day-yard, both of you. I want to try the effect of a bombardment; and I don't want either of you to be in the scrape."

"What art thou about to do, Tom?" said the dear old Daddy; "art thou about to ruin us?"

"Ruin you! you old goose," I said; "you are ruined,—are you not?"

The old man ran off, laughing, into the day-yard, wondering what I was about to do. There was no chair in our day-room; but only a heavy wooden bench, on which we all three were expected to sit. It was very heavy; but I got hold of it, and turning one end unto the inner door, I let go, as a sailor would say—at the door, with all my might, crying "Murder! murder! murder!" Soon came the whole body of turnkeys; and the chief of them, Chidley, who was a large, stout man, opened the door, and cried,

"What do ye mean by this? We'll settle you! Come along—we'll take you to the black-hole!"

They took me to no black-hole; but they locked me up in an empty room, and kept me there till dusk of evening, when they took me to bed without food.

I found my strength sorely lessened by these continued and exhaustive attempts to break down the prison system; and one morning, when the bell rang at half-past five, I felt so weak that I could not rise. Soon came a turnkey, unlocked the door, and threw it open as usual.

"Holloa!" said he; how's this?—why are you not up?"

"I am too weak to get up," I answered; and he closed the door, locked it, and went his way.

In a few minutes, I heard the feet of several persons in the passage, and could tell that they were sweeping it. They drew near the door, and I heard a whispering. Soon one of them whispered through the large keyhole.

"Mester Kewper! dooant yo knaw me? My name's John Smith. I cum thrum th' Potteries; an' I heerd yo' speeak that day, upo' th' Craan Bonk. Dun yo want owt?"

"Want aught?" I said, "why, what can you get me?"

"Some bacca, if you like—or, maybe, the old Daddy would like some."

"But how can you get it, and what are you doing in the passage?"

"Why, we've getten lagged, [*Sentenced to transportation*] yo see; and they setten us to sweep th' passages and th' cells, till we go off. We can get you owt yo like, throo th' debtors. There's a chink i' th' wall where we get things through."

"Can you get me some sheets of writing paper—one large sheet—and a few pens and a narrow bottle of ink ? If you can, I'll give you the money to buy 'em."

And I thrust two shillings under the bottom of the door, for the space was wide; and they promised to bring me what I wanted, if I could be in the same place the next morning.

"I'll take care to be here," said I. And the next morning, when the turnkey found me in bed, as he opened the door, he closed it again, without asking a question, and left me alone as before.

"Can you get me a letter sent out to the post-office?" I asked, as they brought me the ink and pens and paper.

"Yes," they said; if yo conna be here ageean tomorrow morning, leave th' letter under th' mattrass. We shall be sure to get it a few minutes after. We knaw them amung th' debtors that'll see it sent safe to the post-office."

I drew up a petition to the House of Commons on the larger sheet of paper—asking that I might have food on which I could subsist; that I might be allowed to write to my wife and a few friends, and receive letters from them; and that I might be allowed the use of my books, and be also allowed to write what I pleased, for my own purposes, during my confinement.

I also wrote to the great friend of poor Chartist prisoners, noble Thomas Slingsby Duncombe, and told him that I had written out a petition to the House of Commons, and should address it to himself for presentation; that I should put it into the hands of the governor of the gaol on the morrow, and request him to place it before the magistrates. I particularly desired Mr. Duncombe to mark how long it was before he received the petition, and to note that it was dated.

I left the letter under the mattress; and it was safely received by Mr. Duncombe. When the governor made his usual morning call, just as he entered our dayroom, I put the petition into his hands.

"Please to show that to the magistrates," said I; "and then take care that it is sent to Mr. Duncombe, the member of Parliament for Finsbury."

"What is it, sir?" asked the governor, all in a flutter.

"A petition to the House of Commons," said I.

"Take it back sir—take it back—I'll have nothing to do with it," cried the poor governor, trying to push it into my hands.

"On your peril, sir," said I, "lay that petition before the magistrates. Refuse, if you dare, sir! And tell the magistrates if they do not send the petition to Mr. Duncombe, they shall be reckoned with, if I live to get out of this place."

"Where did you get the paper, sir?" he asked; "and the pens and ink?"

"I shall not tell you. If you were to hang me you should not know."

"Well, sir," said he, going away; "I must tell the magistrates all about it; but, depend upon it, you have got yourself into a pretty mess."

"Tell the magistrates they will get themselves into a pretty mess, if they do not forward my petition to Mr. Duncombe," I shouted after him.

CHAPTER XXIII.
CHARTIST PRISONER'S LIFE, CONTINUED: 1843—1845.

FOR many days I asked the governor of the gaol, as he paid us his morning visit, if my petition had been sent to Mr. Duncombe; but his answer was "No." At length it was "Yes;" and, two days after, Governor Brutton suddenly opened the door of our day-room, and, with a really happy look, said,

"Now, come, Cooper, the magistrates want to see you; and do be respectful to them, and you'll get all you want."

"Trust me, governor," said I, "if there be a change of that sort in the wind, I'll be respectful enough."

The magistrates invited me to sit down, after they had said "Good morning, Mr. Cooper;" and I thought that *was* really respectful, and I would be respectful also.

The Hon. and Rev. Arthur Talbot, brother to Earl Talbot, read Mr. Duncombe's letter to me, stating that he had presented my petition to the House of Commons, and had asked the Speaker if it were right and constitutional to detain the petition of a political prisoner nearly a fortnight, as the magistrates had done; and the Speaker had replied that it was neither right nor constitutional. He (Mr. Duncombe) did not wish to make any harsh observations: he simply thought that my requests were so reasonable that the magistrates would deem it right to comply with them.

"I may say," said Mr. Talbot, "that your own conduct in the gaol induced us to detain your petition—but we will say no more about that. With regard to your food, the surgeon has full liberty from us, now, to allow you what he deems necessary for your health. We have also resolved that you shall be allowed to write to your wife and receive letters from her; but all letters must be delivered open by yourself to the governor, and he will open all letters from your wife, before he delivers them to you. In the course of time we may allow you, also, to correspond with two or three of your friends, —so long as they are not political."

"May I write to my wife weekly, and receive a letter from her weekly?" I asked; "you ought to allow me to do that, considering that she seemed so near death when I left her."

My request was granted at once.

"And now, gentlemen," I said, "there is one more favour I must beg of you. Let me have the use of my books, and also be allowed to proceed with my writing. I have an unfinished romance that I want to complete, and some other things I want to do. I hope there will be no objection to my employing myself in a peaceable way. Depend upon it, you shall not have to complain of my behaviour if you treat me reasonably."

"You have no objection to our seeing the books, I hope?" said the Hon. and Rev. Mr. Talbot; "if they be political, we should object to your having them."

"I will open the portmanteau, if you will order it to be brought in," said I; "and you can take out the political books, if you find any; but I do not think you will."

They took out two small books which I cared nothing for, and which I did not know that I had with me; and then they gave up the portmanteau and all that it contained into my possession. I thanked them, and went back to my day-room.

My companions were highly gladdened; for when the surgeon came to visit us, and asked what I wished for in the way of food, he prescribed an equal allowance for them also: so my struggle had won food for all three of us. I asked, first, for coffee; and we had a good allowance of it, and the article was good. We had also a sufficient allowance of sugar, butter, and rice. The surgeon would only allow us a quarter of a pound of meat daily, at first; and this was our worst allowance: it was invariably either a bit of the breast of mutton, or of the "sticking piece" of beef; and became so unwelcome before my two years' confinement was ended, that I often loathed the very sight of the meat. One evil we had to endure was beyond the surgeon's power to remedy. We had to take all the water we drank from a pump in our day-yard; and it was so bad that we had to let the bucket stand a long time that all the unmentionable stuff might settle to the bottom, before we could use the water. I should not forget to say that Mr. Hughes, the surgeon, kindly directed that I should have the use of an arm-chair, so that I could sit by myself to write, at the table, while the old men chose to sit by the fire. The reader must understand that our day-room was not a palace. The floor was stone slabs, and the wind assailed us in every quarter. It was a place to create tooth-ache and neuralgia, daily.

In the course of the first summer, we had an addition to our number; and in the second spring a second companion sojourned with us for a short time. On the 12th of August, 1843, Arthur G. O'Neill of Birmingham, came in to undergo a year's imprisonment; and on the 6th of April, 1844, Joseph Linney of Bilston was transferred from the Penitentiary, London, to complete his term of imprisonment with us. His stay was but short: he left us in twelve weeks.

I was allowed but three visitors, as friends, during my imprisonment: one at the end of six months, another at the end of twelve, and another at the end of eighteen. My dear old friend and benefactor, Dr. J. B. Simpson of Birmingham came first; and my dear departed friend, Thomas Tatlow of Leicester, came last. The other visitor was Bairstow, to whose hands the poor stockingers had committed a little money for my relief; but he kept three-fifths of it for himself. Let me dismiss the name of this depraved, pitiable young man. I had taken him into my house and given himself and his wife hospitality for many months; I had given him money for his journeys; and when I left Leicester, I gave him the care of my business, that he might live out of it, and take care my wife did not want—telling him, in the presence of all the men who crowded round me, as I was departing, that, if my wife died, Bairstow was to consider the business entirely his own.

But he made the house a place of dissipation, invited card-players into it, and ruined the business altogether; so that the house had to be given up, and my wife had to be carried out and taken care of, chiefly by my dear and true friends Thomas Tatlow and William Stafford, who provided her with a kind nurse in her suffering. Bairstow's acceptance with the people as an orator had caused me to keep him at Leicester. He left his wife before the end of my imprisonment; and was never more heard of. He is supposed to have come to his end in some obscure way.

My great business in the gaol has yet to be related. During the first two months I not only could not get at my books, but I had locked up the only copy I possessed of the hundred lines written as a blank verse commencement of my purposed poem, " The Purgatory of Suicides." As I could not recover them, and did not know whether they would ever yield to allow me the use of my books and papers, I thought I could defeat their purpose by composing the poem and retaining it in my mind. So my thoughts were very much intent on making a new beginning,—and on the night of the 10th of June, 1843, when we had been one month in the gaol, I felt suddenly empowered to make a start; and when I had composed the four opening lines, I found they rhymed alternately. It was a pure accident—for I always purposed to write my poem in blank verse. Now, however, I resolved to try the Spenserean stanza. So I struck off two stanzas that night: they are the two opening stanzas of my poem; and they are the first Spenserean stanzas I ever wrote in my life.

The remembrance that Byron had shown the stanza of the "Faery Queene" to be capable of as much grandeur and force as the blank verse of " Paradise Lost," while he also demonstrated that it admits the utmost freedom that can be needed for the treatment of a grave theme, determined me to abide by the Spenserean stanza. When I obtained the use of writing materials, at the end of those two months of struggle, I very soon had a fair copy written of the, perhaps, thirty stanzas I had by that time composed.

The creation of my "Purgatory of Suicides" I have called my "great business" in the gaol. And so it was—for it employed a great part of my thought, and absorbed some mental effort, of almost every day I spent in Stafford Gaol, except one period of three months that I shall have to refer to.

I could revel in Shakspeare and Milton as soon as I got possession of my books; and in Chambers' "Cyclopædia of English Literature" I had portions of almost every English poet of eminence. At an after-date, I had "Childe Harold," and Shelley (the small pirated edition), with Jarvis's translation of "Don Quixote," White's "Selborne," and other books, sent into the gaol. But I set about solid reading. I read Gibbon's great masterpiece entirely through, in the gaol. The reader will remember that this was my second reading of the magnificent "Decline and Fall." In Latin, I read the Æneid and the Commentaries through once more, attended a little to my Greek, and also re-read the volume of German stories, twice or thrice.

O'Neill had been allowed to have some books, and so I read his copy of Prideaux's "Connexion of the Old and New Testament," Milner's Church History, and some other things he possessed. We also formed a purpose of pursuing the study of language together, as O'Neill had been a student in his time. I had copies of the New Testament in several languages, and we read in each, every morning, for a short time; but one of my constitutional periods of passion approached, and I was carried away with it.

I fastened on the Hebrew, with a fine old German-printed Old Testament and the lexicon of Gesenius; and for three months I read nothing, thought of nothing, but Hebrew. I copied out all the verbs, I classified and copied out nouns. I purposed to commit everything to memory. My poem stood still—everything stood still—but Hebrew. At length, I almost raved about it while talking to O'Neill—who kindly and affectionately watched his opportunity, when he saw my health was giving way, and I was becoming incapable; and then he took all my Hebrew books into his own possession, and told me I must give it up, or I should lose my senses. I had common sense enough to perceive, in a day or two, that I was wrong; and so I tore myself away from the study of Hebrew, and never attended to it again, except with great caution, while I remained in the gaol. During the three months my passion had lasted, to the best of my memory, I went through about two-thirds of my Hebrew Bible.

Good old Daddy Richards left us on the 4th of May, 1844; Linney left us on the 29th of June; O'Neill's time of imprisonment ended on the 10th of August; and on the 30th of September, 1844, Capper left me, a lonely prisoner, for I had yet seven months to serve.

I had broken down the stupid custom of sending us to our sleeping cells at six in the evening, before O'Neill came into the gaol; and soon after I obtained leave to buy candles for my use, that I might read or write till nine o'clock, when we were taken to our sleeping cells. Now I was left alone, I began to feel very apprehensive for the consequences, if I should have to sleep another winter on the bag of straw and iron slab, in that cold shivering hole, where the water trickled down the walls in damp weather. I was tormented with neuralgia of the head; I was often obliged to lie on my back a whole day, with neuralgia of the heart; and I told the governor and the surgeon that I believed it would end my life, if I had no better sleeping-place. To my unspeakable relief, the governor said I should sleep in my day-room, so that I could keep the fire in, through the night, if I pleased. Thus, I believe, my life was preserved by Him who has the hearts of all men in His keeping; and whose loving watchfulness has so often shown itself in the preservation of my life.

That "God helps them who help themselves," however, I am fully convinced. If I had not shown both resolution and perseverance, I should never have secured any deliverance from the torturous inflictions of what is called "gaol discipline."

"I admire your pluck, Cooper," said the dear old governor to me one day, in an undertone, a short time before I left the gaol: "your day-room was the dayroom of the Reverend Humphrey Price, the 'good parson of Needwood Forest,' as he was called. He was a clergyman who sympathised, like you, with the poor; and for defending the poor wretched carpet-weavers of Kidderminster, had to pass a year in this prison. But he was never allowed a single privilege. He had to go to bed every night at six o'clock, was never allowed the use of a candle, and had to submit to the common dietary of the prison. The poor man seemed to take it all like a martyr. What he might have gained if he had shown as much spirit as yourself, I cannot tell; but he never seemed to have the spirit to ask for anything."

The magistrates looked in upon me, now and then, when I was left alone. One day, I had a very agreeable and distinguished visitor. It was Lord Sandon, now Earl of Harrowby. He addressed me with so much courtesy and kindness, that I responded cheerfully. After a few minutes his interest increased, and he sat down to talk.

My old German-printed Hebrew Bible (given to me by good Mr. Lumley, the bookseller) happened to catch his eye; and I opened it, and showed him the arrangement of the Chamesh Megilloth (Ruth, Song of Songs, Ecclesiastes, Lamentations, and Esther) immediately after the Torah, or Pentateuch. My noble visitor remarked that he had never seen an arrangement like it—for he had been intent on studying Hebrew at one time himself. We diverged to other subjects; and when the courteous nobleman was gone, I found that nearly half an hour had elapsed since he entered my day-room.

The behaviour of Earl Ferrers was of a different order. He came one day to the little window in the passage, and looked at me through his quizzing-glass. I put on my cap and went close to the window to look at him with a pair of eyes on flame, and that meant, "Who are you, you rude rascal?" He dropt his quizzing-glass, and slunk away!

The chaplain—*not* the reverend gentleman whom I used so roughly at the beginning of my imprisonment—paid me two remarkable visits, but a short time before my term of imprisonment ended. He desired me to walk out into the day-yard with him, as he wished to have a particular conversation with me.

"Mr. Cooper," he said, very suddenly, "you would like to go to Cambridge?"

"To the University?" said I, quickly; "I should think so. What of that, sir?"

"You can go direct from this gaol, on the day that your time expires, I undertake to say—if you choose," he replied.

"Go to Cambridge, from this gaol!" I repeated in wonder.

"Yes: all your wants will be provided for. You will have no trouble about anything—only—" and he stopped and smiled.

"Only I must give up politics?" said I; "I see what you mean."

"That's it," said he; that's all."

"I would not degrade or falsify myself by making such a promise," I replied, "if you could ensure all the honours the University could bestow, although it has been one of the great yearnings of my heart—from a boy, I might say—to go to a University."

The kindly chaplain blamed me for my unwillingness; assured me that all who conversed with me lamented to see me in such a case, and wondered how a man with such a nature and such attachments ever became a Chartist. But he took his leave without accomplishing the purpose for which he had been sent. By whom he had been sent, he would not say, though I asked him during his second visit—when he was still more earnest, and seemed distressed when he found I would not yield. He would not say by whom he had been sent; but I had a shrewd guess about it when I thought of my noble visitor, and our conversation over the ancient Hebrew Bible. I ought gratefully to say that the good chaplain (Rev. Thos. Sedger, now curate of Bracon Ash, near Norwich) presented me with a valuable copy of *Horace de Arte Poeticâ*, before I left the gaol; and, a few years ago, sent me a copy of his translation of *Grotius de Veritate*.

The romance that I mentioned, and which was begun in Lincoln, and the MSS. partially shown to a celebrated author when I first went to live in London, I finished in the gaol; and also wrote several tales to complete a volume, if I could find a publisher. These and my "Prison Rhyme " I took out of prison with me as my keys for unlocking the gates of fortune. I was in rags; for although Leicester friends had impoverished themselves to send me money to pay for my extra fire, candles, washing, and writing materials, I could not expect more of them. A kind friend in London, whom I must not name, sent me ten pounds, fourteen days before my time expired; and so I got a suit of clothes and a hat, and other things I wanted.

I left Stafford Gaol at six o'clock on the morning of the 4th of May, 1845; and reached London, and slept that night at the house of the friend who had sent me the ten pounds.

I must now go back, and enter on the recital I have delayed to begin, and which I dread to touch. But it must be given.

CHAPTER XXIV.
SCEPTICISM IN THE GAOL: LONDON, AND
DISAPPOINTMENTS: 1845.

WHEN I first took upon me to talk to Leicester Chartists, in the little room at All Saints' Open, on those Sunday evenings during the spring of 1841, religion formed the staple of my discourse. I had felt so deep a sense of unworthy treatment when I left the Methodists in 1835, that—as I said at the close of my ninth chapter—"I sought occupation for thought that should not awake tormenting remembrances;"—and so I had avoided religious literature, and conversation on theological topics, as much as possible. And it was not until I began to talk to poor suffering men about religion that I became conscious of any change in my belief, or in the state of my religious conscience—to adopt one of the phrases of the day.

If any one had asked me what I considered myself to be in point of religious belief, six years after I left the Wesleyans, I should have answered that I was a Wesleyan still. But I had not spent many months in talking to the Leicester Chartists, before my "religious conscience" began to receive a new "form and pressure" from its new surroundings. I could not preach eternal punishment to poor starving stockingers. But

when the belief in eternal punishment is given up, the eternal demerit of sin has faded from the preacher's conscience; and then what consistency can he see in the doctrine of Christ's atonement?

Whenever I looked inward—though, alas! I had little leisure for reflection during all the fiery excitement of my Leicester life—I found that I had ceased be orthodox in my belief. Yet I never ceased to worship the perfect moral beauty of Christ; and, thank God! I never ceased to enthrone the goodness and purity and love of Christ in the minds and hearts of the Leicester poor. To the last hour of my teaching in Leicester, I also maintained, in the hearing of the crowds who listened to me, that the miracles and resurrection of the Saviour were historical facts.

But, before I left Leicester, clouds of unspoken doubt began to roll across my reason, of a darker and more horrible shade than even a disbelief of the Gospel records. I gave the reader a hint of what I mean towards the end of my sixteenth chapter. The coarse atheism expressed by some of the stronger spirits among working men, I often felt, found an echo in my own mind, that startled me. When I could not sleep after a day of more than ordinary excitement, atheistic reasonings would arise, as I thought of the sufferings of the poor, the extreme differences in men's condition, and the cruel lot of all in every age who contend for truth and right. These distressing doubts and reasonings for many months passed away when they arose, leaving no conscious lodgment in my mind. Yet they would come again.

It was not until I entered on my last imprisonment—in May, 1843,—that I was conscious of atheistic reasonings becoming habitual. How swift is the process of depravity, even in the understanding, as well as in the heart! How rapidly the mind and heart take up an entrenched position in unbelief, none can tell but those who speak from experience. I believe those two months of torture, at the beginning of my two years' imprisonment, served, most fearfully, to bring my atheistic reasonings to a head. I was conscious of incorruptible disinterestedness in my advocacy of the rights of the poor. I regarded my imprisonment, with its harsh treatment, as a grievous wrong. My tender wife was enduring suffering that brought her near to death. And the poor were suffering still! I had not lessened their evils an atom by my struggles. It was a world of wrong, I now reasoned; and there could not be in it the Almighty and beneficent Providence in which I had all my life devoutly believed. I must give it all up as a dream!

I had never given up the practice of prayer; and I Knelt beside my iron slab and bag of straw, though I hardly felt I prayed—until, one night, I sprang up from my knees, and said, "I'll pray no more!" Nor did I ever kneel to pray again so long as I remained in prison. My angered and distempered mind set itself, now, defiantly to resist the thought of a God. And in the morbid condition of feeling and thought that grew to be natural in the prison, I fell into trains of reasoning about moral evil and the pain I supposed to be so prevalent in creation—such as the reader will occasionally find in my Prison Rhyme.

As the end of my imprisonment drew nearer, my gloom began to lessen and hope to brighten. I felt less inclined to dwell on doubts, and wished I were not troubled with them at all. When the railway train began to bear me towards London, on that beautiful May morning of my release; I burst into tears, and sobbed with a feeling I could not easily subdue, as I once more saw the fields and flowers and God's glorious sun. The world was so beautiful, I dared not say there was no God in it; and the old, long-practised feeling of worship welled up in my heart, in spite of myself.

Nor did I, after my release from imprisonment, yield helplessly to atheistic reasonings. They would arise in my mind, perforce of old habit; but I did not settle down in them. I never proclaimed blank atheism in my public teaching. And I feel certain that I should have broken away from unbelief altogether, had I not fastened on Strauss, and become his entire convert. I read and re-read, and analysed, the translation in three volumes, published by the Brothers Chapman: the translation begun by Charles Hennell, and finished by the authoress of "Adam Bede." I became fast bound in the net of Strauss; and at one time would have eagerly helped to bind all in his net: nor did I feel thoroughly able to break its pernicious meshes, or get out of it, myself, for twelve years.

I was so ill during the first week after my release, that I could not quit my lodging. The kind friend who had sent me pecuniary relief before I quitted prison, still supplied my wants. As soon as I had strength for it, I called on Mr. Duncombe, who was then lodging in the Albany, Piccadilly. He received me with extreme kindness; and asked what I purposed doing. I told him I had written a poem and other things, in prison, and wished he could introduce me to a publisher.

"A publisher!" said he, "why, you know, Cooper, I never published anything in my life. I know nothing of publishers.—Oh, stop!" said he, suddenly, "wait a few minutes. I'll write a note, and send you to Disraeli."

He wrote the note, and read it to me. As nearly as I can remember, it ran thus:

"MY DEAR DISRAELI,—I send you Mr. Cooper, a Chartist, red-hot from Stafford Gaol. But don't be frightened. He won't bite you. He has written a poem and a romance; and thinks he can cut out 'Coningsby,' and 'Sybil'! Help him if you can, and oblige, yours

T. S. DUNCOMBE.

"But you would not have me take a note like that?" I said.

"Would not I?" he answered; "but I would. It's just the thing for you; get off with you, and present it at once. You'll catch him at home, just now. Grosvenor Gate—close to the Park—anybody will tell you the house—now, away with you at once!"

It was Sunday at noon, and away I went to Grosvenor Gate. A tall Hebrew in livery came to the door, with a silver waiter in his hand.

"This is Mr. Disraeli's, I believe?" I said.

"Yes: but Mr. Disraeli is not at home," was the answer, in ceremonious style.

"Then, when will he be at home?" I asked, "as I wish to present this note of introduction to him, from Mr. Duncombe."

"Mr. Duncombe, the member of Parliament?" asked the man in livery. And when I answered "Yes," he presented the waiter, and said, "You had better give me the note: Mrs. Disraeli is at home."

I gave him the note; and he closed the door, I waiting in the hall. He soon returned, saying, "Mr. Disraeli will see you. You understand it was my business to say 'Not at home.' You will excuse me?"

184

"Why don't you bring the gentleman up?" cried a light silvery voice from above.

The servant led me up the staircase; and, at the top, Mrs. Disraeli very gracefully bowed, and withdrew; and the servant took me into what was evidently the literary man's "study"—a small room at the top of the house.

One sees paragraphs very often, now, in the papers about the expressionless and jaded look of the Conservative leader's face, as he sits in the House of Commons. Yet, as I first looked upon that face twenty-six years ago, I thought it one of great intellectual beauty. The eyes seemed living lights; and the intelligent yet kindly way in which Mr. Disraeli inquired about the term of my imprisonment, and treatment in the prison, convinced me that I was in the presence of a very shrewd as well as highly cultivated and refined man.

"I wish I had seen you before I finished my last novel," said he; "my heroine, Sybil, is a Chartist."

I gave into his hands the MSS. of the First Book of my "Purgatory of Suicides."

"I shall be happy to read it," he said; "but what do you wish me to do?"

"To write to Mr. Moxon," said I, "and recommend him to publish it—" if you think it right to do so, when you have looked it over."

"But Mr. Moxon is not my publisher," said he; "and I offered him a poem of my own, some years ago, but he declined to take it. Why do you wish me to write to Mr. Moxon so particularly?"

"Because he publishes poetry; and as he has published poetry of his own—"

"Ah, poet-like!" said the future Prime Minister of England,—"you think he must sympathise with you, because he is a poet. You forget that he is a tradesman too, and that poetry does not sell nowadays. Well, I'll write to Mr. Moxon, when I have looked at your manuscript."

He then directed me to call on a certain day in the week following, when he promised a note should be ready for Mr. Moxon.

I presented the note; and Mr. Moxon smiled, and said, "Mr. Disraeli knows that poetry is a drug in the market. He does not offer me one of his own novels."

Mr. Moxon declined to receive my poem, assuring me that he dared not venture to publish any poem of a new author, for there was no prospect of a sale. He was very courteous, and seemed to wish me to stay and talk. He also showed me a portrait which he valued highly in one of his rooms. I think it was a portrait of Charles Lamb. He also told me that Alfred Tennyson and the venerable Wordsworth had passed an hour together in that room lately. He looked at Mr. Disraeli's note, and read it again; and I gave the manuscript of the first book of my "Prison Rhyme" into his hands; and he read parts of it, and still detained me, to show me something else; and when I left him, he said, —

"I certainly would publish your poem, Mr. Cooper, if I saw anything like a chance of selling it; but I repeat to you, that all poetry is a perfect drug in the market, at present; and I have made up my mind to publish no new poetry whatever."

I wrote to Mr. Disraeli, and told him that I had failed, and desired him to take the trouble to write me a note to his own publisher, Mr. Colburn, as he had offered to do at first.

By the next post, I had the note for Colburn, and soon waited on him. I sent up the note to his room; and on being invited up-stairs was met by the little shrewd-looking publisher himself, and his trusty adviser Mr. Schoberl.

"We publish no poetry whatever: it is a perfect drug in the market," said Mr. Schoberl; "but Mr. Disraeli says here, in his note, that you have written a romance. What is the subject of it, pray?"

I gave him a brief description of it; and, turning to Mr. Colburn, he said, "I think Mr. Cooper might as well send us the manuscript, and let us look at it."

"By all means," said Mr. Colburn.

I took the manuscript; and they kept it a few days, when they sent it back, with a very polite refusal to publish it.

And now I ventured to call upon Mr. Disraeli the second time. He seemed really concerned at what I told him; and when I asked him to give me a note to Messrs. Chapman and Hall, he looked thoughtful, and said,—

"No: I know nothing of them personally, and I should not like to write to them. But I will give you a note to Ainsworth, and desire him to recommend you to Chapman and Hall."

I took the note to Mr. Ainsworth's house, at Kensal Green. He was not at home; but his sweet-looking daughter received Mr. Disraeli's note and my MSS. from my hands very courteously, and assured me she would give them to her father.

I called again two days after, and was invited into the drawing-room, into which Mr. Ainsworth entered from his garden. He was a handsome, fresh-looking Englishman, and showed a very pearly set of teeth as he smiled. He conversed about my imprisonment; and said the poetry was excellent, but all poetry sold badly now, and he was afraid Messrs. Chapman and Hall would not be much inclined to take my poem.

"I think," he said, "I had better give you a note to John Forster of the *Examiner*. They consult him about everything they publish."

So I next took the MSS., with Mr. Ainsworth's letter, to Mr. John Forster, and left my parcel at his office, or chambers, in Lincoln's Inn Fields, for they said he was not in. When I called, two or three days afterwards, I was met by a stout, severe-looking man, who began to examine me with the spirit of a bitter Whig examining a poor Chartist at the bar. He seemed not to hear anything I said, unless it was an answer to one of his lawyer-like questions; and he usually interrupted me if I spoke before he put another question to me. I knew that was the practice of lawyers; but I thought a man with the intellect of John Forster should sink the character of lawyer—should forget his profession—while talking to a poor literary aspirant.

"I suppose you would have no objection to alter the title you give yourself," he said; " I certainly should advise you to strike 'the Chartist' out."

"Nay, sir," I replied; "I shall not strike it out. Mr. Disraeli advised me not to let any one persuade me to strike it out; and I mean to abide by his advice. I did not resolve to style myself 'the Chartist' upon the title-page of my book, without a good deal of consideration."

My offended interlocutor frowned, and bit his lip; and seemed determined to get quit of the thing.

"Well, Mr. Cooper," he said, in conclusion, "I will give you a note to Messrs. Chapman and Hall. There can be no question as to the excellence of your poetry; but I do not know how far it may be advisable for Messrs. Chapman and Hall to connect themselves with your Chartism."

I could not see that any publisher would necessarily connect himself with my Chartism by publishing my poem; but I said no more to the Whig literary man for I wanted to be gone.

Messrs. Chapman and-Hall seemed to take great interest in me, when I went to them. At their own request, I fetched the entire MSS. of my Prison Rhyme, the Romance, and the Tales, from my lodging, and put them all into their hands, that they might form their own judgment of them, as I supposed. But, I have no doubt, the entire parcel was transferred to Mr. John Forster. About a week passed, and I was told my Poem and Romance were declined; but they, *perhaps*, might take the Tales, if I would wait till some volumes they were then issuing, or about to issue, in a series, were published. I turned away, *disappointed*, in this instance; for the eager interest with which Messrs. Chapman and Hall first received me, and the manner in which they requested me to show them all the MSS. I had, had rendered me sanguine that they would really become my publishers.

CHAPTER XXV
DIFFICULTIES AND SUCCESS: "THE PURGATORY OF SUICIDES"
IS PUBLISHED: 1845.

I HAD kept aloof from Chartists and Chartism since my release from imprisonment, for I had learned that O'Connor, in a fit of jealousy, had denounced me. Somebody, it seemed, had filled him with the belief that I meant to conspire against him when I got loose. A few petty subscriptions which had been raised for me in Nottingham, and elsewhere, were withdrawn in consequence of his denunciations of me in his *Northern Star*; and I sent back two or three sums which were sent to me as Chartist subscriptions.

My disgust at O'Connor's conduct was so great that I had resolved never to speak to him again. But I was moved to alter my mind in a way that I could not foresee. I went to call on my old friend Mr. Dougal Macgowan, the printer of the *Kentish Mercury*,—whom I had not seen since I ceased to edit that paper, and left London, in November 1840. He was now printing the *Northern Star*, for O'Connor; for the paper was nearly ruined, like Chartism itself, about this time, and O'Connor had transferred the publication of the paper from Leeds to London, with the hope of restoring its circulation. Mr. Macgowan assured me that O'Connor was sorry for having written against me, and wished I would call on him at his lodgings in Great Marlborough Street, as he wished to apologise to me, and renew his friendship with me. I told Mr. Macgowan that since O'Connor had not signified his recantation in the *Northern Star*, I should decline calling upon him.

About a week after I met Mr. Macgowan, and he was very urgent with me to go and see O'Connor. He assured me that O'Connor took great interest in my poem, and wished me to read some parts of it to him.

"To tell you the whole truth," said Mr. Macgowan, "he affirms that if you will give the manuscript into my hands, he himself will pay for the printing of it. And, surely, if it be printed, we can get it published, somehow. Do go and see him, and hear what he says, that you may judge for yourself."

This occurred the very day after my manuscripts had been sent back by Chapman and Hall, following on the heel of all the other failures. Macgowan's hint seemed to open the way for escape from difficulty to a man who was set fast. It was not the way I wanted my poem to get before the eyes and minds of readers; but when a man is in a strait, he feels he cannot afford to despise any offer of help.

I went and saw O'Connor, and he apologised with great apparent sincerity; and said he would make an open apology in his paper. What rendered me the more ready to forgive him, was the sight of several letters which had been sent him from Chartists for whom I had done acts of kindness at considerable cost to myself. The gratuitous malice of some people would be a puzzling anomaly in the history of human nature, if experience did not show it to be a history of contradictions. I was astonished at what I read. Such a twisting of minute, unimportant facts, and such skill in misinterpreting my motives! I could not have thought the writers capable of such ingenious and profitless wickedness, if I had not known their handwriting.

I had to read parts of my "Purgatory" to O'Connor. He had had the education of a gentleman, and had not lost his relish for Virgil and Horace, at that time of day; and, while I read, he listened, and made very intelligent criticisms. He begged that I would permit him to bear the expense of printing my poem; and that I would put it into Macgowan's hands immediately. As for a publisher, he felt sure, he said, that there would be no difficulty in finding one.

So I took my manuscript to Mr. Macgowan, and soon began to see the proof-sheets. Occasionally, I called on O'Connor, and conversed with him; and he invariably expounded his Land Scheme to me, and wished me to become one of its advocates. But I told him I could not; and I begged of him to give the scheme up, for I felt sure it would bring ruin and disappointment upon himself and all who entered into it. He did not grow angry with me at first, but tried to win me by assurances of his esteem and regard, and of his kindly intentions towards me. I could not, however, be won; for all he said in explication of his scheme, only served to render it wilder and worse, in my estimation.

When Macgowan had got as far as the end of the Fourth Book with the printing of my poem, he proposed that we should take the printed part and try some of the publishers with it.

"Because," said he, "although O'Connor has given me his word to pay the cost of printing and binding five hundred copies, yet the book will need advertising. We ought, therefore, to get some publisher to take the book, that he may advertise it."

So we set out; and as I had a lingering belief that Messrs. Chapman and Hall reluctantly gave up their wish to publish my poem through the influence of their literary adviser, I proposed that we should call on them first. Mr. Edward Chapman, however, did not seem at all favourably disposed; and Macgowan was so much disheartened with our rebuff, that he said he could not proceed further, that day. He returned to Great Windmill Street, Haymarket; and I turned from Chapman and Hall's door, in the narrow part of the Strand, to walk to my lodging in Blackfriars Road. Under the postern of Temple Bar, I ran against John Cleave; and he caught hold of me in surprise.

"Why, what's the matter, Cooper?" he asked; you look very miserable, and you seem not to know where you are!"

"Indeed," I answered, "I am very uneasy; and I really did not see you when I ran against you."

"But what is the matter with you?" he asked again.

"I owe you three-and-thirty pounds," said I; "and I owe a deal of money to others; and I cannot find a publisher for my book. Is not that enough to make a man uneasy?"

And then I told him how I and Macgowan had just received a refusal from the publishing house in the Strand. More I needed not to tell him; for I had told him all my proceedings from the time I left prison, and ever found him an earnest and kind friend.

"Come along with me," said he; "and I'll give you a note to Douglas Jerrold; he'll find you a publisher."

"Do you know Douglas Jerrold?" I asked.

"Know him!" said the fine old Radical publisher; "I should think I do. I've trusted him a few halfpence for a periodical, many a time, when he was a printer's apprentice. If he does not find you a publisher, I'll forfeit my neck. Jerrold's a brick!"

So I went to the little shop in Shoe Lane, whence John Cleave issued so many thousands of sheets of Radicalism and brave defiance of bad governments, in his time; and he gave me a hearty note of commendation to Jerrold, and told me to take it to the house on Putney Common. I went without delay, and left Cleave's note, and the part of the "Purgatory" which Macgowan had printed, with Mrs. Jerrold, and intimated that I would call again in three or four days.

I called, and received a welcome so cordial, and even enthusiastic, that I was delighted. The man of genius grasped my hand, and gazed on my face, as I gazed on his, with unmistakable pleasure.

"Glad to see you, my boy!" said he; "your poetry is noble—it's manly; I'll find you a publisher. Never fear it. Sit you down!" he cried, ringing the bell; "what will you take? some wine? Will you have some bread and cheese? I think there's some ham—we shall see."

It was eleven in the forenoon: so I was in no humour for eating or drinking. But we drank two or three glasses of sherry; and were busy in talk till twelve.

"I had Charles Dickens here last night," said he; and he was so taken with your poem that he asked to take it home. I have no doubt he will return it this week, and then I will take it into the town, and secure you a publisher. Give yourself no uneasiness about it. I'll write to you in a few days, and tell you it is done."

And he did write in a few days, and directed me to call on Jeremiah How, 132, Fleet Street, who published Jerrold's "Cakes and Ale," Mrs. S. C. Hall's "Ireland and its Scenery, etc.," the Illustrated "Book of British Ballads," and other popular novelties of the time. Mr. How agreed at once to be my publisher; and when he learned from me that I did not like the thought of O'Connor paying the printer, and that I meant to repay O'Connor, being unwilling to receive a favour from him, since we had begun to differ very unpleasantly concerning the Land Scheme,—Mr. How immediately offered to go with me to Mr. Macgowan and take the responsibility of the printing upon himself. Mr. Macgowan readily took an acceptance for the money from Mr. How; I think it was £45, being the cost of 500 copies— paper, printing, and binding. It might be a trifle more or less.

The growth of O'Connor's Land Scheme rendered him haughty towards me, when he found he could not reckon on me as one of his helpers—of whom he readily found plenty. I ceased to visit him at last—for I was either told he was not at home, or his bearing was unpleasant to me. I forbear to enter into the recital of the quarrel— the real and fierce quarrel—I had with O'Connor, afterwards, about his land scheme. Any of my readers who wish for information regarding it may consult the "History of the Chartist Movement," by Dr. Gammage of Sunderland. I would have mentioned Dr. Gammage's work earlier and often, if there had not been so many little mistakes in it. Yet I know no person living who could write a History of Chartism without making mistakes. I am sure that I could not; and I endeavour, in this memoir, to keep out of the stream of its general history; and only refer to Chartism when it becomes absolutely necessary for making my narrative intelligible.

My "Purgatory of Suicides: a Prison Rhyme, in Ten Books; by Thomas Cooper the Chartist"—as it was entitled, was published towards the end of August, 1845. Some will think, perhaps, that I have been too minute in narrating the sinuosities of my experience in attempting to get my book before the reading public. Yet I humbly judge that I am simply making legitimate contributions to literary history, by giving the details of my experience. The narrative may be of real service to some poor literary aspirant in the future.

The first trumpet-blast that was heard in praise of my poem was that from the *Britannia* newspaper of August 30th. This periodical had been edited by Dr. Croly and had risen to considerable literary reputation and influence. The criticism on my poem was not written by Dr. Croly, as people have reported; but by the editor who succeeded him, Mr. David Trevena Coulton. Mr. Coulton was a most kind-hearted man, and a great enthusiast in aught that he approved; but his commendation of my poem was too undistinguishing, and was greater than it deserved. William Howitt's generosity led him to write a very enthusiastic eulogy of my "Prison Rhyme" in the *Eclectic Review*; and he also sent a very noble congratulatory letter to me, and I went to see him and good Mary Howitt. Our friendship has continued till I am growing old, and he is really an old man. None of the great or leading periodicals of the day noticed my existence; but the commendations of my book in smaller periodicals were countless; and the 500 copies which formed the first edition were sold off before Christmas.

Mr. How seemed kindly desirous of bringing me before the reading public as fully as possible; and soon proposed to bring out the simple tales I had written in prison. Douglas Jerrold had published one of them—and that, perhaps, the very simplest, "Charity begins at Home"—in his "Shilling Magazine"—for which I also wrote a few other things, in prose and verse. Mr. How thought the Tales I had in manuscript were too numerous for one volume, and persuaded me to give him the fragment of a story which was partly autobiographical, in order to make two volumes. These he issued about eight weeks after the publication of my "Purgatory," and insisted on calling them "Wise Saws and Modern Instances"—

though I wished them to bear the unpretending title of "Simple Stories of the Midlands and Elsewhere."

Next, Mr. How proposed that I should issue a Christmas Book; and I agreed on condition that it should be in rhyme. So "The Baron's Yule Feast" came to be published. But, as it was not brought out till the middle of January, the sale was very slow—for the proper opportunity for sale was lost.

Alas! my poor publisher's money was exhausted. He had spent a nice little fortune on publishing. And now the great printer on whom he had leaned, and from whom he had expected credit—even the millionaire, as he was accounted to be—had gone into the shade, on account of unprosperous railway speculations. In short, my publisher failed; and my seemingly bright literary prospects were blighted!

I received thirty-two pounds from Mr. How for the two volumes of Tales; but not a farthing for the "Purgatory." In fact, though we *talked* of my having £500 for the copyright of it, we never drew up any agreement in writing, for either the "Purgatory" or "The Baron's Yule Feast": so that my poems were still entirely my own when Mr. How failed.

Let no one suppose, however, that my literary labours produced me only disappointment and disaster. One of the first to call public attention to my "Prison Rhyme" was the eloquent W. J. Fox, at that time one of the most popular speakers in London and the country, and afterwards M.P. for Oldham. In addition to his Sunday morning discourses at South Place, Finsbury Square, he was at that period also delivering lectures, on Sunday evenings, on literary and other topics, in the National Hall, Holborn. He made my "Purgatory" the subject of one of these Sunday evening lectures; and said more kind things about me than I can repeat. He also invited me to his house; and from that time honoured me with a most kind, and I might almost say a paternal friendship.

Through the commendation of me by Mr. Fox, the Committee of the National Hall—(among whom were William Lovett, James Watson, Richard Moore, Henry Hetherington, Charles Hodson Neesom, and other well-known Chartists, of the anti-O'Connor school)—invited me to lecture. Among the hearers was Mr. William Ellis, then a plain citizen of London, but afterwards well-known and most deservedly respected as the founder of the Birkbeck Schools. He accompanied me to my lodgings in Blackfriars Road, one night at the close of October, 1845, and wrote me out a cheque on a Lombard Street bank for £100.

I paid brave John Cleave his £33; sent part payment to the lawyer for the expenses of my Trials, "Writ of Certiorari," effecting of "Bail," etc. etc.,—and also sent sums to others to whom I was indebted; and felt happier when I had paid away the £100 than I did when I received it. I had many additional proofs of Mr. Ellis's munificent kindness afterwards.

I was favoured with interviews by the Countess of Blessington—to whom, through Mr. How's persuasion, I dedicated my Christmas Rhyme, or "Baron's Yule Feast;" and also by Charles Dickens, with whom I afterwards corresponded, and for one of whose periodicals I wrote a little. But the most illustrious man of genius to whom my poem gave me an introduction was Thomas Carlyle. I had dedicated my volume to him without leave asked, and from simple and real intellectual homage—in a sonnet composed but a day or two before I quitted the gaol. At first, I meant to prefix a sonnet as a dedication to each book, and I wrote three or four of the sonnets—one to my playfellow, Thomas Miller, another to Thomas Moore (who was then living), and another to Harriet Martineau. But I put this thought aside—fearing it would be deemed too formal (though there is a separate dedication to each book of "Marmion"), and resolved to dedicate the volume to Mr. Carlyle. I sent him the poem; and he sent me a letter so highly characteristic of his genius that I insert it here:—

"Chelsea, September 1, 1845.

"DEAR SIR,

"I have received your Poem; and will thank you for that kind gift, and for all the friendly sentiments you entertain towards me,— which, as from an evidently sincere man, whatever we may think of them otherwise, are surely valuable to a man.

"I have looked into your Poem, and find indisputable traces of genius in it,—a dark Titanic energy struggling there, for which we hope there will be clearer daylight by-and-by! If I might presume to advise, I think I would recommend you to try your next work in *Prose*, and as a thing turning altogether on *Facts*, not Fictions. Certainly the *music* that is very traceable here might serve to irradiate into harmony far profitabler things than what are commonly called 'Poems,'—for which, at any rate, the taste in these days seems to be irrevocably in abeyance. We have too horrible a Practical Chaos round us; out of which every man is called by the birth of him to make a bit of *Cosmos*: that seems to me the real Poem for a man,—especially at present. I always grudge to see any portion of a man's *musical talent* (which is the real intellect, the real vitality, or life of him) expended on making mere *words* rhyme. These things I say to all my Poetic friends, for I am in real earnest about them: but get almost nobody to believe me hitherto. From you I shall get an excuse at any rate; the purpose of my so speaking being a friendly one towards you.

"I will request you farther to accept this Book of mine, and to appropriate what you can of it. 'Life is a serious thing,' as Schiller says, and as you yourself practically know! These are the words of a serious man about it; they will not altogether be without meaning for you.

"Unfortunately, I am just in these hours getting out of town; and, not without real regret, must deny myself the satisfaction of seeing you at present.

"Believe me to be,

"With many good wishes,

"Yours very truly,

"T. CARLYLE."

A copy of "Past and Present" came by the same postman who brought me this letter—containing Mr. Carlyle's autograph. The reader may remember that the motto to "Past and Present" is from Schiller—"Ernst ist das Leben"—*Life is a serious thing.*

I owe many benefits to Mr. Carlyle. Not only richly directoral thoughts in conversation, but deeds of *substantial* kindness. Twice he put a five-pound note into my hand, when I was in difficulties; and told me, with a look of grave humour, that if I could never pay him again, he would not hang me.

Just after I sent him the copy of my Prison Rhyme, he put it into the hands of a young, vigorous, inquiring intelligence who had called to pay him a reverential visit at Chelsea. The new reader of my book sought me out and made me his friend. That is twenty-six years ago, and our friendship has continued and strengthened, and has never stiffened into patronage on the one side, or sunk into servility on the other—although my friend has now become "Right Honourable," and is the Vice-President of "Her Majesty's Most Honourable Privy Council."

At the very moment that I read the *revise* of this chapter, my friend has become about the "best-abused" man in England. But I am so sure of his most pellucid conscientiousness and sterling political integrity, that I fully believe his most determined foes at the present will become his most devoted friends in the future.

CHAPTER XXVI.
JOURNEY FOR JERROLD'S PAPER: INTERVIEW WITH
WORDSWORTH: 1846.

IN spite of the difference between O'Connor and myself, I tried to help the sufferers by Chartism. I had instituted a "Veteran Patriots' Fund," and an "Exiles' Widows' and Children's Fund;" and I endeavoured to keep these funds in existence, until I was driven out of my purpose by sheer abuse. This, however, did not prevent me from ministering to the relief of the sufferers, so far as I was able, myself. I also held it a duty to join in every effort for effecting the recall of those who had been exiled for political struggles. On the 10th of March, 1846, noble Thomas Slingsby Duncombe made a motion, in the House of Commons, for the recall of Frost, Williams, and Jones, together with William Ellis, who had been reckoned my fellow-conspirator. The venerable Richard Oastler, James Watson, Richard Moore, and others, made efforts to win members of Parliament to vote for the motion.

We were eager to learn what success we should have; and I went with Mr. Oastler to the lobby of the House of Commons, and waited till the division was over. We had the promise of a vote from Mr. Disraeli; and at a quarter to twelve we learned the pitiful result, as he came out of the House into the lobby.

"We have polled but thirty-one," said he; "and there were one hundred and ninety-six against us. Macaulay made a most bloodthirsty speech."

In the spring of 1846, Douglas Jerrold informed me that he was about to commence a weekly newspaper, and wished me to contribute to it. He, and his intelligent adviser, Mr. Tomline, at length determined that I should go out for three months through the manufacturing counties, and collect accounts of the industrial, social, and moral state of the people. The *Times* had had its "Commissioner," a short time before, giving such accounts; and it was proposed that I should furnish weekly articles to the new paper. It was June before the arrangements were made for my beginning. I visited the midland and northern English-counties, and sent articles to the newspaper, entitled "Condition of the People of England."

During the first week in September, while at Carlisle, the weather being as fine as in July, I set out to walk through the Lake country; and as I drew near Rydal Mount, I could not resist the desire of making an attempt to see the patriarchal Poet Laureate. I think it better to insert here the "Reminiscence of Wordsworth" I inserted in Cooper's Journal than to write the sketch over again. The reader will please to remember that the article was written and published in May, 1850.

I saw the patriarchal poet who has just departed, in his own home, in September, 1846; and cannot forbear recording, very briefly, the pleasing remembrances of that interview, now that every lover of poetry is dwelling with emotion on the fact of his death. I had set out from my friend James Arthur's, at Carlisle, for a four days' walk through the mountain and Lake country, taking simply my stick in my hand, and a map of the district in my pocket. On the second day I climbed Skiddaw; and on the third, having left beautiful Keswick in the morning, I reached Rydal Lake in the afternoon.

There was a magnet in the very name of Rydal Mount: how was I to get past it without attempting to see and talk with Wordsworth? I asked, at a house by the highway side, where he lived; and was immediately pointed to his cottage, lying upwards and to the left, a little out of the direct road to Ambleside. I began to walk in that direction; but I was somewhat puzzled as to whether my purpose was not too romantic to be carried out.

I had no introduction,—a fact which would have settled the question at once had I been in London, and the wild thought had entered my head of attempting to make a call so unceremoniously on any of the great men of letters living there. But Rydal Mount, thought I, does not come, cannot come, under the same category with London: it is an out-of-the-way place; and many must have come on pilgrimage to it, who had no introduction. Yes,—I reasoned again,—in their carriages they might come, and would then seem to assert their right to be attended to; but what will be said to me, covered with dust, and having nothing to recommend me, except—but I scarcely dared to hope it—the patriarchal Poet Laureate should have heard that a Prison Rhyme was sent forth last year, by a Chartist,—and yet what sort of a recommendation would that be to Wordsworth? That was my forlorn hope, however; and, determined not to fail for want of trying, I boldly strode up to the door, and knocked.

William Wordsworth

1770-1850

Behold, a servant-maid came to the door, and when I asked "Is Mr. Wordsworth in?" and she answered "Yes,"—I was for one moment completely at a loss—for she looked at me from head to foot with an expression which told me she was surprised that I should come there covered with dust, and so plainly dressed. To send in a request, verbally, I felt at once would not do.

" Stop a moment!" I said; took off my hat, drew a slip of paper from my pocket, and resting it on my hat-crown, I wrote instantly— "Thomas Cooper, author of 'The Purgatory of Suicides,' desires to pay his devout regards to Mr. Wordsworth." I requested the maid to present it; and, in half a minute, she returned, and said, with an altered expression of face, "Come in, sir, if you please."

In another half minute I was in the presence of that majestic old man, and I was bowing with a deep and heartfelt homage for his intellectual grandeur—with which his striking form and the pile of his forehead served to congrue so fully—when he seized my hand, and welcomed me with a smile so paternal, and such a hearty "How do you do? I am very happy to see you"—that the tears stood in my eyes for joy.

How our conversation opened I cannot remember and yet I think every word he uttered I can recollect—though not the order in which the remarks came from him. This I attribute partly to our conversation being broken by the visit of a very intelligent and amiable lady—(the widow of a great and good man, the late Dr. Arnold, of Rugby)—accompanied by her little daughter; and also by my being invited to take some refreshment in the adjoining room, and at the kind solicitation of Mrs. Wordsworth,—whose conversation was of too great excellence for me to forget it. It related chiefly to Southey, whose bust was in the room; and for whose genius and industry—in spite of the Toryism of his manhood—I had a deep admiration, to say nothing of the noble strains for freedom written in his youth.

What the great author of "The Excursion" said respecting my Prison Rhyme I shall not relate here; but, remembering what he said, I can also bear the remembrance that the *Quarterly, Edinburgh, Westminster,* and *Times,* have hitherto, and alike, judged it fit to be silent as to there being such a poem in existence.

Nothing struck me so much in Wordsworth's conversation as his remark concerning Chartism—after the subject of my imprisonment had been touched upon.

"You were right," he said; "I have always said the people were right in what they asked; but you went the wrong way to get it."

I almost doubted my ears—being in the presence of the "Tory" Wordsworth. He read the inquiring expression of my look in a moment,—and immediately repeated what he had said.

"You were quite right: there is nothing unreasonable in your Charter: it is the foolish attempt at physical force, for which many of you have been blamable."

I had heard that Wordsworth was vain and egotistical, but had always thought this very unlikely to be true, in one whose poetry is so profoundly reflective; and I now felt astonished that these reports should ever have been circulated. To me, he was all kindness and goodness; while the dignity with which he uttered every sentence seemed natural in a man whose grand head and face, if one had never known of his poetry, would have proclaimed his intellectual superiority.

There was but one occasion on which I discerned the feeling of jealousy in him: it was when I mentioned Byron. "If there were time," he said, "I could show you that Lord Byron was not so great a poet as you think him to be—but never mind that now." I had just been classing his own sonnets and "Childe Harold" together, as the noblest poetry since "Paradise Lost;" but did not reassert what I said: I should have felt that to be irreverent towards the noble old man, however unchanged my own judgment remained.

"I am pleased to find," he said, while we were talking about Byron, "that you preserve your muse chaste, and free from rank and corrupt passion. Lord Byron degraded poetry in that respect. Men's hearts are bad enough. Poetry should refine and purify their natures; not make them worse."

I ventured the plea that "Don Juan" was descriptive, and that Shakspeare had also described bad passions in anatomising the human heart, which was one of the great vocations of the poet.

"But there is always a moral lesson," he replied quickly, "in Shakspeare's pictures. You feel he is not stirring man's passions for the sake of awakening the brute in them: the pure and the virtuous are always presented in high contrast; but the other riots in corrupt pictures, evidently with the enjoyment of the corruption."

I diverted him from a theme which, it was clear, created unpleasant thoughts in him; and asked his opinion of the poetry of the day.

"There is little that can be called high poetry," he said. "Mr. Tennyson affords the richest promise. He will do great things yet; and ought to have done greater things by this time."

"His sense of music," I observed, "seems more perfect than that of any of the new race of poets."

"Yes," he replied; "the perception of harmony lies in the very essence of the poet's nature; and Mr. Tennyson gives magnificent proofs that he is endowed with it."

I instanced Tennyson's rich association of musical words in his "Morte d'Arthur," "Godiva," "Ulysses," and other pieces—as proofs of his possessing as fine a sense of music in syllables as Keats, and even Milton; and the patriarchal poet, with an approving smile, assented to it.

I assured him how much I had been interested with Mrs. Wordsworth's conversation respecting Southey, and told him that James Montgomery of Sheffield, in an interview I had with him many years before, had spoken very highly of Southey.

"Well, that is pleasing to hear," he observed; "for Mr. Montgomery's political opinions have never resembled Southey's."

"That was Mr. Montgomery's own observation," I rejoined, "while he was assuring me that he lived near to Mr. Southey for a considerable time, at one period of his life, and he never knew a more estimable man. He affirmed, too, that when people attributed

Mr. Southey's change of political opinions to corrupt motives, they greatly wronged him."

"And, depend upon it, they did," Wordsworth answered, with great dignity: "it was the foulest libel to attribute bad motives to Mr. Southey. No man's change was ever more sincere. He would have hated himself had he been a hypocrite; and could never afterwards have produced anything noble."

He repeated Mrs. Wordsworth remarks on Southey's purity of morals, and immense industry in reading almost always with the pen in his hand; and his zeal in laying up materials for future works. With a sigh he recurred to his friend's mental decline and imbecility in his latter days—and, again, I led him to other topics.

"There will be great changes on the Continent," he said, "when the present King of the French dies. But not while he lives. The different governments will have to give constitutions to their people, for knowledge is spreading, and constitutional liberty is sure to follow."

I thought him perfectly right about Louis Philippe; and which of us would not have thought him right in 1846? But yet I had mistaken his estimate of the "King of the Barricades."

"Ay, he is too crafty and powerful," said I, "to be easily overthrown; there will be no extension of French liberty in his days."

"Oh, but you are mistaken in the character of Louis Philippe," he observed, very pointedly; "you should not call him crafty: he is a very wise and politic prince. The French needed such a man. He will consolidate French character, and render it fit for the *peaceable* acquirement of rational liberty at his decease."

I remembered the venerable age and high mental rank of him with whom I was conversing, and simply said—"Do you think so, sir?"—without telling him that I thought he scarcely comprehended his subject. But how the events of 1848 must have made him wonder!

He had the same views of the spread of freedom in England in proportion to the increase of knowledge; and descanted with animation on the growth of Mechanics' and similar institutions.

"The people are sure to have the franchise," he said, with emphasis, "as knowledge increases; but you will not get all you seek at once—and you must never seek it again by physical force," he added, turning to me with a smile: "it will only make you longer about it."

A great part of the time he was thus kindly and paternally impressing his thoughts upon me, we were walking on the terrace outside his house,—whither he had conducted me to note the beautiful view it commanded. It was indeed a glorious spot for a poet's home. Rydal Lake was in view from one window in the cottage, and Windermere from another—with all the grand assemblage of mountain and rock that intervened. From the terrace the view of Windermere was magnificent.

The poet's aged and infirm sister was being drawn about the courtyard in a wheeled chair, as we walked on the terrace. He descended with me, and introduced me to her—as a poet!—and hung over her infirmity with the kindest affection, while she talked to me.

When I hastened to depart—fearing that I had already wearied him—he walked with me to the gate, pressing my hand repeatedly, smiling upon me so benevolently, and uttering so many good wishes for my happiness and usefulness, that I felt almost unable to thank him. I left him with a more intense feeling of having been in the presence of a good and great intelligence, than I had ever felt in any other moments of my life.

CHAPTER XXVII.
LITERARY AND LECTURING LIFE, IN LONDON; 1847—1848.

WHEN I returned from the journey on which I had been sent to collect matter for the articles on the "Condition of the People," furnished to Douglas Jerrold's paper, I was told by Jerrold himself that he was very sorry to inform me they had not room for me on the paper: it was sinking in circulation, and they must reduce their staff:

My publisher, Mr. How, had now removed to 209, Piccadilly, and from what he had said to me before I set out on my journey, I had hoped, by the time of my return, he would have been able to publish a second edition of my Prison Rhyme. He requested me not to offer my book to any other publisher, assuring me he should be in a better position soon. I waited long: my poem remained out of print a full year—which was a real loss to myself.

My good friend W. J, Fox, falling ill at the beginning of 1847, he requested me to take his place at South Place, Finsbury Square, till his recovery. I took it without hesitation; and it caused a few severe remarks from some Cockney critics. But I saw no inconsistency in what I did. It was not because I thought I was my peerless friend's equal in eloquence, that I ventured to stand in his place—for he had no equal in England. But I thought I could say something worth hearing, even by Cockneys; and I had not learned to pretend that I feared to supply the place of another speaker, whoever he might be.

My friend was soon well again, and returned to South Place, but intimated to me that he should retire from his post as Sunday evening lecturer at the National Hall; and that he had told the committee he wished me to succeed him. And so I commenced lecturing on Sunday evenings in the Hall, so well known at that time in Holborn.

I had on several occasions seen it right to speak strongly against the old Chartist error of physical force. For the more I reflected on the past, the more clearly I saw that the popular desire for freedom had failed through those errors. One night, the elder Mr. Ashurst, a leading attorney of the city of London, had been among my hearers; and he desired Lovett to ask me if I would deliver two lectures in the National Hall on "Moral Force," as a special theme. I consented; and the "Two Orations against the taking away of Human Life" were first spoken, and then published, in a pamphlet, by the Brothers Chapman, who were then publishers in Newgate Street.

Calling on my old friend and playmate, Thomas Miller, one day, he told me that a series of boys' books was being brought out by Chapman and Hall, and he had written two or three of the books—but other writers were wanted; that, as the books were highly illustrated, Mr. Henry Vizetelly, the engraver, was entrusted with arrangements, and I might apply to him. I called on Mr. Vizetelly, and engaged to write "The Triumphs of Perseverance" for £25. It was but poor pay. But I was waiting still for Mr. How; and the lectures at the National Hall were always suspended in summer: so I was glad to get any employ. Mr. Vizetelly afterwards gave me £10 to alter the "History of Enterprise" which had been written by another person. Eventually, the two volumes were made into one by some other writer, and so published by Messrs. Darton.

During the summer of 1847, I was invited to lecture at the John Street Institution, Tottenham Court Road. It was still held, in lease, by Socialists; and I could not help wondering at the strange changes of my life which had brought me to stand, as a teacher, in the pulpit at South Place, and on the platform at John Street, where I had heard Robert Owen and W. J. Fox, on those two Sundays in 1839.

The last administration of Sir Robert Peel was now broken up, and the general election came on in August. So now, again, I had to take the place of my eloquent friend, W. J. Fox, on Sunday mornings, at South Place, that he might be free to contest the borough of Oldham—for which he was speedily returned M.P.

The political atmosphere, almost everywhere, began now to show disturbance. In Ireland, the writing and speeches of John Mitchell caused considerable alarm. Continental affairs also began to be very unsettled. The really popular course taken by Pope Pio Nono, in the autumn of 1847, created great hope. There were also signs of a struggle for increased liberty in Switzerland. I had no personal acquaintance, up to this time, with the great and good Mazzini; but, at the request of my friend W. J. Fox, I joined a new society which Mazzini had projected. It was called "The People's International League;" and we held our meetings, usually weekly, in the parlour of our secretary, Mr. W. J. Linton, the engraver, in Hatton Garden,— who has, it is feared, settled in America.

Mazzini himself was our great source of inspiration. He assured us—months before it came to pass—that a European Revolution was at hand—a revolution that would hurl Louis Phillippe from his throne, and endanger the thrones of others. He affirmed this as early as in September 1847, when it seemed so unlikely to some of us. But his eloquence and enthusiasm had a marvellous effect upon us. He wished, he said, to rouse intelligent Englishmen to a right feeling and understanding of foreign questions, that we might show our sympathy with the right—when we really understood where it lay.

There were three or four Poles and Hungarians who were members with us, of whom Capt. Stolzman was the chief. In addition to my friend W. J. Fox, and Mr. W. J. Linton and myself, the English members were—the elder and younger Mr. Ashurst, the elder and younger Mr. P. A. Taylor, Mr. James Stansfeld, Mr. Sidney Hawkes, Mr. Shaen, Mr. Richard Moore, Mr. James Watson, Mr. Henry Hetherington, and Mr. Goodwyn Barmby. Dr. (now Sir John) Bowring and my friend William Howitt, were reckoned members— but neither of them ever attended our meetings. The younger P. A. Taylor is now the incorruptible and unsubduable M.P. for my native town of Leicester; Mr. James Stansfeld is the "Right Honourable President of the Local Government Board;" and Goodwyn Barmby is a Unitarian Minister at Wakefield.

The wondrous events of the next year put an end to our meetings; but while they lasted they were deeply interesting. I remember, one evening, Mazzini had been describing to us the strong hope he had that an effective, but secret, movement for the overthrow of Austrian tyranny, was being organized in his beloved Italy. He then made a strong appeal to us, whether English lovers of liberty should not show their sympathy with his patriotic countrymen by subscribing to furnish them with arms.

I ventured to say that I felt doubtful whether it was consistent for some of us who were lamenting the physical force folly of some in our own country, and were often and openly protesting against it, to conspire for aiding another people with arms. Young Peter Taylor followed me on the same side. But before any other could speak, Mazzini sprang up.

"Mr. Cooper, you are right about your own country," he said—and those wondrous eyes of his were lit up with a power that was almost overwhelming; "you are right about your own country. You have had your grand decisive struggle against Tyrannous Power. Your fathers brought it to the block; and you have now a Representation, and you have Charters and Written Rights to appeal to. You need no physical force. Your countrymen only need a will and union to express it, and you can have all you need. But what are my countrymen to do, who are trodden down under the iron heel of a foreign tyranny?—who are watched, seized, and imprisoned before anyone knows what has become of them? What are my countrymen to do, I ask you? They have no Representation—they have no Charters—they have no Written Rights. What must my countrymen do? *They must fight!*"

We were all subdued—for he was unanswerable. And when February brought the French Revolution, it seemed to me as if I had listened to one who possessed a degree of prophetic foresight which is given to few among men. And the wonders that followed, in the year 1848, rendered it the most remarkable year of the nineteenth century,—unless the last year, 1870, be deemed still more remarkable

I resumed my Sunday evening lectures at the National Hall, in September, 1847, and continued them till February, 1848—when I gave offence to Lovett and his fellow-committeemen, by changing the subject of my lecture that I might describe the struggle in France, as the majority of my hearers wished me to do. I was soon solicited to transfer my work to the John Street Institution; and there I continued to lecture for a long time.

We lodged in Blackfriars Road when my Prison Rhyme was published; afterwards in Islington; and then in Devonshire Street, Red Lion Square. But on the 10th of February, 1848, I ventured once more to become a householder; and from that time, for seven years following, I lived at 5, Park Row, Knightsbridge. It was the pleasantest house I had ever had in my life. The access to it was through "Mill's Buildings," a "long square" tenanted chiefly by workpeople and washerwomen, and, therefore, not likely to attract fashionables. But the houses forming "Park Row," though somewhat old, were large and roomy, and must have been tenanted by "considerable" sort of people, formerly. We had no access to Hyde Park, but we looked into it from our really beautiful parlour; and had daily views of the Guards, and Royalty, and great people, passing by, in the Park.

Finding at length that poor How was sinking into greater difficulties, and that I could not hope to see his name again on any book of mine, as the publisher, I yielded to a request which was pressed upon me greatly by working men, that I would let my Prison Rhyme be issued in numbers at twopence each, that they might have it within their power to purchase it. I made arrangements with James Watson to bring it out in numbers; and we were to have shared the profits. But some time after, when I was greatly in want of money, I sold the copyright to Watson for £50. In the year 1860, however, a young intellectual friend (Mr. Thomas Chambers, of H. M. Customs, who possesses the original MS. of my Prison Rhyme) bought back the copyright from him, and presented it to me, so that the copyright of my poetry remains my own. I ought also to say that Watson gave leave to Chapman and Hall, for a fixed sum, to publish a given number of copies, of a superior appearance to his own, or "The

People's Edition." So Chapman and Hall's edition was called the "Third Edition."

Being so thoroughly separated from O'Connor and his party, I was entirely kept out of the "Tenth of April" trouble, and all the other troubles of the year 1848. I was visited, however, by all sorts of schemers, who wished to draw me into their plots and plans; for plotters and planners were as plentiful as blackberries in 1848. The changes on the Continent seemed to have unhinged the minds of thousands. It was not only among O'Connor Chartists, or Ernest Jones Chartists, and the Irish Repealers, that there were plots, open and secret. I got into the secret of one plot of which a grave old politician of great intelligence had become a member. I was amazed at the infatuation displayed by himself and a fine young fellow who lodged with him. I saved them both; but had some difficulty in doing it. I will describe the affair—but must not mention names.

A tall, dark-looking man came to visit me one day, addressing me with an air of amazing frankness: assuring me that he had been in the Detective Police Force, and knew all about their system; but that he hated the government, and wanted to overthrow it and all other tyrannies upon the earth. He was proceeding to tell me what were his plans for a revolution; but I would not hear them. He seemed determined to proceed; but I assured him he had come to the wrong man, and refused to listen. He was evidently maliciously disappointed; and I was glad when he was gone.

I had not mentioned his visit to any one. But, four days after, meeting the grave, matured politician I have already referred to, in Fleet Street,—he drew me into one of the courts, and began to tell me that he had entered into a solemn promise to assist in "ending the present state of things" promise one bold stroke. I asked what he really meant; and he began to inform me that one was at the head of the plot who had formerly been in the Detective Force, and knew all the secrets of the police. I scented the personality he referred to—but let him go on. A young friend of his, he said, had undertaken to be one of five who should fire London, in different places, with a chemical composition which would burn stone itself: nothing could resist it. In the confusion that must arise, the head of the plot that he had referred to would mount a horse and gallop through the town, proclaiming himself the Dictator.

The Irish Confederates, he said, had promised to bring out all their force; and when resistance had been overcome—if any were offered—a Republican government would be formed.

I never felt more astonished in my life than I did at the complete infatuation of the man. I walked home with him; and asked what time his young lodger would be in. "In about another hour," he said, "he would come to his dinner." So I determined to stay and see him, and talked on till he came. The young man seemed more completely infatuated than the older one. The plot was to be executed on the next night but one—and so I knew there was no time to lose. I asked the young man if he knew what the composition was that would burn stone. He instantly mentioned some chemical—the name of which I have forgot, and said if it were placed on a stone, and sugar of lead were put to it, it would burn up the stone. I asked if he had tried it—for I saw I must proceed quietly. He confessed he had not. I said I should like to see it tried: would he go out and purchase the chemicals at two or three different shops? He consented—went out—and soon returned.

We went downstairs, and then into what Londoners call a "back place," which had a brick floor—but there was one large stone in the floor. The young man eagerly put a portion of the chemical on the stone. Then, tying a spoon to a stick, he filled the spoon with sugar of lead; and, standing at a distance from the stone, he stretched out the stick and poured the sugar of lead on the chemical. There was a sudden pink-coloured blaze, and all was over. The stone was scarcely tinged with black. I urged him to try it again; and then to try it on wood,—but it would not fire either!

The young man looked mortified and ashamed; and I took him upstairs to the elder man and communicated the result of our trial; and the elder man looked vexed and ashamed. But I saw now that I had some advantage in talking to them.

"How came you to believe such a wild tale without trying it?" I said. "I can venture my head on the assertion that no man in the world knows of a chemical composition which you can place on the stones of the street and set them on fire—or burn stone houses, or brick houses, either. This scoundrel who has drawn you into this mad plot came to me, before he came to you—"

"Came to you?"

"Came to me, and told me the same tale of his having been in the Detective Force; but I stopped him—although I had to use threatening in order to do it. He seeks to ruin you both."

"I'll shoot him if he plays me false," exclaimed the younger man.

"You had better have no more to do with him; but tell him, when he calls to-night, to walk off."

"Oh no! I shall not do that," said the younger man; "the job will be done to-morrow night, and I mean to go through with it."

The elder man now joined the younger in denouncing my attempt to put them off their foolish scheme. It was time the bad state of things was altered, he said. He had been struggling all his life against bad governments; and now a determined stroke was to be played, he would not draw back.

I left them; but returned at night, and renewed my entreaties. I reminded the elder man that he knew the names of Castles, and Oliver, and Edwards, the old spies and bargainers for "blood-money" in Castlereagh and Sidmouth's time, as well as I did; and he might be sure the brood of such vermin was not extinct yet. As the fellow did not come at nine o'clock, according to promise, the younger man said he would go out, and try to find him.

"Nay," I said; "you had better stay. Let him come, and let me confront him."

Ten o'clock struck; but he did not come. No doubt he had seen me enter the house; and so felt it would destroy his scheme to meet me, if I had not destroyed his scheme already. I told the two deluded men that the fellow most likely knew that I was in the house, and would not come in. The younger man jumped up, and said he should like to know if it were so, and would go to the house of a friend who lived near, and ask if he had called there.

The young man returned, but not with any news of the whereabouts of the mysterious would-be Dictator. Yet he had learned that the Irish Confederates had signified they could not "come out" the next night: so, most likely, the thing would be put off for the present.

I went again the next day, and found that a night's reflection had produced a change. Neither the young man nor the elder one talked so confidently as before. They seemed greatly to wonder that their chief had failed to call.

"If he has been laying a lying information against us, and means to visit us to-day and bring some of the Force with him," said the elder man, "he can prove nothing against us."

"He could only assert that he had visited you in your houses," I said; "and it would be strange evidence to give against you—though you were unwise to listen to him. I feel sure you are in no danger from him, if you refuse to let him enter your house when he calls again; and tell him you will have nothing more to do with him."

They did not promise—but I saw they would take my advice. So long as the old politician lived, he never met me without a blush.

Let me add another reminiscence—but of a very different character—before I conclude this chapter. I mentioned the fact that I met my old Italian instructor Signor D'Albrione on the day of the riot in the Potteries; and in the latter part of 1845 I found him again, in London. We agreed that he should resume his old office as my French and Italian teacher; and we kept the agreement till I went out into the North of England for Jerrold's paper in 1846. When I returned, as we went into a new lodging, he failed to find me; and as I had no knowledge of where he lived—for he was always reticent about it—I could not find him.

One forenoon in the close of 1847, I was passing over Blackfriars Bridge when I caught sight of a tall figure, almost in rags, bending over the parapet, with such a look of misery that, at first, I did not recognize in it the noble face of the brave old Carbonaro and soldier of Napoleon. Believing it to be the face of D'Albrione, I called him by his name. He did not speak, but turned upon me a glance of despair that I can scarcely describe—while he sobbed, and the tears rolled down his cheeks.

"My good friend," I said, "what are you doing here?" He pointed significantly to the river beneath.

"Oh, nay, come away," I said, "come away, and tell me about yourself—don't think of that!"

He told me his dark tale of distress, and it was dark indeed. His teaching had fallen off, till, at last, he could not get food, and his strength sank; and when he had pawned everything but the rags he wore, he did not feel strength or courage to apply for employment in his profession as a teacher of languages. I helped to keep him on his legs—though his constitution was gone—until the political earthquake came in 1848; and then he asked me to raise him a little money, and give him an introduction to Mazzini, who, he felt sure, would complete the means of getting him home to his native Turin. The noble heart of Mazzini was touched with the misfortunes of his countryman, and he effectually opened the exile's path back to his birthplace. Doubtless the poor wanderer has long since been borne to his rest on his native soil.

CHAPTER XXVIII.
LITERARY AND LECTURING LIFE CONTINUED: 1848—1850.

IN the year 1848, I think, Chartists were wilder than we were in 1842, or than the members of the First Convention were in 1838. Experience had rendered me a little wiser than to suffer myself to be mixed up again with any plot, however plausible: so I kept out of them all. If the reader would know the wild Chartist history of 1848, and learn how imprisonment, and death in prison, were the lot that fell to some of its victims, he can consult Dr. Gammage, as I told him before. As I had nothing to do with the monstrous "National Petition," or the meeting on Kennington Common, or the "glorious 10th of April," or any of the "monster meetings" of the year, I am cut off, happily, from the later Chartist history of violence and failure.

Mention of that memorable "10th of April" calls up one agreeable reminiscence. On the evening before the day, I was kindly invited by my highly intelligent friend Dr. Garth Wilkinson to join a party, in his house at Hampstead, to meet Emerson, the illustrious American. He was the only American in whose company I ever felt real enjoyment. The few Americans I have ever met displayed too much of my own native mood—the imperative—to render them pleasant companions. I met Margaret Fuller twice, during the time she was in London—once at W. J. Fox's, and the other at Hugh Doherty's; but felt only a modified pleasure in her company. She talked in a nasal tone, and lifted up her head to shout, so as to be heard by all in the room—behaviour so utterly foreign to an Englishman's notions of womanliness! Emerson did not talk in his nose; and why any American should, I cannot see. Why do they not master the bad habit? Emerson's talk was gentle and good; and his manners were those of a quiet English gentleman. I walked into London with him—as he had intimated a wish to walk. It was Sunday evening; and he made observations on a host of subjects, as we gently walked on—for he would not hurry. Religion, Politics, Literature—ours, and America's: he seemed eager to learn all he could, and willing to communicate all he could. He seemed to think and talk without pride or conceit, and with remarkably good common-sense, so far as my humble judgment went.

I could say anything to him—but I could not talk to Margaret Fuller. I remember that my friend. Mr. Fox left his arm-chair to come to the opposite side of his drawing-room, and remind me that I had not yet spoken to his American guest. And if he had not done so, I do not think I should have exchanged words with her—though my friend Willie Thom stood and conversed with her a long time.

Poor Willie Thom! how melancholy it seems to look back upon the close of the history of the weaver poet of Inverury! especially when one calls to mind what his natural endowments were, despite his lowly condition. Mr. Fox used to say that Willie Thom had the richest powers of conversation of any man he had ever known; and Mr. Fox had been intimate with Leigh Hunt, and Macready, and Pemberton, and Talfourd. And, indeed, it required an effort to free yourself from the conviction that you were conversing with a thoroughly educated man when you talked with Willie Thom. The *thought* in every word he used was wondrous, even on the commonest subjects.

And then he sang so sweetly! We got up a weekly meeting, at one time, at the Crown Tavern, close to the church of St. Dunstan's-in-the-West, Fleet Street; and it was chiefly that we might enjoy the society of Willie Thom. Julian Harney, and John Skelton (now Dr. Skelton), and old Dr. Macdonald, and James Devlin, who wrote "The Shoemaker," and Walter Cooper, and Thomas Shorter, and a few others were members of our weekly meeting. Willie Thom usually sang us his "Wandering Willie," or "My ain wee thing:" and sometimes I sang them my prison songs, "O choose thou the maid with the gentle blue eye," and "I would not be a crowned king."

The poor poet's singings soon came to an end. After the publication of his first and only volume, he was induced (as he always said, by Gordon of Knockespock) to come and settle in London, under false promises. Money had been subscribed for him by Scottish merchants in India and others—I think to the amount of £400. But he made no proper use of it. He yielded to people who urged him to sit up singing and drinking whisky the whole night through. And although he had some constitution left when I first knew him, it soon faded. Again and again, I carried invitations to him, from Douglas Jerrold, to contribute to the *Shilling Magazine*, and also from William Howitt, to contribute to his periodical; but it was in vain.

"Nay-nay!" he used to say, with an air of wretchedness; "I can do nae such thing as they ask, although they promise me siller for it. I threw off my lilts o' the heart in auld time, when I had a heart; but I think I've none left, noo!"

At last, he was reduced to absolute starvation, in London. He had married his servant after the death of his first wife; and when she was in a condition that needed some amendment of life, they were at the lowest. She actually brought forth her child without any help from a medical man, her own husband in the room,—and they were without food! George Jacob Holyoake, living near them, was the first to learn the fact; threw them his last sovereign, and ran out to seek the proper help the poor woman needed.

I went to Mr. P. A. Taylor (the present M.P. for Leicester) so soon as I heard the sorrowful facts; and he promised to renew the help he and his friends had formerly rendered the poor poet. It was perceived, however, that there was no hope for him in London. So, by the interest of Sir Wm. Forbes, £40 was obtained from the Literary Fund, and he was sent down to Dundee, under a promise that he would return to the loom. He lived but a few months, and his wife but a few months after him; and they lie buried together in Dundee Cemetery, not far from the grand river Tay.

During the stirring year of 1848, I kept on at my lecturing work, on Sunday evenings, at the John Street Institution. I had large audiences, to listen to history and foreign and home politics, mingled with moral instruction. One great charm of these evenings, for myself, was the music. There was a good organ, and I strove to direct the taste of the choir to Handel and Mozart and Haydn and

Beethoven; and the result was that we soon had some thorough good chorus-singing.

I had crowds to listen to me in the winter of 1848-9. And I might have done great good if I had continued simply to teach history, and to deal with the stirring politics of the time. But I had now become a thorough adherent of Strauss. I believed his "Mythical System" to be the true interpretation of what was called Gospel History. So, in my evil zeal for what I conceived to be Truth, I delivered eight lectures, on successive Sunday evenings, on the teachings of the "Leben Jesu." I soon repeated them in the "Hall of Science," City Road—for I began in October, 1848, to lecture, alternately, at that place and at John Street. There is no part of my teaching as a public lecturer that I regret so deeply as this. It would rejoice my heart indeed if I could obliterate those lectures from the Realm of Fact. But it can not be. We must bear the guilt and take the consequences of all our acts which are contrary to the will of Him Who made us, and Who has a right to our service.

In December, 1848, Mr. Benjamin Steill, of 20, Paternoster Row, asked me if I were willing to conduct a weekly penny periodical, to be devoted to Radical politics and general instruction. I answered "Yes;" for I could have no doubt that the original publisher of Wooler's *Black Dwarf* and I would well agree in our political views. Mr. Steill allowed me to choose a name for the new serial; and, without knowing that Hazlitt had formerly conducted a periodical, or rather published a series of papers under that title, I determined to call it "THE PLAIN SPEAKER."

Mr. Steill gave me but two pounds per week, and expected me to write the greater part of the contents. But with the third number he introduced Wooler, the aged editor of the famous old *Black Dwarf*, of the times of Hunt and Cobbett. Yet Wooler did not help me effectually.

"He was, at one time, the finest epistolary writer in England," said Mr. Steill in his commendation. But the stilted style of the *Black Dwarf*, however it had been relished by the men of a former generation, was not in favour with the men of my generation, and they could see no resemblance to "Junius" in him. Nor was Wooler's conversation more animated than his style: it was "flat, stale, and unprofitable."

The best papers I wrote in the *Plain Speaker* were my "Eight Letters to the Young Men of the Working Classes." They were afterwards published as a sixpenny pamphlet, and sold in thousands. I do not think I ever wrote anything that was instrumental of so much real good as those Letters.

Letters to Richard Cobden, the Duke of Grafton, the Bishop of London, Joseph Hume, Lord Ashley, the Duke of Beaufort, Lord John Russell, the Earl of Carlisle, the Earl of Winchilsea, Sir Robert Inglis, Sir Robert Peel, the Archbishop of Canterbury, James Garth Marshall of Leeds, Sir E. N. Buxton, John Bright, Benjamin Disraeli, the Marquis of Granby, R. Bernal Osborne, Sir Joshua Walmsley, Lord Stanley, the Duke of Rutland, Lord Brougham, and others, all more or less political, form the staple of my writing for the *Plain Speaker*. But the letters to the "Right Reverend the Lord Harry of Exeter" were considered to be the most amusing part of the series.

In the spring of 1849, I lectured in Birmingham, Sheffield, Manchester, Liverpool, Bolton, Newcastle-on-Tyne, Shields, Sunderland, Carlisle, Leeds, and York; and still kept up my writing for the *Plain Speaker*. In the month of May, the kind and true friend to whom Thomas Carlyle showed my Prison Rhyme, asked me to go over with him to Paris. I hesitated; but my dear wife said I should, perhaps, never have such another offer in my life; and when I consulted Mr. Steill, he said I could write from Paris. So I consented. Under the titles "Five Days in Paris" and "A Sunday in Calais," I gave a sketch of my experiences, in the current numbers of the *Plain Speaker*. That was the only time I was ever on the Continent; and I feel myself under lasting obligations to my friend for affording me the opportunity of seeing Paris, and Versailles, and St. Denis, and Calais with my own eyes.

I went over to Leicester in 1849, and addressed meetings, at the request of several old friends, who wished me to present myself again as a candidate for the representation of my native town in Parliament. I speedily gave up the project, clearly discerning that no poor man, unconnected with aristocracy, or powerful local influences, can succeed in such a purpose. During this year I also lectured at Cheltenham and Northampton, and other towns.

In August, 1849, I ceased to write for the *Plain Speaker*. The paper was not got out at the proper time of the week (the proprietor not being able to buy the materials), and so the circulation sank. To enable Mr. Steill to cope a little better with difficulties, I gave up half of my salary as editor; but he still was too late in the week with the publishing; and, seeing no hope of amendment, I withdrew. Wooler and he struggled on with the paper to the end of the year.

I cannot close my account of the year 1849 without recording a slight incident connected with the memory of a man of real genius. My friend George Searle Phillips (or "January Searle ") was on a visit to Ebenezer Elliott, and, in my name, presented him with a copy of my " Purgatory of Suicides," and also intimated my wish to see him. The poet (who died very soon after) sent me his mind in a note which is, at once, so characteristic of the man, that I present it to the reader:—

"*Hargate Hill, near Barnsley,*

"*9th September*, 1849.

"DEAR MR. COOPER,

"Stone deaf, as I am at present, and agonized with unintermitting pain, I could not welcome a visit from Dante himself, even if he brought with him a sample of the best brimstone pudding which may be prepared for me in the low country. But if I should recover, and you then happen to be in my neighbourhood, you will need no introduction but your name; and I will promise you a hearty welcome, bacon and eggs, and a bed.

" I am, dear sir,

"Yours very truly,

"EBENEZER ELLIOTT."

Before the end of the year, I was strongly urged by all my friends to commence a weekly penny periodical on my own account; and so on Saturday, January 5th, 1850, the first number of *Cooper's Journal* was published by James Watson, who lived then at "3, Queen's Head Passage," one of the passages between Paternoster Row and Newgate Street. I regret deeply that I was persuaded by my freethinking friends to publish my Lectures on Strauss's "Leben Jesu," in the new periodical. I had many misgivings about it; but some of them urged it so strongly, that I committed myself to a promise, and then felt bound to fulfil it.

Of course, I had to furnish the greater portion of writing for each number; but I was kindly assisted by friends in filling up the weekly pages of *Cooper's Journal.* My best contributors of poetry were Gerald Massey (some of whose earliest pieces first appeared in my periodical), J. A. Langford (now Dr. Langford) of Birmingham, and poor William Jones of Leicester. There were scattered pieces of rhyme by W. Moy Thomas (now editor of *Cassell's Magazine*), William Whitmore of Leicester, and others. My best and most productive prose contributor was Frank Grant—a young man of very considerable powers of mind, but an invalid for years, by paralysis of his lower limbs. He was the son of an excellent clergyman in the Staffordshire Potteries, but was a free thinker—and that most conscientiously. Other contributors were my beloved friend Samuel M. Kydd (now a barrister-at-law), George Hooper (author of "The Battle of Waterloo," and an active member of the London newspaper press), my very old intellectual friends, J. Yeats of Hull, and Richard Otley of Sheffield, Thomas Shorter (secretary of the Working Men's College), and a few more.

There were sold, altogether, of the first number, 9,000; but the sale soon began to decline. At the end of June I suspended the publication, by announcement, for three months. But the recommencement, in October, was so unsuccessful, as to lead me to close the publication entirely at the end of that month.

During the months of January, February, March, April, and May, 1850, I lectured, on Sunday nights, alternately, at the John Street Institution, Tottenham Court Road, and the Hall of Science, City Road. And during these months I also lectured, on other nights of the week, in several of the smaller Institutes of London. The months of June, July, and August were devoted to travelling—when I lectured at Coventry, Hull, Newcastle-on-Tyne, Sunderland, North Shields, Alnwick, Carlisle, Stockton-on-Tees, Middlesborough, York, Leeds, Keighley, Wakefield Huddersfield; Bradford, Sheffield, Rotherham, and Doncaster, together with Pudsey, Heckmondwike, Cullingworth, and other smaller towns in Yorkshire; and afterwards at Cheltenham, Norwich, and Southampton. The subjects on which I lectured in these journeyings were—the Lives and Genius of Milton, Burns, Byron, and Shelley; the Genius of Shakspeare; the Commonwealth and Cromwell; the Wrongs of Ireland; and sometimes I lectured on the political changes at home and on the Continent.

CHAPTER XXIX.
LECTURING IN IRELAND AND SCOTLAND: FUNERAL OF "THE
GREAT DUKE."

THE opening of the " Great Exhibition Year," 1851, found me at
what had now become my settled employ on Sunday evenings—the
lectures at John Street and City Road. During the year, I delivered
ten lectures on the History of Greece, and seventeen lectures on the
History of Rome. But my London lecturing, be it observed, was
interrupted for six months of this year. Living so close to Hyde Park,
I saw them dig the fountains and mark the ground for the "Great
Exhibition," and I saw the Queen go, in procession, to open it. Our
house, we soon found, had lost all its pleasantness. On Sundays,
especially, we seemed to live in the midst of a fair. They were crying
"Oranges, fine oranges" in our ears, all the daylight hours after ten
in the morning; and the grass of the beautiful park disappeared
beneath the feet of the thousands that frequented it. The hurly-burly
and noise were insufferable. So we began to wish to get away. I had
often received invitations to lecture in Scotland, and now came one
to lecture in Ireland. So I let the house for the summer—my dear
wife went to her sister's, at Lincoln—and I went down into the
Staffordshire Potteries to commence my six months' lecturing tour.

After a stay of nearly three weeks in the Potteries, I spent a fortnight
in Manchester; then took the packet at Fleetwood, and went over to
Belfast. I delivered eight lectures (Shakspeare, Milton, Burns, Byron,
Shelley, French Revolution, Civilisation, Cromwell) and remained
fourteen days in Belfast. I liked the town, and I liked the
neighbourhood; and I experienced the most perfect kindness from
the friends who invited me. But I did not feel "at home" in Ireland. I
felt as I lectured that I never got hold of the Irish mind or heart. It is
true, I went over to the Green Isle at an unfavourable time. The
names of "John Mitchell" and "Smith O'Brien" were in the ascendant
then in the affections of Irish working men; and I was no friend of
either of those great professors of patriotism.

The last lecture I gave at Belfast was on the Poet Shelley; and such commendation as I gave his beautiful poetry seemed to excite ten times the applause I received when I had eulogized our glorious Shakspeare, or Milton. I took the opportunity to tell them that I was glad to awaken their sense of approval, for I had really been disappointed with my reception in Ireland. It had ever been the lesson taught in England, I assured them, that Irish nature was warm, generous, and easily excited to sympathy; but I had felt my audience cold, critical, and unsympathising, compared with an English audience. I said I could not account for this. There seemed to be no natural separation between English and Irish, to my humble perception. Our features were pretty much alike—their country seemed like ours, for I had found the daisies and buttercups of my childhood in their fields—and I hoped we were very much alike in our love of freedom.

"We don't want to be like the English," shouted a young Mitchellite, with all his power of lungs.

"Then, what do you want?" I asked.

"Nationality!" was the thundering reply, followed by clapping of hands and thundering of feet on the floor, from nearly all the younger members of the audience.

"Nationality!" I resumed, so soon as silence was restored; "and if you had what you call 'Nationality'—that is, entire separation from England—today, what would you have to-morrow? I will tell you. Intestine war and bloodshed—fierce war between Protestant and Catholic—and finally, domination by some foreign power, whether French or American; and while the new conquerors used you to mortify Old England, you would be no happier yourselves, and would soon desire to unite with us again."

The elder part of my audience cried "Hear, hear," vociferously; but the younger cried "No, no!" and I speedily brought the meeting to an end. I may briefly say that I have never felt any uncontrollable desire to re-visit Ireland.

From Belfast I sailed, by steamer, to Ardrossan, and thus first set foot on the shore of Scotland. I lectured six times in Glasgow, four times at Paisley, twice at Hamilton, once at Kilbarchan, once at Barrhead, four times at Aberdeen, thrice at Dundee, twice at Dunfermline, six times at Edinburgh, twice at Dalkeith, once at Lasswade, twice at Galashiels, and twice at Hawick; and re-entered England, as I always do, gladly—but with a very different feeling from that with which I left Ireland. I was "at home" from the first moment while addressing a Scottish audience; and I freely declare that I would choose to address some such audiences as I have addressed in Scotland, sooner than any English audience I could name. I know no people so keenly appreciative of the value of thought as the people of Edinburgh; and I would sooner lecture to an Edinburgh audience than any other audience in the world.

While I was at Edinburgh, two of its literary people—(Dr. Black, and Mrs. Crowe, the authoress of " Susan Hopley ") attended one of my lectures, and kindly stayed to speak to me at the close. They learned that I had to lecture at Lasswade, and urged me to go and see Thomas De Quincey, who, they said, lived by the river Esk, about a mile beyond Lasswade. And I did go to see him, presented him with a copy of my Prison Rhyme, and was very kindly received by him.

One of the daughters of the man of genius—(there were two of them at the table)—manifested bad behaviour, as I thought. Her father showed true courtesy in speaking to me on political subjects— although we were on different sides. This did not suit the elder daughter—a really fine-looking young woman; and so she proudly chid De Quincey for not "maintaining his sentiments with dignity."

He remonstrated with her, very gently; but the proud girl only denounced my Chartism the more.

"My dear," said her father, whose small slender frame shook with feeling, "do not talk so, I beseech you—you will insult Mr. Cooper."

"But I am not insulted," said I.

The daughter caught my glance, bit her lip, and was silent. Her father kindly walked along the Esk with me, back to Lasswade, and conversed most delight fully. I left him with regret, and found my audience had been waiting for me full half an hour, to hear my lecture on Robert Burns. It was the only time in my life I ever neglected to meet an audience at the right time; and I found my Scottish hearers forgave me when they learned I had been with Thomas De Quincey.

Before returning to London for the winter, I lectured in Alnwick, North Shields, Newcastle-on-Tyne, Hexham, Carlisle, Blackburn, Padiham, Oldham, St. Helen's, Staleybridge, Wigan, Colne, Wakefield, Huddersfield, Halifax, Bradford, Leeds, York, Hull, Sheffield, Keighley, Batley, Birstal, and some smaller towns in Yorkshire. I was so disabled, bodily, by the time I got into Yorkshire, that my good and kind friend—my right honourable friend, as I will call him, henceforth—when I reached his house at Rawdon, insisted on putting me under the care of Dr. Macleod, of the Hydropathic Establishment, Ben Rhydding, and paying all the expenses. I remained at that most delightful place three weeks, and gratefully left it with a degree of health and strength that I had not felt for some years.

I lectured at Leamington, on my way to London, and went over, with a few friends, to see sweet Stratford-on-Avon, and to worship, intellectually, at Shakspeare's shrine. Before the close of 1851, I also lectured at Norwich, Leicester, Hastings, Portsmouth, Southampton, Winchester, and Salisbury, and had the indescribable pleasure of seeing mysterious Stonehenge—a sight I had longed to see for many years.

After giving but four lectures on Sunday evenings, at John Street, at the beginning of 1852, I thought it better to leave that Institution for a time. So I lectured at the Hall of Science only, on Sunday evenings, for the rest of that year. I went out of town, however, sometimes, on the other days of the week, to lecture; and thus visited Devonport, Bristol, Cambridge, Peterborough, Coventry, Lincoln, Louth, Keighley, Barnsley, and Todmorden; my subjects being

"Shakspeare," "Milton," "Burns," "Byron," "Cromwell," "Civilisation," "Washington," etc., etc. At the Hall of Science, during the year 1852, I delivered a series of eleven lectures on the French Revolution, five on the British Poets, six on the life of Wellington, besides miscellaneous lectures.

This was the death-year of the Great Duke—the " Iron Duke," as we so often called him. Living in Knightsbridge, about a quarter of a mile beyond Apsley House, I had to pass by his dwelling every time that I went into the heart of London; and saw him, sometimes, every day for weeks together. What a fascination, what an irresistible attraction there was about that grand old man! How all the memorable doings of our century seemed to gather around him, as you looked at his rigid, stern figure! I often walked close by his horse, for half a mile out of my way, marking his bearing, and noting the uniform "military tip," of his forefinger towards his forehead, that he gave to all those, great or little, who took off their hats to him; and there were usually scores who did this.

I remembered how Radicals employed the rough side of their tongue—to quote an old Lincolnshire phrase—when they described "the man who helped Castlereagh to carry up the Green Bag to the House of Lords," for the prosecution of poor Queen Caroline—I remembered the laughter of old Rads when they described the fierce, exultant hurrah that they gave at the door of Westminster Abbey when the body of "carotid-artery-cutting Castlereagh " was taken out of the hearse, and the Duke held up his hand, and said, "Hush!"—I remembered his opposition to Reform, in the later time, and the caricatures of him as a hook-nosed coachman on the box, and King William the Fourth inside, with the inscription beneath: "The Man wot drives the Sovereign "—I could not forget the barricades to his house put up during the Reform struggle, for I saw them every day; they were never taken down till after his death. But all this had passed away; and Wellington had become not only the great pillar of State and most valued counsellor of his Queen; but, next to her, the most deeply respected and most heartily honoured person in the realm.

Everybody liked to see "the Duke"; and no one would hear a word against him. Soldiers—old soldiers—they idolized him. They regarded him as the very personification of English valour and English sagacity. Politicians—they all had a glance towards him when they contemplated new measures. He was an institution in himself. We all felt as if we lived, now *he* was dead, in a different England. The very elements were held to sympathize with the national loss. It began to rain on the day that the Duke died, and it continued to rain—rain—rain!

Some may be still in the habit of crossing Hyde Park from the Marble Arch to the Albert Gate, and may remember a tall old man who kept the spring at the head of the Serpentine, and who used to hand a glass of water, as a morning draught before breakfast, to his customers, who remembered him with a sixpence now and then. I often tarried to talk with him, and learned that he had undergone the Peninsular campaign with Wellington; and that he had at the time been both soldier and servant to General Lygon, who had secured him the little post at the spring in Hyde Park, in addition to his small pension.

"Still very rainy, my friend," I said to him one morning, about three weeks after the Duke's death.

"Yes, sir:—there will be no more fair weather till the Duke is buried," said he, very solemnly.

I stared at the old man—who kept solemn silence.

"Not till the Duke is buried!" I said. "What makes you think so, my friend? It will be three more weeks before the Duke is buried."

"I don't care for that, sir," said the old man ; "I tell you there will be no more fair weather till he is buried."

And he drew himself up very statelily, and turned to wait on the next comer to the spring. I walked on—thinking about the word "superstition," which any fool can employ as readily as the wisest man; and thinking also of history's multitudinous records, of the storm all round the English coast on the night of Cromwell's death—of the storm that seemed to threaten to tear St. Helena from its foundations in the Atlantic, on the night of Napoleon's death—on the natural convulsions at the death of Julius Cæsar, and others—and saying to myself, "What do I know about it? If there be a Future State, what strange discoveries it may unfold to us! What do we know about the sympathies of nature? How largely they may exist without our knowing it in our present state!"

The funeral of the Great Duke was the most impressively grand spectacle I ever beheld. The morning was fair—the first fair morning for six weeks! The bright sun seemed something new: the luminary seemed to have come out to grace the splendid show; and to do honour to him in death whom the nation had honoured in life. I witnessed the passing of the entire funeral procession, and the greater part of it twice. First, I got a place on the south side of the Green Park, near the Duke of Sutherland's, and saw the procession come up the Mall, from the Horse Guards. Then I crossed the Park, and got a standing-place opposite the Duke of Cambridge's—the house in which Lord Palmerston afterwards lived—and saw the slow march along Piccadilly. The pomp of the "Dead March in Saul" was varied by some of the regimental bands playing "Sicilian Mariners," and others Handel's "Old Hundred-and-Fourth." The varied costume of the English regiments mingled with the kilted Highlanders, and Lancers and Life Guards with the Scotch Greys, rendered the vision picturesque as well as stately.

But it was upon the huge funeral car, and the led charger in front of it, that all eyes gazed most wistfully:—above all, it was upon the crimson-velvet covered coffin, upon the vast pall—not covered by it, borne aloft, on the car, with the white-plumed cocked hat, and the sword and marshal's baton lying upon the coffin, that all gazed most intently. I watched it—I stretched my neck to get the last sight of the car as it passed along Piccadilly, till it was out of sight; and then I thought the great connecting link of our national life was broken: the great actor in the scenes the Peninsula and Waterloo—the conqueror of Napoleon—and the chief name in our home political life for many years,—had disappeared. I seemed to myself to belong now to another generation of men; for my childhood was passed amid the noise about Wellington's battles, and his name and existence seemed stamped on every year of our time.

CHAPTER XXX.
LITERARY AND LECTURING LIFE CONTINUED: W. J. FOX AND
TALFOURD; 1852-1854.

I SAT up the whole night preceding the day of the Great Duke's funeral to finish the writing of what was intended to be a three-volume novel. I remember well tying it up, getting my coffee, and then hurrying off to the Green Park to see the funeral spectacle, with the intent to take the manuscript to a publisher when the sight was over. I had been trying my hand at novel-writing, by intervals, for more than a year. After the appearance and popular reception of Charles Kingsley's "Alton Locke," I had a conversation with Mr. Edward Chapman, of the firm of Chapman and Hall, when he said to me,—

"Why, I should think you could write a Chartist novel, and a successful one. You see Kingsley has succeeded; and you ought to know a deal more about Chartism than he can possibly know."

"Would you publish a Chartist novel if I were to write one?" I asked; for I remembered well how my poor Prison Rhyme had been rejected by this very house, because they were advised "to have nothing to do with the Chartism in it."

"If the novel suits us, we will publish it," replied Mr. Chapman. "Of course we never publish anything unless we think it worth publishing. But I should think you could hardly fail to write a good Chartist novel."

"You mean, then, that you will take such a novel of me, if I can write one?"

"Yes," was the reply; and I said, "Then I'll try."

And try I did; and took my manuscript to Mr. Edward Chapman, and left it in his hands. This was in the latter part of 1851, or in the very early part of 1852. I very soon had a reply. The house could not publish my novel, because their literary adviser—who was, of course, Mr. John Forster of the *Examiner*—advised them not, declaring that "evidently, prose fiction was not Mr. Cooper's *forte*." The reader will be sure that I was not surprised at this—coming from the eternal extinguisher of all my literary hopes, Mr. John Forster of the *Examiner*.

But neither was I discouraged. I had made up my mind to write a novel, or more, that some publisher would take. So I threw aside the rejected manuscript, and commenced an entirely new story, which I finished on the morning of the Great Duke's funeral, and entitled "Alderman Ralph." I took this manuscript to Mr. Edward Chapman, and asked him whether he would look it over and tell me whether he would publish it. He consented to receive it for c-o-n-s-i-d-e-r-a-t-i-o-n. It was rejected, of course. I quite expected that; but was determined that Mr. John Forster should exercise all the power he could to extinguish me. I regarded him as a bitter personification of Whiggery that was natively instinct with hatred of everything like Chartism, living or dead.

My novel was put into the hands of Messrs. Routledge, and they received it, and published it, in 1853. Their reception of "Alderman Ralph" made me resolve to compose another novel; and in this new novel I embodied some part of the story of my former Chartist novel, but burnt the Chartist part of it. I suppose about a third of the new novel was composed of my older one. I gave my new novel into the hands of Messrs. Routledge, having first entitled it "Cain Colton; or, the History of the Great Family Feud of the Uphams and the Downhams." But when they made up their minds to publish it, they determined to style it simply "The Family Feud." They brought out this novel at the beginning of 1855; and gave me £100 for "Alderman Ralph," and the like sum for "The Family Feud."

Not long after the publication of "The Family Feud," I commenced another novel, which I purposed calling "The Wharfedale Beauty." But events put a stop to my novel-writing; and I have never resumed it, and never shall.

I forgot to chronicle one notable event at the beginning of 1852. A person who called himself "Edward Youl" obtained introduction as a literary contributor to William Howitt's journal, and other periodicals, and wound himself into the position of a visitor at Mr. Howitt's, and also at my humble home. At the close of the year 1851, he intimated that he was leaving London; and we saw him no more. But within a few days, first came a letter from Lord Brougham to William Howitt, expressing a hope that himself and Mary Howitt were better, and regretting that he was only able to send them so small a sum on, their late application for money! Mr. Howitt wrote to Lord Brougham to learn the meaning of the strange letter; and soon discovered that Youl had pried into the affairs of his family that he might write a counterfeit letter in William Howitt's name, and so obtain money from Lord Brougham.

My friend W. J. Fox having called on his friend Serjeant Talfourd about this very time, was informed by the Serjeant that his (W. J. Fox's) friend Thomas Cooper had applied for help in his affliction, and he (the Serjeant) was happy in having been able to send Mr. Cooper twenty pounds!

"Affliction!" exclaimed Fox—"what affliction? The man is in jolly good health, I assure you. He called on me only yesterday; and I never saw him look better. There must be some mistake."

"Well: here is his letter, however," said Talfourd; "read it for yourself."

"I don't think this is his writing," said Fox, "though it looks like an imitation. But the tone of the letter is so unlike him. Will you lend me this letter for a day or two? I suppose you have heard of the villainous trick played by a man called Youl"—and he then related what he knew of the counterfeit letter to Lord Brougham.

Serjeant Talfourd consented that Mr. Fox should take the letter, and Mr. Fox soon summoned me to his house in Charlotte Street, Bedford Square. He acted cautiously.

"You were ill when you called on me the other day," said he; "why did you not tell me?"

"No," said I, "I was not ill. What makes you think I was ill?"

"But you have been very ill of late?"

"Nonsense!" said I, and I burst into laughter.

"Have you not been ill, and written to Serjeant Talfourd for money, and received twenty pounds from him?"

"Good God!" I exclaimed, "what do you mean?"—for my laughter had changed to alarm, seeing my good friend's serious look.

"Look at that letter! Is it not your own handwriting?"

"My handwriting? No," I cried, after I had run over a part of the letter with a sense of choking; "why this is another trick of that insidious fiend Youl, that you were talking about the other day!"

"Then you must inform Talfourd instantly; and then see Howitt, and try if you cannot find out where the foul thief has hidden himself, and have him brought to justice."

By the assistance of the police we found that the fellow had quitted London for Liverpool, the police having had their eye upon him for some time,—we little suspecting that we were harbouring a well known and practised thief, who wore different dresses, could put on a wig, wear false eyebrows, and even change his voice, so as to pass for several different persons. Mr. Howitt went off to Liverpool; but the police had there lost sight of him. Lord Brougham thought it would be a waste of money to employ a skilful search for him; and so pursuit was given up.

I went to Serjeant Talfourd's house in Russell Square, to assure him that I had never written a line to him; and to inform him that several expressions in the letter to which my name was appended by a false signature, made me feel sure the letter a& dressed to him was written by the villain who had made himself known to Mr. Howitt and myself as "Edward Youl." Serjeant Talfourd received me with the most solicitous kindness. He cared nothing about the loss of the £20, he said, if I would only accept £20 from him. He feared I was not getting rich by authorship: and he pressed me so hard to take the money, that I consented; and he immediately wrote out a cheque on Coutts' bank, which I found was for £25.

I called again at Mr. Fox's, and showed him the cheque. He threw himself back in his chair and burst into laughter all over—for every part of his body seemed always to partake in his laughter—and exclaimed,—

"Ho—ho—ho! He has done it to ease his conscience! He wanted to ease his conscience in the same substantial way, I have no doubt, when I asked you to call upon him, and you wouldn't."

My friend Mr. Fox was alluding to a confession he had drawn from Serjeant Talfourd. During the discussion in the House of Commons, on the 20th of June, 1848, upon Mr. Hume's motion for the enlargement of the franchise, Mr. Fox pleaded, in behalf of the working classes, that there were men of intelligence among those who had suffered imprisonment for their Chartism—witness, William Lovett, who had written his book on "Chartism" in the gaol, and Thomas Cooper, whose noble poem, "The Purgatory of Suicides," was brought before the reading public chiefly through the recommendation of the honourable gentleman opposite (Mr. Disraeli). This drew Talfourd to his feet to plead *against* Mr. Hume's motion, in order to support the Whig ministry. His friend Mr. Fox had spoken of Thomas Cooper, the Serjeant said; and he did not yield to his friend or to the honourable gentleman opposite in their intelligent admiration of that magnificent poem "The Purgatory of Suicides;" but who was Thomas Cooper? He (the Serjeant) had been one of the counsel for the prosecution of Thomas Cooper, and he felt compelled to state the truth, that Thomas Cooper had delivered harangue upon harangue to the people in the Potteries, and the speeches of Thomas Cooper were followed by deeds of violence.

My friend Fox was indignant at this; and, as he could not speak a second time in the debate, he requested Richard Cobden to get up and reply to Talfourd in my behalf. And illustrious Richard Cobden did reply. He felt surprised, he said, that the learned Serjeant should have spoken of Mr. Cooper in the way that he did; for everyone who knew Mr. Cooper believed he had never advised or counselled violence, and no one regretted the occurrence of the violence alluded to more than did Mr. Cooper himself.

A few days after this scene in the House of Commons, Fox was present at a soiree in Serjeant Talfourd's house in Russell Square. The Serjeant, he thought, seemed to lack the hilarity with which he usually received guests; and during a part of the evening when everybody seemed to be busily engaged in conversation, he observed the Serjeant slily beckon him to a vacant sofa. Fox took his seat by Talfourd's side.

"My friend," said Talfourd, in a low tone, and, as Fox declared, with a most lugubrious face, "I feel so uneasy about the words I uttered in the House of Commons about your friend Cooper. I don't believe he advised the violence committed; I have told you so before, and I wonder that I uttered the words I did. It was a moral obliquity I cannot account for."

"Moral obliquity!" said Fox, bursting into laughter—"I say moral obliquity too. You spoke not for conscience, but for the Ministers. You meant a judgship!" ended Fox, sticking his elbow into Talfourd's chest.

"Don't—my friend—don't!" cried Talfourd; "but I deserve it all. Only, now I want you, if you please, to give my best and heartiest regards to Mr. Cooper, and tell him that I wish to see him here, as soon as ever he can make it convenient to come. I want to see him particularly."

"I'll tell him," said Fox; and indeed he told me all about it from first to last, and urged me to comply with Talfourd's request. But I refused, and did not enter his house till I had to defend myself against Youl's mischief. Talfourd always shook hands with me if he met me in the street, and at different times gave me other sums, which amounted altogether to nearly one hundred pounds. This was very noble conduct on the part of one who had been the leading barrister against me at my long second trial. But Talfourd's unlimited kindness to poor Pemberton ("Pel Verjuice") and others, is so well known, that those who are acquainted with his life will not be surprised at what I have related.

My good friend Charles Kingsley also assures me that my last judge, the Hon. Thomas Erskine, always spoke of me with the utmost kindness, and immediately sent out to buy a book of mine, when he learned that I had written another. I said, a good many chapters ago, that I could never make money. Well, but, thank God! I can make friends. And when sometimes I fall into the vein of musing on the rough usage I have met with now and then, in the course of my pilgrimage,—turning to the better side, I think of the many noble hearts who have shown me sympathy and friendship, and feel that I am as rich as Rothschild.

CHAPTER XXXI.
LITERARY AND LECTURING LIFE CONTINUED: RELIGIOUS
CHANGE: 1852—1856.

IN November, 1852, I commenced a series of Sunday evening lectures on the "History of England," and continued them till the end of May, 1853; then resumed them in October, 1853, and continued them to the beginning of May, 1854; I recommenced them in October, 1854, and concluded them in the middle of April, 1855— making fifty-one lectures; the longest series of lectures I ever ventured on in my life. I had crowds at my audiences, almost to the end of the time. In the intervals of the series I delivered other lectures at the Hall of Science, and, among them, seven on Schools of Painters—Italian, Dutch, Flemish, Spanish, French, and English— pointing out to working men, who listened, the chief features of excellence in our National Gallery, the Bridgewater Gallery, the Dulwich Gallery, the Galleries at Hampton Court, etc.—for I had spent unnumbered hours in each of these Galleries, and my passion for pictures, at one time, was almost as great as my passion for music.

At the John Street Institution I began again to lecture on Sunday evenings at the beginning of May, 1853; and, thenceforward, lectured alternately at that Institution, and at the Hall of Science, to the end of 1853, through the whole year 1854, and to the middle of April, 1855. The lectures on the Schools of Painters were also given at John Street, together with eight lectures on the Life of Napoleon, four on the Life of Wellington, two on the Life of Nelson, and six on Russian History.

Besides the lectures I have mentioned in different chapters, I delivered also, during these years of Sunday evening lecturing at the John Street Institution, the Hall of Science, and the National Hall, Holborn, discourses on the following subjects: the Lives of Luther, Mahommed, Cobbett, Paine, Kosciusko, Raleigh, William Tell, Rienzi, Howard, Oberlin, Neff, Bernard Gilpin, Latimer, Washington, Sir William Jones, Dr. Johnson, Major Cartwright, William Godwin, Louis Philippe, George Fox, Rousseau, Voltaire,

John Knox, Handel, Haydn, Mozart, Mendelssohn, Beethoven, Defoe, William Pitt, Columbus, Sir Isaac Newton, Cortez, Pizarro, Thomas à-Becket, Sir Robert Peel, Sir Charles J. Napier, Wickliffe, Calvin, Sir Thomas More, Wesley, Swedenborg, Pythagoras, and Beau Brummell,—Negro Slavery, Church Establishments, Taxation and the National Debt, Mental Cultivation, the Age of Chivalry, the Middle Ages, Wrongs of Poland, the Gypsies, Athens under Pericles, Conquests of Alexander the Great, Ancient Egypt, Histories of Italy, Switzerland, Hungary, etc., Pio Nono and the Italians, Genius of Pope, Dryden, Scott, Cowper, etc., the Peterloo Massacre and Henry Hunt, Monarchy, Aristocracy, Democracy, Early English Freethinkers, Philosophy of Lord Bacon, Philosophy of Locke, Gulliver's Travels, Astronomy, Geology, Natural History, the Vegetable Kingdom, the Baltic Nations, and many other subjects. The reading which was necessary in order to enable me to deal with such a variety of themes, and to render my lectures attractive to crowds of intelligent hearers, was, of course, very great. At John Street, especially, I was surrounded by scores of the really elite of the working classes: the pianoforte makers of Marylebone, and others. The Library of the British Museum was my great resort for solid reading; while in Westerton's Circulating Library, which was near me, I had ready access to the periodicals and new publications of the day. Except in those devoted days of my youth, I never read so many books as I read in the few years I lived at Knightsbridge.

In September, 1854, I left my beautiful house in Park Row, Knightsbridge, and went to live in the Green Lanes, Stoke Newington. I had not above half the money to pay for rent at my new house, and I had a garden. But I had no longer the grand outlook on Hyde Park; and there were so many associations connected with my seven years' residence in Knightsbridge that I left it with regret. It had been the scene of frequent visits by my kind friends John Elliotson and John Ashburner—two very noble medical men who honoured me with their friendship, often stayed a long hour with me for converse, and insisted on the gratuitous performance of medical attendance either on myself or my dear wife. And there I often gathered round me, in evening hours, young eager aspirants for literary distinction, W. Moy Thomas, and George

Hooper, and Neville Burnard the sculptor—who is a true poet as well,—and some who have passed away.

One night—and only one night—I persuaded my old playmate Thomas Miller to come; and then secured Willie Thom to meet him. We had a merry meeting, for there were a round dozen of us; and as Willie Thom *mellowed* he began to pour out his wondrous words of thought till Miller grew silent, kept the pipe in his mouth (we were all smoking that could smoke)—and fixed his eyes on Thom in amazement, till he broke our with,—"Why the d— don't you *write* such talk? It would bring you gold!" "I dinna think it's e'en worth siller," said Willie, very innocently.

Before I pass on to a new step in my changeful life, let me say that my novel of "The Family Feud" drew a handsome critique in the *Examiner* from Mr. John Forster—for a wonder! I may as well tell how it came about. I went to 5, Cheyne Row, Chelsea, one evening, with the intent of spending a couple of hours with my illustrious friend Thomas Carlyle. But I had not been with him more than half an hour when Mr. John Forster was announced. I met him, as the reader may suppose, without any high degree of pleasure. And although there was no treat on earth I could have desired more than to listen to the interchange of thought between two such intellects as those of Carlyle and John Forster,—I felt inclined, with the remembrance of the past, to "cut my stick!"

And I certainly should have decamped hastily, had it not been for an incident worth mentioning. A loaded truck stopped at the street-door—there was a loud knock—and the maid-servant ran upstairs, breathless, to say that a huge parcel had been brought. Mr. Carlyle seemed all wonder, and muttered, "A huge parcel! *what* huge parcel?—but I'll come down and see." And, somehow or other, we all went down to see—for there was a large wooden case, evidently containing a picture. A hammer and a chisel were soon brought, and I offered to take them, and open the case—but, no! my illustrious friend would open it himself.

"It's doubtless the picture from that old Landor," said he; and he worked away vigorously with his implements till there was revealed a very noble picture indeed, with its fine gilded frame. It was a portrait of David Hume, in full dress—the dress he is said always to have worn when he sat down to write: so strangely were his polished style and his full-dress associated!

"Only think of that old Landor sending me this!" broke out Carlyle again and again, as we all stood gazing on the portrait with admiration.

This incident served to "break the ice" so far that I joined a little in the conversation that followed; and when Mr. Carlyle quitted the room to fetch a book he wanted to show his friend, Mr. John Forster said to me, in a marked tone,—

"You have just had a novel published by Routledge—do you happen to know whether a copy has been sent to the *Examiner*?"

I replied that I did not know; but I would inquire.

"Take care that it is addressed to me, will you?" said Mr. Forster; you understand what I mean? Take care that it is addressed to me, personally and he nodded, and smiled.

"Thank you, sir," said I; "I will address a copy to you, myself "—for I thought I did understand what he meant.

I rose to go soon after, and my illustrious friend, with the perfect kindness he has always shown me, would go with me to the street door to say "good night." So I whispered to him, in the passage, and requested him to strengthen the good intent there seemed to lie in John Forster's mind towards me. Carlyle gave me one of his humorous smiles, and squeezed my hand, as an assurance that I might depend upon him. And so the favourable critique on my "Family Feud" appeared in the *Examiner*.

The reader will observe that, in the beginning of this chapter, I said that my lecturing on Sunday evenings was continued both at the Hall of Science and John Street to the middle of April, 1855. But there it terminated. I had remained in London two whole years— taking no summer lecturing tour, as usual—on purpose to write novels; but I was so little satisfied with my success, although it was not despicable, that I determined on getting into the country once more. There was another stimulant to my wish for change. I felt myself to be in the wrong place at the John Street Institution; the managers of it seemed to have lost their approval of my teaching; and I wished to break off my connection with them. I dare say the wish was mutual; and so no offence was taken when I told them I should leave them.

Before I could make any arrangements for revisiting old friends in the country, my course was utterly changed by an unexpected occurrence. My friend W. J. Fox said to me one day, when I called to borrow a book,

"I had a conversation with Mr. Wyld, of the 'Great Globe,' in the House of Commons the other day about yourself; and he wishes you to call upon him."

I found that the proprietor of the "Great Globe," who was at that time advertising his "Model of the Crimea and Sebastopol," for exhibition, was getting casts of it made, with the purpose of sending them into some of the great towns. The reader will remember that 1855 was the most exciting year of the Crimean War. Mr. Fox said that Mr. Wyld was disposed to remunerate me well, if I would take charge of one of the models and lecture upon it.

I called on Mr. Wyld, and agreed to take charge of a model, to be exhibited first at Birmingham. We did not stay many weeks, however, there. Mr. Wyld next directed me to remove to Manchester; and there I remained many weeks, lecturing thrice and sometimes four times in the day, with the model before me, on the Crimean War. I threw my whole nature into my work, as usual— fought the dashing Light Cavalry charge and the Battle of Inkerman, till the crowds who listened to me almost thought they were in the fight themselves; and, as the war progressed, described the attack on the Redan and the winning of the Malakhoff, with fiery reality— often feeling myself so completely exhausted, after the last evening effort, that I could scarcely crawl to the Clarendon to get my mutton-chop.

In consequence of an offer of £70 being made by a party in Burnley for the exhibition of the model in that town for a fortnight, we left Manchester too soon. The fall of Sebastopol occurred when we reached Burnley; and thus the crowning success we should have had in Manchester was lost. I was wearied with the Model, and so gave up my engagement with Mr. Wyld, and he had it taken back to London. I was invited, however, to lecture on the Crimean War, in several towns, with the aid of pictures on large canvas, sketched by my talented young assistant, Mr. Charles Dyall, now of the Liverpool Walker Institute. After visiting Preston, Haslingden, Wigan, Duckinfield, Staleybridge, Leigh, Bury, Rochdale, Blackburn, Manchester, Tamworth, Congleton, and Burton-on-Trent, I returned to London.

I had left it in the beginning of May, and I returned to it in November, 1855. But the six months' absence had wrought a signal change in me. I felt as if all my old work were done, and yet I knew not how to begin a new work. My heart and mind were deeply uneasy, and I could hardly define the uneasiness. I felt sure my life for years had been wrong. I had taught morals, and taught them strictly; but the questioning within, that would arise, day by day, and hour by hour, made my heart ache. "Why should man be moral? Why cannot he quench the sense of accountability? and why have you not taught your fellowmen that they are answerable to the Divine Moral Governor, and must appear before Him in a future state, and receive their reward or punishment?"

It was not a conviction of the truth of Christianity, of the reality of the Miracles and Resurrection, or of the Divinity of Christ, that had worked the change in me. I was overwhelmed with a sense of guilt in having omitted to teach the right foundation of morals. I had taught morals as a means of securing and in creasing men's happiness here—but had left them without Divine sanctions for a moral life. I had ignored religion in my teaching.

I commenced the year 1856 at the Hall of Science, with the aid of a large map of Europe, and signified that I should occupy the Sunday evenings by lecturing on the various countries, their productions, people, habits and customs. I delivered the first lecture on the 6th of January, "Russia and the Russians;" but on the 13th, when I should have descanted, according to the printed programme, on "Sweden and the Swedes," I could not utter one word. The people told me afterwards that I looked as pale as a ghost, and they wondered what was the matter with me. I could hardly tell myself; but, at length, the heart got vent by words, and I told them I could not lecture on Sweden, but must relieve conscience—for I could suppress conviction no longer. I told them my great feeling of error was that while I had perpetually been insisting on the observance of a moral life, in all my public teachings for some years, I had neglected to teach the right foundation of morals—the existence of the Divine Moral Governor, and the fact that we should have to give up our account to Him, and receive His sentence, in a future state.

I used many more words in telling the people this; and they sat, at first, in breathless silence, listening to me with all their eyes and ears. A few reckless spirits, by degrees, began to whisper to each other, and then to laugh and sneer; and one got up and declared I was insane. A storm followed,—some defending me, and insisting that I should be heard; and others insisting on speaking themselves, and denouncing me as a "renegade," a "turncoat," an "apostate," a "traitor," and I know not what. But as I happened to have fought and won more battles than any or all of these tiny combatants put together, I stood till I won perfect silence and order once more; and then I told them, as some of them deemed me insane, we would try that issue. I then gave them one month for preparation, and challenged them to meet me in that hall on the 10th and 17th of February—with all the sceptics they could muster in the metropolis—to discuss, first, the Argument for the Being of God; secondly, the Argument for a Future State.

The time came, and they had got Robert Cooper, the Atheist, and a band of eager sceptics to do battle with me. Amidst the dense crowd and the almost frantic excitement of some, I maintained my ground. And when it was demanded that I should maintain my challenge also for two Sunday evenings at the John Street Institution, I assured them I was very willing so to do. So on the 2nd and 9th of March the combat came off again, with Mr. Robert Cooper as chief champion on the Atheist side. He challenged me, in conclusion, to a separate discussion with himself. I intimated that I had no confidence in his ability, and declined to meet him. So he announced that he should expose my errors in two or three lectures at John Street. He published these "exposures;" and it will be a sufficient proof of his super-eminent ignorance to record that they contain this idiotic declaration: "Mr. Cooper says that Man has a Moral Nature, and that proves the existence of God as the Moral Governor; and I say that Man has also an Immoral Nature, and that proves the existence of God as an Immoral Governor!"

They had no wish to hear any more from me at John Street; and Mr. Bendall, who rented the Hall of Science, City Road, wished to close the place entirely, until the next autumn, for thorough repair and re-decoration. So I had an enforced silence of six months before me, unless I chose to travel, as I had been wont to do, in the finer part of the year.

But I could not travel. I felt it was the silence that I wanted. Yet how to get bread was the question. Before I went out of London with Mr. Wyld's model, I had asked the publishers of my "Family Feud" and "Alderman Ralph" if they would advance me a little money while I set on to write my purposed "Wharfedale Beauty." But they declared they never did anything of the kind. So if I had tried to go on with the novels, I had no prospect of help. But neither could I have written the novel if I had tried. My mind and heart were too ill at ease.

CHAPTER XXXII.
LECTURING LIFE CONTINUED: CONTRIBUTIONS TO THE "REASONER." 1848—1853.

I AM often, I must confess, extremely mortified by some descriptions of myself given by religious friends. They tell the people, in words spoken, or in print, that I am the "Converted Infidel Lecturer;" that, "after having once done *all in my power to oppose and overthrow the faith of Christ*, I am now," etc. etc. Now I have no taste for being exhibited as a recovered reprobate. It affords me no pleasure, but much sorrow, to remember my scepticism; and there is really a deal of untruth in these announcements. I was never an "Infidel Lecturer," in the common sense of the term. The eight lectures on the "Leben Jesu" of Strauss, delivered at the John Street Institution, and repeated at the Hall of Science, City road, formed the only deliberate and systematic attack I ever made on orthodox Christianity. And even in those lectures I again and again insisted on the perfect and worshipful moral beauty of Christ.

My unbelief, even when I was most completely fascinated with the "Mythical Theory" of Strauss, never made me happy; and so I felt no peculiar pleasure in spreading it. And I never went about the country as an "Infidel Lecturer." With the one exception of Newcastle-on-Tyne, there was not a place out of London where I openly broached sceptical opinions. My subjects were the Poets, History, Politics, and Morals. I saw no good, nor should have felt "at home," in peregrinating the country as an "Infidel Lecturer."

I do not make this statement with the wish to back out of really truthful charges that may be brought against me for past errors. I think I have displayed sufficient moral courage in life to warrant me in saying that I have never shrunk from uttering my conscientious convictions, nor from paying the penalty for uttering them. But I see no reason why a man should suffer real aspersions to be made upon his character, and be silent, when his silence can do no good. God knows, I have sins enough to answer for; but I do not feel covetous of suffering for sins I have not committed.

I have strong reason for believing that charges of "atheism" were made against me by some parties in mistake. It was *Robert* Cooper these parties had heard, and not my humble self. His teaching was avowedly atheistic and materialistic, and unchangeably so. I was guilty, at times, of enunciating sceptical thoughts, incidentally, while lecturing on historical themes at John Street and in the Hall of Science, City Road. But often I did not utter any such thoughts during a whole lecture; and, I repeat, the lectures on Strauss (which were delivered at John Street and repeated at the Hall of Science, and—with the exception of the eighth lecture, which was on the character of Christ—were printed in *Cooper's Journal*) formed the only studied and determined attack I ever made on orthodox Christianity.

I often wrote out from memory a sketch of part or parts of the miscellaneous lectures I delivered in London, and gave them to my friend George Jacob Holyoake, as helps to increase the sale of the *Reasoner*. I call him my friend, for he is my friend still. I never break friendship with sincerity, uprightness, and real nobleness; and these qualities are personified in my friend. If I were to do so in order to please even the religious friends that I love most deeply, I should feel myself to be a contemptible sneak. I gave the sketches I have mentioned to my friend, and he inserted them in the well-known periodical with which he was so long identified. The following passage from one of these sketches has often been quoted against me in a malicious way—although, in one of the lectures I have been in the habit of delivering for these last dozen years and more, I have shown that I was mistaken in both my facts and inferences as to the amount of pain and suffering endured by the animals:—

"The Universe is so beautiful, says the philosophic thinker: it is, in a large degree, so wondrously adapted for happiness, and its main provisions show so triumphantly that the Designer, if there be one, *could* have filled it with happy beings only,—that the very fact of there being adaptations in it for pain and misery makes me doubt that it had any Designer at all. Wisdom raises admiration, until the fruition of its supposed contrivances is perceived to be, in great part, pain and destruction. Then, it is that reason revolts, and exclaims,

'This is not worshipful, for goodness is not supremely united with
it.' We are not here to-night to solve these doubts: we only announce
them, and proclaim that the priests of no religion have ever yet
solved them; nor can they so long as the hawk and the eagle and the
vulture remain the slaughterous sovereigns of the feathered tribes;
so long as the lion remains the king of the forest, and makes the stag
and antelope quake by the thunder of his roar, even when miles
distant; so long as the pike pursues the gliding eel through the
inland waters, and the shark is the tyrant of the ocean; so long as the
spider weaves its web, and drains the blood of the captive fly. It is a
universe—with all its glories of resplendent suns and mighty
systems of millions of stars—with all its grandeur of mountains and
verdure of vallies—with all its luxuries of fruits, and hues and
perfume of flowers—it is a universe of pain and death, of murder
and devastation. Man is in awful keeping with the scenery of the
picture in which he is the chief figure: he becomes the hawk and the
vulture, the lion and the wolf, to his own species." (*Reasoner*, No.
117.)

I add a passage from another lecture—for I wish it to be understood
what I really did say, occasionally and incidentally, in my historical
and miscellaneous lectures.

"Why is the term 'First Cause' ever employed? If no cause could
produce the universe from nothing,—if the universe has ever been in
this 'Cause,' or He in it,—then, to speak of the *Eternal cause* may be
consistent; but the term 'First Cause' is a misnomer, for there was no
first cause. Since matter in its organized forms has consciousness,
from the worm (for it shrinks when touched) to Man, I may not take
upon me to deny that the infinite universe has One All-pervading
Consciousness. I may not deny that; but I do not know it. I may not
deny it, for I behold adaptations—I use not the word 'contrivance,'
because nothing in nature really resembles Man's inventions, since
Man never contrives anything that can produce its like—I behold
adaptations, on every side, wherever I look on nature; and I am
impressed with the presence of Power and Wisdom while
contemplating them, and often with the presence of Beneficence.
But, is it always thus? Watch the beautiful spider which, just at this

season, is so common in your gardens, the *Epeira diadema*, a beautifully marked and diademed insect, that weaves its wheel-formed webs from bough to branch with wondrous nimbleness—for it will renew its web ten times a day if you destroy its work—and with consummate art. What manifest adaptation! But, for what? That web will have a fly entangled in it soon. Hark at its cry of pain, for the diademed fly-butcher runs to drain its blood.

"Glance from an insect to a lion, with its massive bones and powerful sinews, its formidable teeth, and prickles leaning backwards on the tongue with which it can lick off the flesh from a limb, and its gastric juice that will digest flesh and bruised bone, but not grain or grass. Look through all nature, and see murder, pain, destruction, in the midst of life, pleasure, renewal of existence.

"What says the priest, while we take the survey? That he cannot explain why there is pain in the universe, except by the fable of Man's fall from primeval innocence; and that the continuance of pain is now a part of God's government, and we must bow and adore where we cannot understand. Nay, priest, but I will not. How can my heart worship Power, or even Wisdom, if it be not conjoined with Goodness? I tell him, as in my humble prison-song,—

'I cannot worship what I cannot love.'

Nay, more : if even *thy* Deity exists, I cannot conceive that He would do otherwise than reject my worship, were I to tender it to Him without love. He could not look for an acknowledgment from any of His intelligent creatures that the production of pain, by however wondrous a display of skill, was worshipful. Pay Him worship for beneficence, if thou wilt, priest, and that wherever it is found; but do not expect me to offer it wherever I discern adaptations in nature for the production of pain." (*Reasoner*, vol. iii., page 523.)

The erroneous thinking in these extracts will be discerned even by sceptics who are acquainted with Combe's "Constitution of Man." There are no "adaptations in nature for the production of pain" *for the sake of pain*—to speak plain English. Beneficence is traceable in all such adaptations: they are means for preserving happy life, and often for preserving life itself. Better acquaintance with the facts of zoology convince me that there is a widely-prevailing mistake in people's minds as to the amount of pain and suffering experienced by the lower animals. Even men of considerable reading do not come at the real truth on these subjects; but suffer their judgments to be misled by their mere sensibilities, as I did for a long time.

"But what did you call yourself during the twelve years you were sceptical?" some may ask: "you evidently object to being classed as an atheist." Yes: because I never dared to say "There is no God," nor could I ever reach such a conclusive thought. Indeed, I never remained long in any one state of belief or unbelief on the subject of the Divine existence during my sceptical time. Perhaps I was near Pantheism, sometimes; while at other times I was a Theist. I feel *now* that I was indeed "without hope and without God in the world," for I had ceased to seek communion with Him, and to love Him; but I did not sink into blank atheism and glory in it, as some did who taught at John Street and the Hall of Science. The great error was in mixing myself up with such teaching. I ought to have known better; but, like others, I feel, the older I grow, what a blunderer I have been. I never could learn to "take care of my reputation," like some people; and I doubt if I could learn to do so, even if I could enter on life anew.

I have said that I never ceased to worship the moral beauty of Christ; and this was a frequent theme with me, in my sceptical time—yet, as I became more and more imbued with the spirit of Strauss, the more I strove to make it out that there was nothing above humanity in Christ's excellence. The following extract will make my meaning more plain:

"Do you ask me whether this elevated teaching does not prove the supernatural mission of Christ? I answer, No. It is but the natural revelation of the human heart drawn from its deepest fountains. Christ needed no inspiration, in the priestly sense of that word. If he were inspired, so was Confucius, who taught the great precept—'Do unto others as ye would they should do unto you,' 500 years before

Christ. But neither was that an inspired discovery of the Chinese sage. The heart had uttered it, and, doubtless, thousands of tongues had proclaimed it, ages before Confucius lived. If Christ were inspired, so was Socrates; so was Homer and Eschylus and Sophocles; so was Shakspeare and Milton; and all who have astonished and elevated the human mind by the great products of poetry. If Christ were inspired, so was Phidias and Canova, so was Raphael and Michael Angelo, so was Handel and Mozart, so was Copernicus and Galileo and Newton, so was Bacon and Locke, so was Davy and Watt, so were all who have revealed to humankind the wonders of art and music, of philosophy and science. Nature produces her own great children, in her own time; and she endows them for their mission, and impels them to its fulfilment, whatever may be their apparent disadvantages of circumstance.

"Was it more wonderful that that young man of Nazareth, that despised carpenter's son, should be born with an organisation to discern moral beauty, and be girt up to proclaim love, and pity, and mercy, and goodness, even to the death—than that Shakspeare, with all his capacity for fathoming and depicting the human heart, and for universal creation, should be born in a woolstapler's shop? Perish the false, idolatrous, and enslaving forms in which Priestcraft clothes that glorious Galilean Peasant! Let him stand forth in his simple moral beauty; and he is more worshipful than in all his mythical and fabulous garniture! Stripped of the tinselled rags of miracle and imaginary godship, the heart cleaves to him, loves him with intensity, as the noblest of human brothers, as the One who has shown most loftily what it is that Man may become in moral perfectibility, and how he may learn to love goodness, and triumph over the passions of hatred and revenge, until he can expire breathing out forgiveness, even for his murderers!" (*Reasoner*, vol. iii., page 507.)

I give another extract from one of my John Street lectures, of the same tendency:—

"The doctrine of Equal Rights was often enunciated by Christ; but he could not show that knowledge would lead to their acquirement.

His 'Heavenly Father' had commissioned him to introduce the 'Kingdom of Heaven.' He, the 'Son of Man' would 'come in the clouds of heaven, clothed with glory and surrounded with his holy angels, to bring it. His glorious worship of goodness led him to wish that the 'kingdom of heaven' should be established on earth; his highly religious mind could not disrobe itself of the national belief entirely, and he personified the goodness he worshipped as the 'Jehovah,' though with widely different attributes to the ancient Jehovah; and taught that the Universal Father, as He became under Christ's teaching, would institute the Universal Brotherhood.

"Christ taught no sciences. How, where, when, was he to learn them? Christ inculcated no education, in any such sense of the word as we accept it. He never recommended the cultivation of the powers of the mind, either to his disciples, or to the multitude. How was it possible? Education, in his country and time, consisted in a knowledge of the Mosaic law, the precepts of the Rabbis, and the foolish traditions and silly ceremonies of the Doctors. His grand nature soared above the ridiculous teachings of the latter, it shrank from the fierceness and cruelty of the first; and it distinguished and selected what was excellent in either the Rabbinical precepts, or those of the older scriptures.

"Christ saw the world was wrong. He thought to right it at once— believing his own glorious enthusiasm. But the experience of eighteen hundred years has proved to us that his goodness was more truthful than his enthusiasm. Dethrone Christ? Dost thou say, priest, that I am seeking to dethrone him? I tell thee, my worship of him is as ardent as thine. I tell thee that thou hast crucified him afresh— thou and thy dark tribe—these seventeen hundred years; but that science will prepare his throne; that his 'kingdom of heaven' was no dream, save in the mode of its realisation; but that universal knowledge will bring it. Not as Millenarian fanatics tell: not as orthodox teachers prophesy. I speak of no 'coming in the flesh,' or 'coming in the clouds, but of the universal recognition of the great law of goodness and brotherhood—of the reverence and love of the name of that lowly young man of Nazareth as the highest of moral teachers—and, above all, as the grandest example of the triumph of our moral nature, the common nature of man." (*Reasoner*, vol. iii., pp. 547—549.)

While thus intent on convincing myself and others that there was nothing above humanity in the moral perfection of Christ, and that science and mental progress would eventually bring in the reign of such moral perfection, I did not perfectly succeed in convincing myself. Every fresh glance at the pure spirituality of the New Testament teaching threw me back; and so I had to fence with these difficulties again and again, by endeavouring to show that the Pauline teaching was super-induced on Christ's teaching, and was impracticable. How hardly I battled to establish this point will be seen in the following extract from another John Street Lecture—though I believe the thoughts were first uttered in my friend Fox's pulpit, during the time he was absent from London securing his election for Oldham:—

"How the simple teaching of Jesus of Nazareth—this yearning of a large and grand and beautiful nature—became mixed up, almost at the onset, with superstitious imaginings—the natural consequence of its reception amidst ignorance, old creeds, oriental tendencies—I need not repeat. The creed was most simple, and but very few outward observances were inculcated in the outset. The first Christians were chiefly remarkable for their refusal to be soldiers, for their contempt of wealth and show, and for the firmness with which they underwent martyrdom for their faith, whereby the admiration of the polytheists was deeply excited, and, not seldom, their conversion was secured, The idea which Pliny himself, in the letter to Trajan, gives us of Christianity at the end of the first century, is borne out by the language of the Epistles in the New Testament. Being not conformed to this world—praying without ceasing—counting the present life nothing, but the future, on which they might enter at any unlooked-for moment, everything,—*that* is the true Apostolic Christianity: the Christianity of the Epistles. In late times, such deeply sincere, enthusiastic, and self-sacrificing men as Wesley and Whitfield, Brainerd and Swartz and Eliot, Fletcher and Bramwell, have been exemplars of this Apostolic Christianity.

"This religion of Paul, however, is more ascetic and mortifying, and less rational, than the religion inculcated by Jesus himself, so far as my humble investigation of the subject enables me to form a conclusion. Christ frequently rebukes the narrow spirit of asceticism; and the ever-fertile burthen of his teaching is goodness and mercy, love and brotherhood. Yet his own views of a 'kingdom of heaven,' here, argue great unacquaintance with the laws of nature. Had Jesus understood those laws, he would not have looked for the immediate institution of that 'kingdom of heaven' upon earth (for such were his views in the beginning of his ministry) nor, had Paul and the Apostles understood those laws, would they have inculcated the ascetic precepts which abound in the Epistles.

"Where would civilisation have been, if all had become Christians after the model of these precepts? Where painting, music, poetry, statuary, architecture? Where the invention of arts, where the discoveries of science and adventure? Where commerce, manufactures, machinery, and the convenience of food and clothing? What, if Shakspeare had 'prayed without ceasing,' should we have had his Macbeth and Lear and Othello? What, if Michael Angelo and Wren had thought of nothing but of being 'not conformed to this world,' and of being 'transformed by the renewing of their minds,' would the magnificent domes of St. Peter's and St. Paul's ever have attracted the wonder-stricken gaze of men, in Rome or London?

> 'Nothing is worth a thought beneath,
> But how I may escape the death
> That never, never dies.'

is a modern embodiment of Apostolic religious thought. Where would have been the discoveries of Cook, or the inventions of Watt and Arkwright, if they had been ascetics after this model? To what a state the world would have been reduced by an entire devotion to such a religion, may be seen in the examples of Simeon Stylites and many of the early Christian eremites, while the melancholy diaries of. Halyburton, and other modern pietists, confirm the truth that ascetic religion would cover the world with a funeral pall, and shut up the human mind in the gloom of the sepulchre." (*Reasoner*, vol. v., pp. 262-3:)

Thus I thought and spoke and wrote; but not all the thinking and speaking and writing could destroy the latent wish that rapt communion with God were again mine. I might call it "asceticism," and give it other hard names; but the remembrance of it would return, in spite of all the corruption of the heart and the wandering of the mind to which I had yielded.

I have again mentioned the name of my friend W. J. Fox, and will now say my last words about him. He was as kind and tender to me as a father; and I loved him. I saw but little of him in his closing years, being so much out of London after 1857. He died in June, 1864, while I was lecturing in Staffordshire. I should have left my work to attend his funeral, if I had been able to do so; but I was not. The difference in our religious views had become very great; but I should have paid the tribute of heartfelt regard to his memory, had it been in my power.

CHAPTER XXXIII.
ENTRANCE ON THE RIGHT LIFE: THE LIFE OF DUTY.
1856—1872.

IMMEDIATELY after I had obeyed conscience, and told the people I had been in the habit of teaching that I had been wrong, I determined to open my mind fully to my large-hearted friend Charles Kingsley. He showed the fervent sympathy of a brother. We began a correspondence which extended over many months: in fact, over more than a year. I told him every doubt and described every hope I had; and he counselled, instructed, and strengthened me to the end.

But, as I said before, bread was to be earned, and where was it to come from? I had many friends ready to help, and they did help nobly; but a man cannot live honourably in idleness, and I asked on all sides for some employment. So my friend the Rev. F. D. Maurice, and three barrister friends, Mr. Hughes, Mr. Ludlow, and Mr. Furnivall, after conferring with my now Right Honourable friend W. E. Forster, besought Mr. W. F. Cowper, M.P., President of the Board of Health, to find me some employment under that Governmental Department.

Mr. Cowper (now Lord Mount-Temple) named a time for me to wait on him, and I went. He said he wished much that he could offer me anything better but the only thing he could offer me was that I became a copyist of letters, etc., at a low remuneration: he thought it was seventy words for a penny. I told him I would take the employ, if it were seventy words for a halfpenny. So I went down into the *cellar* of the Board of Health—for that is the truest name for the room; and there I was almost a daily worker, every week for ninety-seven weeks—not finally quitting my post till the end of May, 1858.

This humble post brought me the hearty and valuable friendship of another man of genius,—Mr. Tom Taylor, who was Secretary of the Board—which is now become the "Local Government Board." It brought me, too, the kind and friendly attention of the Under

Secretary, Mr. Campbell, cousin of the Duke of Argyll, and son of Campbell of Islay.

I am glad, too, that I served in that *cellar* of the Board of Health, because I had there to copy out the letters of several hundred eminent medical men, and otherwise humbly assist Mr. Simon, the highly intelligent Physician to the Privy Council, in the completion of his masterly "Report on Vaccination." The letters were from the most eminent foreign as well as British physicians and surgeons. The reading of them, as well as of all other papers I could reach on the subject, left in my mind a most ineffaceable conviction that Jenner's discovery was a real blessing to mankind; and that the scourge by which I suffered so much when a child, and by which hundreds are now suffering, might be swept out of existence, if all children were duly and efficiently vaccinated.

My enforced silence of six months, and all its inner experiences, found me a still more completely changed man when September came, and I applied to Mr. Bendall to know if he would let me recommence my Sunday evening lectures at the Hall of Science, and teach what I pleased. He granted me leave to occupy his room as I chose. So I re-commenced, and simply taught Theism—for I had not advanced farther yet in positive conviction.

I confess I am very incredulous respecting sudden conversions from the habitual scepticism of years. I had been twelve years a sceptic; and it was not until fully two years had been devoted to hard reading and thinking that I could conscientiously and truly say, "I am again a Christian"—even nominally. The deep conviction which first arose within me, that I had been very guilty, as a public teacher, in not courageously and faithfully presenting the great truth of God's existence as the Moral Governor before men, gradually merged into the deeper and more distressful conviction of my own personal life of sin: the remembrance that I—I myself—had been living without God, and without teaching men the worship of the God that I had loved in my early manhood, and Who had then given me to feel His love, day by day, and hour by hour.

My conviction of personal sin deepened to such a degree, in the hours of reflection during the silent six months, that I dared not pray; and my wife said I never smiled for those six months. I told my dear friend Dr. Jobson, who was ever trying to strengthen and help me, that I believed God would shut me up in judicial darkness; that He would never suffer me to live in the "light of His countenance" again, as a penalty for my great sin in deserting Him because I thought men ill-used me.

"No, no!" said my dear friend; "I don't believe it. God will bring you to the light yet, and fill your soul with it!"

I told my friend Charles Kingsley, in our correspondence, that while I diligently read "Bridgewater Treatises," and all the other books with which he furnished me, as a means of beginning to teach sceptics the truth from the very foundation, that the foundations themselves seemed to glide from under my feet; I had to struggle against my own new and tormenting doubts about God's existence, and feared I should be at last overwhelmed with darkness and confusion of mind.

"No, no!" said my faithful and intelligent friend, you will get out of all doubt in time. When you feel you are in the deepest and gloomiest doubt, pray the prayer of desperation; cry out,—'Lord, if Thou dost exist, let me know that Thou dost exist! Guide my mind, by a way that I know not, into Thy truth!' and God will deliver you."

But I dared not pray, as I said before. This bondage of dumbness of spirit was suddenly broken, one morning, as I awoke, by the words running through my mind that had been familiar to me when I was a Bluecoat boy, and stood in the aisle of Gainsborough church,—"Almighty and most merciful Father, I have erred and strayed from Thy ways like a lost sheep; I have followed too much the devices and desires of my own heart; I have offended against Thy holy laws,"—and it went on to the end.

"The words running through my mind," did I say? Oh, was it not the Holy Spirit Himself, in ineffable condescension and love, leading my mind by a way that I knew not? The words came again, as I awoke, morning after morning, till at last I felt I could pray in my own words. I had no more awful gloom of mind; but I was far yet from getting back to Christ, and receiving Him as my Saviour.

I have said that, at the end of my six months' silence, I began to teach Theism to sceptics in the Hall of Science. My subjects were,—"The Design Argument substantiated from the Sciences," and I occupied an hour each Sunday night, for many weeks, with this theme, illustrating it from Natural History, (Man—the Mammalia,—the Birds,—the Fishes, etc.,) from Chemistry, Geology, Light, etc. After my hour's lecture, the discussion began; each speaker being allowed ten minutes, and I ten minutes in reply, if necessary. The absurd wrangling and ignorance of some disputants were very wearisome, and the fierceness and intolerance of others were still more distressing. I sometimes went home at eleven o'clock at night from these discussions, so completely worn down and enfevered that I thought I would give up my task. But I no sooner got on my knees than I felt I dared not. I was bound to go on, and atone for my errors, if it were possible; and I should be a guilty coward to desert that championship for the truth I had taken upon myself from a sense of bounden duty.

I advanced to treat the Moral Government of God more exhaustively, my subjects being "Man's Moral Nature," "Pain, Prey, and Physical Suffering," "Moral Evil," "The Soul and Future State," "Materialism and the Spiritual Nature of Man," "Evidence and Responsibility"—and, at last, I ventured on "Prayer a Duty." In the very next lecture I announced a series of discourses on the "Evidences of Christianity." I felt much hesitation in doing this. My mind was not fully clear—my reason and understanding were not fully settled on the order of the "Evidences;" but my heart wanted Christ, and I felt, if I did my work imperfectly, still I was bound to do it.

For months I placed the Christian Evidences before my audiences in every possible form—I mean the external evidence from history, miracles, etc.,—and then I advanced to doctrines, the Atonement,

Faith, Repentance, etc. The opposition became most bitter when I had advanced so far; and it seemed that a considerable number of sceptics entered into a new scheme: they made every effort to dissuade people from coming to hear me, so that I often lectured to a comparative few. But I persevered, and defeated their scheme. At their demand I also took up Paine's "Age of Reason," and in five lectures showed them its errors, while they as stoutly defended it. Next I took up Robert Taylor's "Diegesis," and dealt with it in like manner.

At the beginning of September, 1857, I formed another newspaper engagement. It was to furnish a series of articles—similar to those I had written for Douglas Jerrold's newspaper on the "Condition of the People"—to a weekly paper called *The People*, the property of a well-known Christian philanthropist, John Henderson, Esq., of Park. My engagement lasted only nine months; and the paper itself did not continue long, though it was said Mr. Henderson spent several thousands in trying to establish it.

With the beginning of 1858, I began to receive very urgent requests from old friends, in the country, that I would come out of London and talk to them on my new subjects. So I went and lectured at Sheffield, and York, and Norwich; and soon found I should be compelled to go to other places—nay, the duty of giving up my entire life and time to the work of lecturing on the "Evidences," and in every part of the kingdom, began to dawn upon me. This conviction was deepened into a resolution by an act of most gracious Providence that I must describe.

I had engaged to deliver six lectures on the Evidences, in St. George's Hall, Bradford Yorkshire; and was to be the guest, for the week, of my beloved friend Dr. Jobson, who was then stationed at Bradford, but had come over to London on a preaching visit. On Saturday, the 8th of May, my friend called on me and said,—

"I have to be at Brixton to-morrow; and I fear I shall be in danger of being late on Monday morning. So be sure to get to the Euston

Square Station in good time yourself, and take your place in a carriage, and beckon me as I come up, that we may travel together."

So on Monday morning, the 10th May, 1858,—a day I trust I shall remember, and shall thank God for His especial mercy as long as I live and the 10th of May returns,—I got early to the Euston Square Station and took my ticket. I opened a door in the second carriage behind the engine and tender; and was about to step into it, when a porter, who was an utter stranger to me, took hold of my portmanteau, and said,

"Don't go in there, sir! go a little lower down."

I yielded to the man, but felt a little surprised at his motion. I had just put my portmanteau under the seat of the carriage, lower down, and was looking out for my friend Dr. Jobson, when I saw him about to get into the very carriage I had left. I shouted to him and beckoned him, and he came and got into the same carriage with me, but expressed his surprise when I told him how the porter had particularly led me to enter it.

It was a first-class carriage, and soon four persons, whom we easily discovered to be barristers going to the Liverpool Assizes, joined us in it. But before we started, a barrister (who was killed between two and three hours after) came and called one of our companions out— as it proved afterwards, to have his leg broken. It was a short express train, and we went on rapidly but steadily till we came within about a mile of Nuneaton. There was now a bend in the line, and a bridge over the bend, so that neither engine-driver or guard could see any danger till they passed from under the bridge.

A cow had had her calf taken from her, and, becoming unruly, got upon the line and was driven off several times. But now she could not be driven off. A man, who had been trying to drive her off, stood in a field close to the railway line and waved a red flag. The guard put on the drag, which was afterwards said to be an error, for that the express train unchecked would have crushed the cow to death and passed on without the human passengers suffering any harm. And the cow was crushed to death; but the shock and check put upon our motion broke the coupling chain whereby the carriages were fastened to the engine and tender. The engine and tender went on—but the carriages rebounded back; and first one went off the line and rolled over the ten feet of descent, then a second, a third, and a fourth. Next, the coupling chain of ours, the fifth carriage, was broken, and the whole carriage of three compartments was removed from one line of rails to the other, as if supernatural beings had lifted it up, and placed it down again!

Both the lines of rails were so much broken that for some hours the trains that came up, either way, had to disgorge their passengers, reload, and return the way they came. Very soon there were hundreds of persons on the spot; they seemed to come across the country almost flying, in gigs, on horseback, and on foot.

The glass was broken in our carriage, but not a hair of the head of any person in it was injured. In the other carriages there was not a passenger without injury of some kind, and three were killed. The whole action had been so sudden, and seemed so stupefying, that I did not feel all the awful sense of deliverance I ought to have felt, till I observed a circle of persons gathered in a field, and was told the dead were in their midst. I went to gaze, and as I saw the three figures in their clothes and boots, lying side by side, with a cloth covering their faces, I said to myself,—

"I and my friend might have been two of these three; but Thou, Lord God, hast preserved us! Oh, take my life which Thou hast graciously kept, and let it be devoted to Thee. I have again entered Thy service; let me never more leave it, but live only to spread Thy truth!"

It was, indeed, a vow to consecrate my future life to God's service and God's work; to have no more fervours or passions diverting me from it; but to perform His work only. I have kept my vow feebly; but, thank God, I have kept it! I told my dear friend, before I left Bradford, that I should leave my employ at the Board of Health, should return to the pulpit and preach every Sunday, and should peregrinate the whole land to lecture on the Evidences of Natural and Revealed Religion.

At the end of May, resigning my situation at the Board of Health, and bidding farewell to the Hall of Science, I left London, my dear wife remaining behind. I did not return home till the end of August, and then only for one week; I then went out again, and did not return till January, 1859; and immediately went out again, and did not return till November, 1859. My dear wife felt it like widowhood to be thus deserted; but she did not begin to travel with me till January, 1861. From that time to the present she has been often my winter companion, and has always been with me in summer. And through deep love of the pursuit, as well as to preserve health, we have taken advantage of our wide wanderings over England, Scotland, and Wales, to gather the darling wild-flowers everywhere. My dear wife has preserved a fine collection of flowers; and I have kept a register of our gatherings that occupies several volumes.

I have said that I vowed to have no more fervours or passions diverting me from what I considered to be God's work. And if our study of Botany had tended to divert me from my great life-duty I would not have pursued it. I gave up the thought of advancing in the knowledge of languages, when I entered on my present work; and except that I make my Greek Testament, as much as possible, my daily companion, I have seldom read a page in any other language than my own since that 10th of May, 1858. And my reading, even of English, has been very much restricted. Of course I read every book I can get hold of that proclaims the new tendencies of scepticism—its Darwinism, and dream about "Evolution," and other dreams—for I strive to show the error of these new tendencies; but I have now little time, indeed, for general reading.

I was much beset by solicitations to join religious societies when I began again to preach, which I did on the first Sunday in June, 1858, at Sheffield. But I could not easily make up my mind. I felt my old love for Methodism return; but I could not bring my mind to return to the old body of Methodists. I might have joined the United Free Methodists, for I had many good friends among them; but I knew it would lastingly grieve my dear and faithful friend Dr. Jobson, and I could not be guilty of such ingratitude towards him as to grieve him.

If I could conscientiously have connected myself with the Established Church, I should at once have accepted the kind and generous offer of a venerable clergyman—Dr. Hook, now Dean of Chichester, but at that time Vicar of Leeds. I had been describing to him the real good which had been done in Sheffield by my friend Dr. Sale, the vicar, through the agency of a band of Scripture-readers—some of them Methodist local preachers—which Dr. Sale had organised.

"Will you come and live at Leeds?" said Dr. Hook to me; "will you come and select me just such a band of Scripture-readers, and be yourself their captain? I will make it worth your acceptance if you will fill such a post. And I also promise you that you shall be free to go out, often, on the great errand that you believe to be your duty. Do not say 'No,'—consider of it."

The nobleness of the work, and the noble tray in which the offer was made, moved me much; but I felt compelled to decide against it.

One day a few sensible questions were put to me, at a tea-table in Barnsley, by the very intelligent wife of a Baptist minister. I could not answer them; and reflection soon made me a Baptist in conviction, and on Whit Sunday, 1859, my old and dear friend Joseph Foulkes Winks immersed me in baptism in Friar Lane Chapel, Leicester. Dr. Price, the well-known Baptist minister of Aberdare, was present at the performance of the rite, and assisted in the celebration of the Lord's Supper in the evening. I forthwith joined the General Baptists; not with the intent to confine myself to preaching and lecturing in the chapels of any one particular body of Evangelical Christians, or of being directed by any, as to how, and when, and where I should do my work of duty; but to make the full, outward sign which I think every true Christian man is bound to make, that he belongs to Christ's Church.

267

One esteemed Christian friend thought a committee had better be formed to direct my motions, and secure me support, when I commenced my present itinerant work in 1858; but I begged of him to give up the thought. I felt it was far better for me to have nothing to do with committees, but to go forth with God only as my director, and with the belief that I was simply performing the duty to which. He had summoned me. I could not doubt that He would provide for me.

CHAPTER XXXIV.
RENEWED PREACHER-LIFE; AND LIFE AS A LECTURER ON
RELIGIOUS EVIDENCE. 1858—1866.

FROM June, 1858, to the month of November, 1866, I kept on, without stoppage, at my new work, preaching usually thrice on Sundays, and lecturing on the Evidences of Natural and Revealed Religion, usually every night of the week. In addition to the lectures I delivered in 1858 at Sheffield, Norwich, York, Bradford, Leeds, Sunderland, North and South Shields, Newcastle-on-Tyne, Hexham, Stockton-on-Tees, the Hartlepools, Nottingham, the Staffordshire Potteries, Barnsley, Halifax, Keighley, Darlington, Leicester, Bilston, Cardiff, Devonport, and Exeter, I entered Cornwall for the first time, and preached and lectured at Falmouth, Penryn, Penzance, Redruth, and Truro.

During the year 1858, I also held public discussions with George Jacob Holyoake: four nights at Norwich, five nights at York, and one at Nottingham. My friend was gentle and temperate, conscientious and straightforward. I could not convince him, and he could not convince me; nor did the discussions disturb our friendship and mutual regard. I had discussions in after-years with big and little champions of Atheism; but their proceedings seemed to me crooked and unprincipled, and I shall therefore pass them by without recording even their names. My clear conviction is, that public discussions on the Evidences of Christianity never do any good, but often do great harm. The sceptical champion, and his friends too, generally come up to the encounter to win, by fair means or foul: they are in too great a heat to hear the truth; it cannot get any fair entrance into their minds. On the other hand, young fresh minds, unused to these inquiries, are often caught by the new and startling words they hear, and become doubters; perhaps, eventually, confirmed unbelievers.

For the first few years, I was also in the habit, at the end of almost every lecture, of inviting sceptical hearers, if any were present, to ask questions, or make observations in the way of objection, if they had any. But I gave up this habit, as well as the practice of public discussion; for I found that the persons who rose to ask questions were often so much disposed to turn the meeting into a scene of disturbance and bad feeling, that they destroyed the good I had been endeavouring to effect.

One week of excitement, at the end of January, 1859, often comes to my memory. I spent it at Northampton, where I had lectured in the old Chartist times; and where the swarms of shoemakers were known to be sceptical, and were eager for the fray. I preached there on the Sunday, and they came in crowds far too great for the chapel to hold them. I lectured on the six nights following, and they rose up and disputed; but, with very slight exceptions, they manifested so much good-humour and regard for their old democratic champion, that I felt something like regret because I could not stay longer among them. In this year, 1859, I revisited Manchester, Birmingham, and Coventry; was largely employed in Yorkshire, Lancashire, and Staffordshire; and lectured and preached in various town of Essex, Norfolk, Huntingdon, Cambridge, Lincoln, Derby, Cheshire, Durham, and Northumberland.

I ventured into Scotland in 1860, as a preacher and lecturer on the "Evidences;" and was so well received by ministers and people at Edinburgh, Glasgow, Aberdeen, Dundee, Paisley, Stirling, and many smaller towns, that I very heartily promised to renew my visit. In this year, 1860, I revisited Bristol, Cheltenham, Leamington, Worcester, Chatham, Sheerness, Macclesfield, and Carlisle,—preached and lectured for the first time at Kendal,—was extensively employed again in Lancashire, Yorkshire, and Devonshire,—and performed my work of duty in numerous towns of Derbyshire, Nottinghamshire, Leicestershire, Lincolnshire, and Norfolk.

In the earlier part of the year 1861, I revisited Northampton and Bristol, and had a week of lecturing in Liverpool, and afterwards revisited towns, and performed my work in towns I had not before visited, in the counties of Warwick, Worcester, Bedford, Stafford, Derby, Leicester, Nottingham, Lancaster, York, Durham, and Northumberland. In the middle of August, 1861, I again entered

Scotland, and remained in it till the 7th of January, 1863—a period of one year and nearly five months. During this period, I preached and lectured in nearly every town in Scotland which has a population of over two or three thousand. I was twice through the whole length of the country, from the Border to Inverness; and revisited some of the principal towns several times over. Almost everywhere, ministers of every denomination received me with welcome, and many with great kindness, while the people came readily to hear, and listened with eagerness. The hearty welcome I received rendered me willing to prolong my stay among the grandeur of its mountains, the music of its rivers, and the association of its great names; and I am glad that the time is near when, if spared by the providence of God, I am to return to dear auld Scotland.

Re-entering dear old England in January, 1863, I lectured during that year at Lancaster, Preston, Manchester, arid Shrewsbury; revisited some towns in Worcestershire and Staffordshire; and was afterwards busily employed in Durham, Northumberland, Yorkshire, Lincolnshire, Norfolk, Suffolk, Bedfordshire, and Hertfordshire. The months of November and December, 1863, together with January and parts of February and March, 1864, I devoted to preaching and lecturing in London.

In the year 1864, I lectured and preached in several parts of Kent, Hertfordshire, Bedfordshire, Northamptonshire, Warwickshire, Leicestershire, and Staffordshire, and again devoted a week to the important town of Birmingham. July and half of August were devoted to the principal towns of South Wales. I saw beautiful Tintern on leaving the principality, and after lecturing at Gloucester and ancient Tewkesbury, made my way across the kingdom, and spent September in Essex and Suffolk. The months of October, November, and December, 1864, I devoted entirely to London, with the exception of one week, which I spent most delightfully in preaching, lecturing, and seeing the sights in classic Oxford.

The months of January, February, and March, 1865, were devoted almost entirely to London; and during these months I delivered a series of eight Lectures on the Evidences of Christianity to the students of Mr. Spurgeon's College. I never enjoyed my work more in my life; and I believe the enjoyment of the students was as great as my own. I wish I could more often be employed in a similar way. Telling the "Evidences" to a crowd of young men who will have to preach Christ to thousands, seems like doing several years' work in an hour. Quitting London in April, I went on to Brighton, and preached and lectured in the chapel of my beloved friend Paxton Hood. The remainder of this year was spent, very delightfully, in itinerating through all the beautiful south of England, and in preaching and lecturing in nearly all the towns of any importance in Kent, Sussex, Hampshire and the Isle of Wight, Dorsetshire, Devonshire, and Cornwall.

I commenced the year 1866 in the charming region of Devonshire; and afterwards preached and lectured in Salisbury and many of the Wiltshire towns; revisited Portsmouth, Southampton, and the Isle of Wight, and had a week's work in ancient Winchester; spent many weeks in making a thorough working tour through the pleasant county of Somerset, seeing ancient Glastonbury, Wells, and the Cheddar rocks; went over to the Channel Islands, and had eighteen days' preaching and lecturing in Jersey and Guernsey; spent one week at Bath, another at Windsor, and ten days at Woolwich, and then went on into Kent, with the intent to finish my year's work in that county—though I had had symptoms of illness, now and then, for several weeks.

At last, I broke down seriously. And, perhaps, none will wonder that I broke down so soon, but rather that I did not break down sooner, when it is considered that, within these eight years and a half, I had preached 1,169 times and lectured 2,204 times—in other words, I had delivered 3,373 discourses; had visited every county of England, and many counties of Scotland and Wales, and also the Channel Islands, for the fulfilment of what I felt to be my work of duty; had preached or lectured in every considerable town in Great Britain, and in some of them many times; had travelled unreckonable hundreds—I may say, thousands—of miles; and had kept up a voluminous correspondence with an ever increasing number of friends and acquaintances.

In November, 1866, my dear wife, who travelled with me constantly for nearly six years, feeling that she could no longer sustain exposure to the weather in winter, left me to take refuge with her sister in Sheffield—for we had entirely broken up our home in 1861, and have never had one since. So when I fell seriously ill at Ramsgate, at the end of the month just mentioned, I was alone. Nor could I remove till Christmas, when I crept on to the house of an old favourite scholar at Croydon; but could not join my wife at Sheffield till February, 1867.

I made several attempts to preach, but it was only to expose myself to renewed suffering; and it was seven months from the time of my falling ill at Ramsgate before I could get back to my work again. The brain would not let me sleep, and the heart threatened to stop; and frequently, for hours together, I expected life would cease the next moment. Providentially, I had the kind and gratuitous help of an excellent physician, Mr. Walford of Ramsgate, when I had the first seizure, or I might never have recovered at all. The nervous horrors of my nights were more torturous than any mere bodily pain I ever knew in my life. The ever-recurring thought was, "I shall go mad—I must go mad sooner or later—for I can get no sleep!" How glad I was always to see the light of the morning, and how often I dreaded the act of lying down in bed at night!

The frightful nervous horrors of those months have served to warn me against all attempts to work at more than human speed. I have never dared to preach more than twice on Sundays,—and have limited myself to three or four lectures in each week, since my recovery. And now I am on the way to sixty-seven years of age, I must never think of trying to return to the old passionate speed of working. But I hope to keep in harness to the end; and never give up my Work of Duty, save with my life.

Let me most gratefully record the fact, that, all unexpectedly to myself, my friends made my illness the occasion for raising me help for life, in the shape of a little annuity. My Right Hon. friend first suggested the proposition; my beloved friend Dr. Jobson assented to it; and he and Mr. James Harvey of London,—so well known, among

Baptists, for his ready and munificent help in every scheme for good,—forthwith met Samuel Morley, M.P., a name identified with Christian philanthropy, and laid their purpose before him, when he at once put down his influential name for £100. My Right Hon. friend, and my old friend Charles Seely, M.P., with Mr, James Harvey, followed, each with £50, and my dear friend, Dr. Jobson, with £20, and then the proposition was placed before the public. Among the principal contributors were Mr. Bass, M.P, for Derby, Mr. Colman, now M.P. for Norwich, Mr. Mitchell, Provost of Montrose, my kind and good friends, Mr. Crosby of Stockton-on-Tees, and Mr. Abram Bass of Burton-on-Trent; and, above all, let me not forget my illustrious friend Thomas Carlyle, who sent his £10.

Mr. Harvey, with a kindness I know not how to describe, took upon himself all the drudgery of receiving subscriptions; and, eventually, £1,300 was raised, and an annuity of £100 was purchased at the National Debt Office, for myself and my dear wife, and for the survivor, whichever it may be. Of course, they deduct Income Tax half-yearly, when I receive my payment; but, even with that deduction, which an old Radical does not relish very sweetly, I feel grateful for what kind and numerous friends have thus secured for me for the term of my own life, and also for my dear wife, should she be the survivor.

CHAPTER XXXV.
MY LIFE AND WORK FOR THE LAST FEW YEARS:
CONCLUSION. 1867—1872.

I RECOMMENCED my work with June, 1867, and have continued to perform it,—although in May, 1868, I was reported to be dead—dead and buried!—and columns of somewhat spurious biography were published in the Midland newspapers. The death, at Manchester, of Robert Cooper, the Atheist lecturer, gave rise to this imagination, no doubt. During the year 1867, I lectured and preached in various towns of Bucks, Beds, and Berks; Hants, Surrey, Leicestershire, Derbyshire, Lincolnshire, Yorkshire, and Nottinghamshire. The pleasantest visit of the year was to delightful Stratford-on-Avon-a town in which I should certainly go to reside for life, if I were a man of fortune, and had "nothing to do." In 1868, I performed my work again in towns where I preached and lectured in 1867, and also visited towns in Cheshire, Staffordshire, Lancashire, Oxfordshire, Herefordshire, Shropshire, and Worcester: I also spoke in Newtown and Wrexham (North Wales) for the first time.

The first four months of 1869 I devoted entirely to Lancashire— lecturing and preaching in Oldham, Heywood, Staleybridge, Rochdale, Manchester, Bolton, Liverpool, Wigan, Chorley, Lancaster, Preston, Blackburn, Clitheroe, Over Darwen, Padiham, Accrington, and Burnley. When I passed, very hastily, through Lancashire in 1863, the "Cotton Famine" was raging. I thought I would return now prosperity had returned, and see what improvement the people had made. I found the towns vieing with each other in the erection of new town-halls, and in their superior style of erecting houses of business; and I also found working men had bettered their physical condition considerably. But I confess, with pain, that I saw they had gone back, intellectually and morally.

After revisiting several Yorkshire towns, I made my way, in July, to the north-western sea-coast corner of England, and preached and lectured, for the first time, in Whitehaven, Workington, Maryport, and Ulverstone. I spent a few rapturous days at sweet Keswick and in the neighbourhood, and then went on to work again at Kendal; and took my way into other parts of Lancashire—determined to re-examine my painful problem. So I preached and lectured at Blackpool, Haslingden, Ramsbottom, Bacup, Bury, Farnworth, Hindley, and Warrington; and, passing into Cheshire, talked at Crewe, Hyde, and Stockport, and thus finished the year.

With 1870 I returned to my inquiry, and devoted January, February, March, and April again to Lancashire—renewing my work chiefly in the towns I had visited a year before, and entering a few new places. My sorrowful impressions were confirmed. In our old Chartist time, it is true, Lancashire working men were in rags by thousands; and many of them often lacked food. But their intelligence was demonstrated wherever you went. You would see them in groups discussing the great doctrine of political justice—that every grown-up, sane man ought to have a vote in the election of the men who were to make the laws by which he was to be governed; or they were in earnest dispute respecting the teachings of Socialism. Now, you will see no such groups in Lancashire. But you will hear well-dressed working men talking, as they walk with their hands in their pockets, of "Co-ops" (Co-operative Stores), and their shares in them, or in building societies. And you will see others, like idiots, leading small greyhound dogs, covered with cloth, in a string! They are about to race, and they are betting money as they go! And yonder comes another clamorous dozen of men, cursing and swearing and betting upon a few pigeons they are about to let fly! As for their betting on horses—like their masters!—it is a perfect madness.

Except in Manchester and Liverpool—where, of course, intelligence is to be found, if it be found anywhere in England,—I gathered no large audiences in Lancashire. Working men had ceased to think, and wanted to hear no thoughtful talk; at least, it was so with the greater number of them. To one who has striven hard, the greater part of his life, to instruct and elevate them, and who has suffered and borne imprisonment for them, all this was more painful than I care to tell.

From Lancashire I passed into Yorkshire, revisiting some old scenes, and then into Westmoreland, and so on to the new rising port of Barrow-in-Furness, where they are shipping the hœmatite iron. Again to Whitehaven and the sea-coast towns of Cumberland, and Carlisle; and then crossed the country, and began to lecture and preach among the Northumberland colliers. They heard me eagerly. I always like to talk to the poor colliers; and wish they were better cared for. After renewing my work in Newcastle, Sunderland, and other large towns, I turned to the eastern sea-coast, and lectured and preached at Whitby, Pickering, Scarborough, Bridlington, Driffield, and Beverley, and so ended the year.

The last year (1871) I commenced with the East Riding of Yorkshire, and then passed into the West. With the exception of one fortnight devoted to Manchester, I worked in the West Riding to the end of April, and then passed into the North Riding. The whole month of June I passed in romantic Westmoreland; and commenced this autobiography. In July, after revisiting Barrow-in-Furness, I re-entered Yorkshire, and in August resumed my work in the busy counties of Durham and Northumberland, once more among the poor colliers. In November I re-entered the West Riding, and remained in it till near the close of the year; and I am looking over the last proofs and revises from the printer of this autobiography, at Leeds, the capital of the West Riding, in the month of February, 1872.

"And now you have chronicled your labours so fully," some reader may say, "tell us whether you have reason to think that they have been of any value to the audiences you have addressed." I am not in the habit of publishing the results of my labour. I have no taste for it. God knows best, and most unerringly, what degree of good I may have effected. I would rather tell into the ear of some good Christian man how scores have come to me, or written to me, during these last dozen years and more, and told me how they have been recovered from sceptical wandering, by hearing my lectures, and have found their way to Christ as their personal Saviour. If I were to take upon me to pronounce in what direction I judge that I have been the most instrumental of good, I should say it has been in the checking of incipient scepticism in the minds of young men, members of religious families, and regular attendants on public worship. I invite the hearing of such young men wherever I go; and direct my teaching most earnestly to them. If such young men can be preserved from sceptical error, and be persuaded to become active members of Christian churches, it will be productive of great blessings to the next generation.

I do not, however, as I have already said, labour as intensely as I did at first. I cannot do it; and, finding my force decay, I have yielded to the desire so often expressed by hearers of my lectures, and have begun to write them down, and publish them. If the little volume brought out for me, by the publishers of the present volume, a short time ago—entitled "The Bridge of History over the Gulf of Time," embodying in a popular form the Historical Evidence for the Truth of Christianity—be successful, I hope to have life and strength remaining to issue my other discourses on the Evidences in a printed form.

Ten years ago, I hoped to produce a large volume instead of a small one, on the Historical Evidences: I meant to have the picture of a bridge for the frontispiece, and to fill the arches with inscriptions of contemporary names; and I purposed to have the volume stored with engravings of every kind that would illustrate the subject,—the chair of Venerable Bede, and the coffin of St. Cuthbert, and the coins of Constantine, and the arch of Titus, with the figure of the golden candlestick, etc. etc. I imagined I might get a month, now and then, to sit in the British Museum Library, and work at such a book; but I must leave it now to be accomplished by some other humble and earnest worker whom God may raise up. It is the very volume on the Historical Evidences that is wanted; but it could not be done in a hurry. It should form a cyclopædia of Christian literature and history; and would take one man's whole strength—and a strong man's, too—to accomplish it worthily.

One feat I hope to be able to accomplish, though I cannot accomplish this. I promised myself, when my "Purgatory of Suicides" was issued twenty-six years ago, that I would write another poem, of about the same length, and in the same stanza, to be entitled "The

Paradise of Martyrs." I have written three books of it, and hope, if I have health and strength, to get it finished.

In the present year, 1872, I have, as I said, to revisit Scotland, in which I spent the whole year 1862. But I keep in mind that our purposes are not always accordant with the purposes of our Maker, even when they are founded on convictions of duty. So I do not make myself sure that what I purpose will be fulfilled. I only ask that if God should call me from earth ere these purposes are fulfilled, I may be with Him in heaven, for Christ's sake!

I have no doubt, while I write this, that I shall be with my Saviour in heaven. I never harbour the fear, for a moment, that I shall not be with Him. I love Christ. I never lost my love for His moral beauty, and never ceased to worship that, even when Straussian errors had the strongest possession of me. But my love for Christ now springs from other grounds. I have accepted Him as my Saviour; and through faith in Him and His atonement for sin, and in the everlasting love of the Father, I feel God has accepted me. Living or dying, I am His; and trust to have this confidence until He shall call me home.

My work is, indeed, a happy work. Sunday is now a day of heaven to me. I feel that to preach "the unsearchable riches of Christ" is the most exalted and ennobling work in which a human creature can be engaged. And believing that I am performing the work of duty, that I am right, my employment of lecturing on the Evidences of Natural and Revealed Religion, from week to week, fills me with the consoling reflection that my life is not being spent in vain, much less spent in evil. I often regret that scores of men, who might easily fit themselves for this work, are not employing themselves in maintaining and defending the evidences for the truth of Christianity. I cannot help thinking that the Christian world will awake to the necessity of sending out champions for the truth, ere long. If the next generation are to be saved from the deluge of unbelief, this championship should be entered upon. I wish one hundred intelligent, studious, pious, and courageous young Christian men would resolve to enter upon it. May God, in His wisdom, select the instruments, and call them to their work, for the glory of His Holy Name!

If the summons to such work have already reached the heart and conscience of some whose eyes may light on these pages, one word in their ear. Do not enter upon your work as a mere genteel profession. Do not stipulate for so many guineas fee before you open your choice lips, and pour out your precious treasures of instruction. Let others live that kind of sugar-candied life that choose it. Doubtless they will have their reward.

But go you forth as the servant of your Divine Master, asking nothing but alms in your poverty. Places for the delivery of your discourses you will find, after a time, without great difficulty, if people feel you are in earnest. Let all come in to hear you, free. Sell no tickets, take no monies for admission, have no practices that may leave a hair-breadth's room for Christ's enemies to charge you with selfishness. Have a collection at the end of your discourse, on the ground that you cannot live on the air, and pay expenses of lodging, and travelling, and printing, from an empty pocket. Make this simple appeal to your countrymen, and they will not fail to respond to it, generally.

You must not expect to "make money," and have thousands in the bank. But you cannot starve, if you have industry, and brains, and honesty of purpose. As to saving, unless you have children to come after you, you had better not be bothered with the thought of it. Saving money seems to make many people miserable. Don't be troubled with it. You had better, if you have any money to spare, give it away to relieve the wretched; they abound on every hand. Give yourself up to your work, and live for that only. Go and sell all you have and follow your Master, and you shall have treasure in heaven.

POSTSCRIPT: April, 1873.—I take the opportunity afforded by the issue of the "People's Edition" of this book, to say that I did revisit Scotland last year; and was received both by preachers and people, with unspeakable kindness. Since the present year commenced, I have been at my preaching and lecturing work in the West Riding, in the Staffordshire Potteries, and in the "Black Country." In literature I have been so far active that, last September, my publishers issued my "Plain Pulpit Talk," a volume containing seven of the sermons that I have often preached; and while I write this Postscript, they are publishing the first half of my long-purposed poem, "The Paradise of Martyrs."

T. C.

THE END.

Lightning Source UK Ltd.
Milton Keynes UK
175161UK00001B/34/P

9 781409 965916